The Rising Middle Classes in China

Chief Editor: Li Chunling
Translator: Rupert Campbell

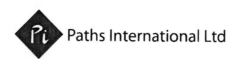

Paths International Ltd

社会科学文献出版社
SOCIAL SCIENCES ACADEMIC PRESS (CHINA)

Preface

China's rapid economic growth has led to a rapidly growing middle class. Especially since the start of the century of capitalism, the size and scale of China's middle class have clearly grown. While the proportion of the middle class within China's population as a whole is relatively small, the number of middle class members is still a huge quantity of people because of the enormous size of China's population. So, according to conservative estimates by scholars and analysts, in China today there are 100 million members of the middle class. Some scholars in China predict that the middle class will likely reach 30~40% of China's population in the coming decade, or 400 million people. In China's social, economic, cultural, and political spheres, this widespread, rapidly growing social group is displaying its influence. In the consumer market, China's middle class has already showed its huge power as one of the main forces pushing forward China's economic transformation (transforming from an export-based to domestic consumer-based economy), and is the key target consumer group of transnational corporations. In the socio-political sphere, the middle class is constantly making its voice heard as well, and its stance will decide the direction of Chinese society. The values and lifestyle of the Chinese middle class will also likely influence China and, beyond this, global resource consumption structures, ecology, and the environment. Such an important group has drawn the attention of many scholars, analysts, policy makers, and businesses, yet to this day no authoritative work has conducted holistic description and analysis of the situation of this group.

This book embodies the newest research results of China's foremost scholars on the middle class carrying out in-depth exploration of the middle class's background, process of formation, state of development, key characteristics, socio-economic status, and socio-political function. Of note, this book analyses conceptual definitions of the middle class, its scale of development, values it identifies with, social attitudes, income, and consumer characteristics. This book is divided into four parts: Observing China's Emerging Middle Class in Multiple perspectives; The Definition, Composition and Size of China's Middle Class; Identity and Attitudes of China's Middle Class; The Socioeconomic Status of China's Middle Class. The four chapters in Part One introduce the social, economic and political backgrounds to the creation of China's middle class, as well as the formative roles of state, market, public media, and cultural elites in this process. The three chapters in Part

Two discuss definitions of the middle class, and estimate the size and scale of the middle class in China based on national survey data, as well as the differences within this social group. The three chapters in Part Three analyze the middle class's socio-political outlook, exploring in particular the possible role of the middle class in pushing forward democracy in China. The three chapters in Part Four describe the income and consumer conditions, lifestyle, and approach to social relations of the middle class. The vast majority of chapters in this book rely on extensive survey data and case studies as the bases for analysis, while only a few rely on publications. Based on extensive statistical description and analysis this book explains in detail the process of creation and basic situation of China's middle class, predicting the future direction of the middle class and its influence on socio-political change.

CONTENTS

List of Contributors

He, Jin. Associate Professor, Political College of Youth of China

Li, Chunling. Professor, Institute of Sociology, Chinese Academy of Social Sciences

Li, Lulu. Professor and Director, Department of Sociology, Renming University

Li, Peilin. Professor and Director, Institute of Sociology, Chinese Academy of Social Sciences

Li, Shen. Doctoral Student, Department of Sociology, Renming University

Liu, Xin. Professor and Director, Department of Sociology, Fudan University

Liu, Shuo. Doctoral Student, Department of Sociology, Chinese University of Hong Kong

Lui, Tai-lok. Professor, Centre of Asian Studies, University of Hong Kong

Qin, Chen. Doctoral Student, School of Social and Behavioral Sciences at Nanjing University

Rocca, Jean Louis. Research Fellow, Centre d'études et de recherches internationales, (Paris School of Political Science); Professor, Department of Sociology, Tsinghua University; Director, the Sino-French Centre of Research in Human and Social Sciences

So, Alvin Y. Professor, Division of Social Science, Hong Kong University of Science and Technology

Wang, Yu. Doctoral Student, Department of Sociology, Renming University

Zhang, Yi. Professor, Institute of Population Studies and Labor Economics, Chinese Academy of Social Sciences

Zhou, Xiaohong. Professor and Dean, School of Social and Behavioral Sciences at Nanjing University

Part I   Observing China's Emerging Middle Class in Multiple perspectives

Changes in Theoretical Directions and Interests of Research on China's Middle Class

Li Chunling

At the beginning of this century, especially in the first three to four years, China's middle class became a hot topic in the realm of public opinion. Likewise, it became an important research interest in sociology, especially within the study of social stratification. The emergence of China's middle class as a result of economic growth was of course the force behind this change. In other countries we see that sustained rapid economic growth, industrialization, urbanization, and the emergence and growth of the middle class have all caught the attention of public media and scholars, leading to heated debates on questions of the middle class. However, because of varied social, political, environmental, and economic contexts, as well as being at different stages of development, academics in different countries choose different theoretical directions, and represent very different points of interest. In China, academic analysis and public debate of the middle class both receive certain degrees of influence from Western theories. In particular, industrial and post-industrial discourse on the "new middle class", and postmodern concepts of consumerism relating to middle class consumer tastes and lifestyles, have had considerable influence on China's study of the middle class. Sometimes China's scholars and public both take China's newly-forming middle class and compare it to Europe and America's middle classes, as these Western living conditions, lifestyles, and values have become the model of China's middle class, or rather the goals that they pursue. Comparatively, Western neo-Marxism and its theories of the middle class – including Erik Olin Wright's research on the middle class – have had only a slight influence on the Chinese academy. The theorist that academics and social critics in China utilize most of all is American sociologist C. Wright Mills, particularly his 1950's work *White Collar: The American Middle Classes* (C. Wright Mills, 2006), which already has several translations available in China.[1] Additionally,

---

1 In international sociological studies of middle classes, this work is seldom referred to or utilized.

in studying issues of middle class culture and consumerism, Pierre Bourdieu's work *Distinction: A Social Critique of the Judgment of Taste* (Bourdieu, 1994) and Paul Fussell's work *Class: Style and Status in the USA* (Fussell, 1998) are also frequently used by academics and critics, as Chinese translations are available for both. Even though Chinese academics studying the middle class often refer to these works and theories, the interests and directions of China's middle class research are essentially very different from mainstream social stratification research in Euro-American sociology. The emergent middle class phenomenon is a quintessential phenomenon of globalization, but the drive and direction of China's research has particular Chinese characteristics. This paper examines the changes in the development and interests of research on China's middle class over the last decades, and discusses the interconnected relationship between changes in Chinese society, economy, and politics with changing scientific research objectives. Moreover, this paper considers and analyzes the characteristics and directions of current research on the middle class, finally raising some proposals for the development of research on the middle class in the field of sociology.

1. The Rise in Interest in Research on China's Middle Class

Chinese sociologists began to take notice of China's middle class in the second half of the 1980's, following the rapid emergence and increase in size of this social group. Following this increase, people's discussion of the middle class also increased, which can be seen clearly in Graph 1, below. Diagram 1 lists the number of articles found on a search of China's national journal database for all results with 'middle class' in the title. Before 1986 almost no articles on questions of the middle class existed, but towards 1990 a rapid increase occurs. This increase peaks quickly as a result of 1989's political turmoil, where research on the middle class became a politically sensitive topic censored by the government, creating a decline in the research field. There is only a small number of articles towards the end of the 1990's, but these articles are mostly introductions to the state of foreign middle classes, with very few analyzing China's. The year 2000 represents a significant turning point, as there is a clear increase in articles on China's middle class, especially in the three years since 2004. It is during this time that the middle class became a hot topic across China, and it is the time that a few sociologists, economists, and government statisticians used survey research data to study and analyze China's middle class, doing more than just presenting some ideas or introducing new theories like past articles. Furthermore, during this time the subjects of discussions surrounding China's middle class began to diversify: the size and structure of the middle class had been the main topics of interest, but people began also to look at its different characteristics (such as income, consumerism, culture, political stance, etc.) and its social influence.

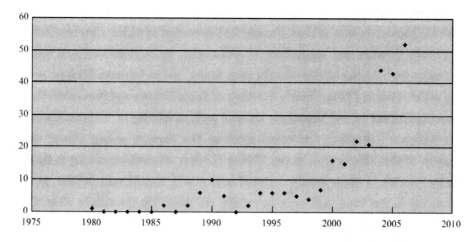

Graph 1   Number of Articles in the National Journal Database with "Middle Class" in the Title

In discussing questions of the middle class, Chinese academics utilize a lot of related discourse from Western theorists, but generally speaking their research interests and related theoretical explanations come from the researcher's reaction to the reality of Chinese social changes and issues. Thus the starting point, force behind, and focus of such research are very different from theories of the middle class from Western sociology. Furthermore, while China's research on the middle class has not been developing long, different time periods will have different theoretical inclinations and different points of interest.

2. Early Interests in Middle Class Research: Class Analysis Perspectives and Democracy

After the 1980's, a small peak in discussion of questions of the middle class occurred (graph 1), before this quick peak, very few people discussed China's middle class. The only exceptions are Marx's "petty bourgeoisie" and Mao's "national bourgeoisie" mentioned by researchers of Marxist-Leninist and Maoist thought. In terms of current understanding, Marx's petty bourgeoisie refers to the middle class of capitalist society, between the bourgeoisie and the proletariat, and with wavering political inclinations. Similarly, Mao's national bourgeoisie refers to the also politically wavering, but more likely to support the proletariat and revolution, class between land-owning warlords, bureaucrats and comprador capitalists, and factory workers and peasants of the proletariat of pre-1949 China. In that era, this group was designated as China's middle class by government officials – that is, small and medium sized land-owners, and petty bourgeoisie. After the mid-1980's, a new wave of Western thought entered Chinese theorizing, during a time when Neo-Marxism was popular in the West. Thus Neo-Marxist debates on the middle class, and alternations to traditional Marxist theories of class, became the key content of middle class research.

China's theorists and researchers, in philosophy, political science, and sociology, came under the influence of Neo-Marxist class theory, and so began to focus on questions of the middle class in China. China's Academy of Social Science and Humanities Research Institute carried out several large-scale research projects relating to "Chinese Social Class Order Structure", of which researchers (such as Dai Jianguo, among others) were all supporters of Neo-Marxist class theory. During this time, discussions relating to the middle class by theorists in China mostly occurred in step with Neo-Marxist debates on middle class theory in the West, and were essentially the same. On the middle class, Chinese theorists and researchers find themselves in one of two groups: supporters of traditional Marxist class theory (the theory of the two extremes, bourgeoisie and proletariat), or those who think the emergence and formation of a middle class has altered the original class structure. This second group considers the Chinese middle class to mainly consist of intellectuals, private businessmen, and small business owners. Additionally, during this time a few radical supporters of middle class theory also vehemently advocated democracy. They thought that the middle class – whom they considered to be primarily business people – would be the impetus behind democratic political change. After the political storm of 1989, these "middle class theorists" came under criticism from the government. Some government thinkers claimed that Western "middle class theory" (from industrialization theory and Neo-Marxism) was anti-Marxist, as it opposes Marx's theory of the bourgeoisie, and attempts to cover up class conflicts in capitalist society. They claimed that 'developing the middle class' was a euphemism for cultivating China's bourgeoisie, and thus changed the social essence of socialism. A famous sociologist of the time pointed out, "Socialist China cannot allow a 'middle class' to appear", "a minority is attempting to create what is known as a 'middle class' in China, which they are relying upon to overturn our socialist system." "This cannot be allowed; this plot is doomed to fail." "Middle class theory exists in the West to cover up the issue of class conflict, to gloss over, protect, and homogenize the reign of capitalism. In socialism, the theory of the middle class divides the proletariat class, separating business people and intellectuals from the proletariat, creating a subversive force within socialism."

In conclusion, theorists and researchers from this era bring clear analytical perspectives in debates on questions of the middle class. Whether it is supporters of so-called Western "middle class theory" or their critics, they all take a class-based analytical perspective when approaching these issues. At the same time, it is very clear that middle class issues are not just academic questions, but most critically are also political problems. 1989 was a watershed year, before which Neo-Marxism was pursued, but after which traditional Marxist class theory returned in an official capacity. Around this time, research on the middle class with a classist analytical perspective ended, and afterwards entirely new theoretical directions on China's middle class were adopted.

3. Research on the Middle Class Moving Forward: Research on Policy Directions Becomes Mainstream

After middle class theory came under criticism post-1989, discussion of questions of the middle class entered a low. During the early- and mid-1990's very few academics discussed middle class issues, and research on such topics was considered politically sensitive–in standard theoretical and academic publications, middle class-related vocabulary was also forbidden. In the late-1990's however, a few influential sociologists began to look at middle class issues once more, and they predicted that economic growth, industrialization, and marketization would be followed by the development of a middle class, which would become the main social subject. Yet at that time, due to severe restriction on the publication of "middle class" related language, and the ideologically polarized nature of middle class theory, these academics used alternative vocabulary with similar meaning to indicate 'middle class', such as 'middle level', or 'middle class' but using different characters. In using these words, they emphasized the characteristics of different classes, not the characteristic of their relationships to each other. They did not define the middle class within the framework of class relations, but within a social ranking structure. According to this understanding, the middle class are those found in the middle sector of society based on a multi-dimensional differentiation (particularly regarding income). For example, "middle class indicates the social group with a middle-level standard of living and material wealth in society" (Li Qiang, 2001). Such an understanding of the concept of the middle class shows that China's theories and directions in research on the middle class are totally different from those of the earlier period. No longer is the discourse of social ranking used, but of social ranking and differentiation. The conflict of the earlier period between the theory of the bourgeoisie and petty-bourgeoisie (that of the Neo-Marxists) and traditional Marxist class theory has been completely skirted. Only by also skirting the ideological conflict of this debate was significant sociological research on China's middle class – in the heated political climate of the time –able to survive and develop.

Most importantly, during this time sociologists called for research on China's policy directions relating to the middle class. A number of senior sociologists published arguments on the influences created by government policies, attempting to change the government's ideological misgivings and fearful attitude towards the middle class by demonstrating from various perspectives how China's middle class has progressive social function, and. These sociologists especially emphasized the importance of China's middle class towards maintaining political stability and economic development, and how socio-political stability and economic development are the government's two main priorities. In the 1990's, the government's focus on socio-political stability surpassed even its desire for economic development, and sociologists especially emphasized that the formation of China's middle class is beneficial to this end. Professor Li Qiang is a representative advocate of this kind of middle class theory. His ideas are particularly representative, and also very influential: "In any society, the middle class is the most important force in maintaining social stability. Firstly, the middle class is a cushion between the upper and lower classes, so when they become the subject of society, conflicts between the upper and lower classes are kept in check, thus social conflicts will be mitigated – this is the political reason for social stability. Secondly, the middle class represents socially moderate and conservative ideologies. When these ideologies hold influential position, extremist ideologies and conflicting ideas struggle to find a market, and this is the ideological reason for stability. Third, the middle class is the key social group in leading consumer society, so when the middle class becomes the majority, their middle class lifestyle ensures a broad and stable consumer market. This is the economic reason for stability" (Li Qiang, 2001). A lot of sociologists, including some scientific researchers, endorse these ideas, that the formation of the middle class is beneficial to political stability and economic development. Aside from this example, other influential sociologists (such as Lu Xueyi and Li Peilin, etc) raised ideas for adjusting the social structure – changing Jin Xuepei's current ideas of social class structure to the olive-shaped social class structure. The 'olive-shaped structure' is where the middle class is the main social group, and is the only social structure that can maintain long-lasting peace and stability. Based on this conceptual approach, these sociologists raised policy suggestions, that the government should utilize corresponding policies to foster and strengthen the middle class.

This kind of research on middle class policy direction made a huge impression. Sociological perspectives on the middle class received recognition in the realms of both academic and public discussion, and the greatest success of these sociologists was to gradually change government policy makers' attitudes and policies towards middle class issues. The government no longer looked on China's middle class as a political threat. An indication of the government's changing attitude was on the 11th of November, 2002, at the Sixteenth Plenum of the National Congress, when Central Committee Secretary Jiang Zemin clearly raised the need to "raise the proportion of the middle-income group", after which fostering a strong "middle-income group" was established as one of the government's objectives. Academic understanding of this new slogan is that the fostering of a strong middle-income group had become a government policy objective. A lot of people think that "middle-income people" are just China's "middle class". The government may use the term "middle-income group" rather than "middle class" because they can only accept a term that refers to income alone, and which does not define the middle class in terms of any other meaning or stance. In recent years, China's middle class has displayed huge potential as consumers, becoming the primary force fueling domestic demand. This actually proves the immense help the development of this group is to national economic growth, while at the same time public criticism of inequality in China has increased as each day passes, also forcing the government to consider broadening the middle-income group in order to control trends in rising inequality extremes.

4. The Surge in Research on the Middle Class: Middle Class Income and Consumption Trends Research

Research on the middle class and policy directions created a resurgence in research on China's middle class, and also led to such research receiving a degree of legal recognition, and an increase in discussion of middle class issues. Yet it certainly was not research on policy directions that led to the huge surge in discussion of middle class questions. Research on the middle class and policy directions is a theoretical debate left to the academic world, but what made middle class questions go viral in Chinese society were product producers, sellers, and service providers, as well as related people in mass-media, who caught on to the rise of the middle class in China. At the end of the 1990's and the beginning of the 2000's, in a number of relatively high-end product advertisements and promotional products, "middle class" vocabulary became the linguistic tool used to beguile the public. For example, real estate advertisements refer to their "middle class homes" or "middle class neighborhoods"; mid- to high-end car advertisements say their sedans are specifically made for "middle class" or "professional" owners; mid- to high-end furniture and daily use product promotions call their products of middle class taste and style; and an internet retailer promotional slogan is "our goal is to become the number one brand for urban middle class neighborhood resident daily products". All of a sudden "middle class" became a prevalent word in advertising and media, yet in the world of academia and theory, especially sociology, "middle class" was still censored. As such, a few commercial journalists, economic critics, and corporate CEOs published "The Rise of China's Middle Class" (Xu Jiang, 2001) and "The Surfacing of China's Middle Class" (Chen Xiaoya, 2002). Business people not only sold their products to the "middle class", but also through all kinds of advertisement and promotions created an image of China's middle class in the eyes of the public – which included ideas of what houses they should live in, what cars they should drive, where they should travel, and where they should go to shop and have fun. Surrounded by such commercial and media blazoning, this image of the middle class was firmly established in the imagination of the public, becoming the goal towards which Beijing youths strove. At the same time, 'middle class' became a word often on the lips of the public. However, people retained a lot of doubts regarding this new language. Recently in newspapers, magazines, and online posts a common phrase is "Are you middle class (*ni zhongchan le ma* 你中产了吗)?" or "Who is middle class (*Shei shi zhongchan* 谁是中产)?", "What kind of person is middle class (*Shen me yang de ren shi zhongchan* 什么样的人是中产)?" and "Am I middle class (*Wo shi bu shi zhongchan* 我是不是中产)?" Debates on such questions and doubts are a hot topic in the Chinese public today. Businesses, media, and the public all display increasingly strong interest in China's middle class. It is as if the whole society is frantically seeking information and knowledge about this social group, and sociologists have become the object of this pursuit. Researchers of social stratification are constantly hounded by media, businesses, and laypeople asking questions about the middle class, and the two questions asked most frequently are: 1) what conditions define the middle class? 2) How big is China's middle class? Four or five years ago, when questions of the middle class were just emerging, people were still asking: "does China have a middle class or not?" But nobody asks this anymore; China's middle class has already emerged – a fact that there seems to be no need to question, although people still question whether this group of people have formed a proper social group.

Regarding questions raised by businesses, media, and the public, while sociologists have still not done any complete studies, they have researched enough for them to respond to these questions. Over the long-term, sociological research on the middle class has mainly used policy research directions, theoretically demonstrating the importance of the middle class to political stability and economic development. Research collecting actual data and evidence on this social group is relatively scarce. Given the constant pressure from the public and media on questions of the middle class, sociologists have begun to align their research interests with these questions, such as: what exactly is the middle class (establishing a concept of the middle class), what criteria define the middle class, and how big is the middle class in China? Over the last one or two years, the majority of debates on the middle class between sociologists have been on these questions. Table 1 shows the number of middle class people estimated by sociologists and the criteria by which they chose to define the middle class.

Table 1 Estimated Size of Middle Class and Defining Conditions

Year	Author	Source	Proportional Size of Class	Urban Middle Class	Criteria	Survey Results and Method
1997	Zhang Jianming, et al	"The Current and Future Development of China's Middle Class", *People's University of China*, 1998(5)	----	48.5% (Beijing)	Socio-economic index (cultural level, income, and career)	Sampling in Beijing with statistical analysis
2000	Xiao Wentao	"The Current and Future Development of China's Middle Class", *Sociology Research*, 2001(3)	20%~25%	....	Income and household financial assets	No survey, based on subjective estimation
2001	Zhou Xiaohong	"China's Middle Class: Fantasy or Reality?", *Tianjin Sociology*, 2006(2)	----	11.9% (large cities)	Economic criteria, career and cultural level	Telephone survey in five major cities with statistical analysis
2001	Li Chunling	*Cleavage and Fragmentation: An Analysis Empirical Analysis of the Social Stratification of Contemporary China*, Social Sciences Academic Press, 2005	4.1%	12% (large cities)	Career, income, and consumer factors, and subjective self-identification	National sampling survey with statistical analysis
2003	Oxford Analysis	"China: The Middle Class", *Money China*, 2004(4)	4.5%	8%	Income and real purchasing power	National sampling survey with statistical analysis
2004	Liu Yi	"Methods and Measures for Determining the Middle Class-- China's Pearl River Delta as an Example", *Open Times*, 2006 (4)	----	23.7% (Pearl River Delta households)	Income, career and consumption factors	Pearl River Delta sampling survey with statistical analysis
2005	Li Qiang	"On the Status and Theories of China's Middle Class", *Society*, 2005 (1)	15%	....	Employment	Subjective analysis, no survey
2006	Li Peilin	"The Scale and Recognition of China's Middle Class", China Annual Sociology Conference, 2007, "Middle Class International Comparison Colloquium" Compilation	Core Middle Class 3.1% Middle-Middle Class 8.9% Peripheral Middle Class 20.9%		Employment, income, and cultural level	National sampling survey with statistical analysis

Looking at the information in Table 1, the conditions chosen by sociologists to define China's middle class are relatively similar, mainly including employment, income, cultural level, consumption, and subjective self-identification. But looking at the estimates resulting from these conditions, there is large disparity in the size of China's middle class. The estimates of middle class size across China range from 3.1% to 25% of national population, while urban middle class estimates range from 8% to 48.5%. Generally speaking, subjective estimates are quite high, perhaps because those making subjective estimates are strongly influenced by current feelings of the rapid growth of this class. Additionally, those estimates that used a single criterion – especially employment or career criteria – to define the middle class are extremely high, while those with multiple criteria are typically quite low.

5. New Research Interests on the Middle Class: Class Culture and Politics

These past two years, while sociologists were still concerned with defining the conception, structure, and size of the "middle class", in the cultural sphere, cultural critics discovered clear characteristics of the middle class – unique lifestyle, aesthetic tastes, and outlook. In the 1990's, a number of young authors started a wave of middle class literature. Representative works include *Shanghai Baby*, *Ziben Aiqing Xianzai Shi* (资本爱情现在时), *Coming and Going*, *Parvovirus* (*XixiaoBingdu* 细小病毒), among others. So-called "middle class literature" uses middle class aesthetics in its narrative, and is absorbed with displaying middle class lifestyles and tastes. It promotes what is known as "the essence and values of middle class-ification"[2]. These works in particular project gregarious consumerism. Characters display unfettered pursuit of brand name commodities, expensive food and clothing, and use valuable brand names to symbolize and show their class position, achieving further cultural division between classes. Another aspect of this literary genre is a heightened focus on the small details of everyday life. To the middle class, details not only show, but represent one's taste. This genre further emphasizes the concept of "elegance" (*youya* 优雅): "elegant" aesthetic taste, "elegant" literature, and so on. As they put it, "elegance" is a kind of lifestyle, a daily mood and taste, and a kind of outlook on life (Xiang Rong, 2006). This kind of outlook shows playfulness, creating and pursuing vogue, and an interest in the decay of pragmatic compromise for the sensuality of hedonism (Zhang Qinghua, 2006). Literary critics refer to this wave in literature as "petty bourgeois sentiment" and "middle class taste" (He Ping, 2005). This wave of middle class culture not only localized to the literary world, but also exists in the worlds of art, fashion, film, media, and public culture. These literary works narrate and promote middle class lifestyles,

---

2 *Zhongchanhua de jingshen lichang he jiazhi xiangdu* 中产化的精神立场和价值向度

aesthetic tastes and worldviews, and also allow their authors to fulfill their own middle class lifestyles. For both of these reasons, these authors are known by many as the "middle class authors". These authors and their works often achieved great market success, as a great many urban youths followed this wave. The flourishing development of this literary wave lets us experience the existence of middle class ideas in contemporary Chinese culture, and further show just how disparate the middle class described in cultural works is from that statistically defined by sociologists. It also shows how much these fictional depictions are much closer to the public's imaginary of the middle class than more accurate, specific sociological descriptions. Yet sociologists have not been able to give this middle class cultural phenomenon enough attention. A major focus of research is what political influences or consequences the rise of the middle class in China might have. At the end of the 1980's, China's theorists and researchers had just begun to be interested in questions of the middle class, and this was their primary interest. Some theorists thought that the middle class would be a force for democracy, as a foundation for democratic politics, and from a political perspective, that the middle class appeared to be an unstable political factor. In the late 90's, the research on policy directions and the middle class advocated by sociologists tended to emphasize the role of the middle class as the basis of political stability, as this social group is politically conservative, supportive of gradual reform and opposed to rapid change. When these two viewpoints were raised, the middle class had not yet formed in China, in other words, the middle class had not yet become a social force. Meanwhile, due to the degree of political sensitivity attached to such questions, conducting research was made extremely difficult, as a result, research on the middle class was always lacking, despite many theoretical concepts and perspectives.

In recent years, following the increasing emergence of China's middle class, each day the existence of a middle class has become clearer, and a few researchers discovered that, regarding the two above perspectives, middle class political leanings are not homogenous. In other words, using these two perspectives to explain the rise of the middle class is overly simplistic, possibly leading to socio-political consequences. Some scholars think that the middle class's political stance is currently one of indifference. Zhou Xiaohong calls it the "consumer vanguard, political rearguard"[3] middle class (Zhou Xiaohong, 2005), while other academics think the political attitude of China's middle class is one of "politicization"[4] (Zhang Qinghua, 2006). There are further academics who have displayed keen interest in

---

3   *Xiaofei qianwei, zhengzhi houwei* 消费前卫、政治后卫
4   *Qu zhengzhihua* 去政治化

the special political leanings of middle classes across industrializing East Asian countries, and they suggest that China's middle class will share some qualities with these foreign groups. But the political aspects of East Asian middle classes are also dissimilar from China's,[5] as in certain countries and areas the middle class has shown relatively strong feelings for civil society and democratization, while the middle class in other countries and areas have shown special adherence to the status quo and the nation. A few Chinese sociologists, interested in new social movements, are starting to do research on middle class-led social movements, such as owner committees, consumer movements, and environmentalist movements. Yet what has been disappointing is that in contemporary Chinese society, what have flourished and drawn the most attention are movements centered on the lower classes (migrant workers, landless farmers, displaced residents, and so on), movements and collective action focused on economic profits, while movements centered on the middle class or worthwhile objectives have not nearly flourished enough.

6. Conclusion: Developing Sociology Research on China's Middle Class

The development of research on China's middle class closely followed the rise of this class. Researcher interests and theoretical directions followed the characteristics and changes of the different stages of the middle class's development. Before the middle class had clearly emerged, researchers discussed the socio-political meaning of the middle class in theoretical debates. When the middle class phenomenon became clear in the areas of income and consumption, research interests switched to income and consumption characteristics, and the social influence of this class. Currently, as the middle class is beginning to show its own culture, values, and possible political leanings, this will likely incite continued and deeper research into these questions. Current sociology research on the middle class has received huge impetus from policy and market demand trends. These two powerful factors have helped push forward the development of research on the middle class, but at the same time have possibly funneled research perspectives to a certain area. Recent

---

5 See: Tang Jing: "Zhongchan jieji de xingqi yu dongya shehui zhuanxing" [The Rise of the Middle Class and Social Transformation in East Asia], *Changjiang Luntan*, 4 (2006); Wang Xiaoyan: "Hanguo, Xinjiapo, Zhongguo Xianggang he Zhongguo Taiwan: Zhongchan jieji zhengzai jueqi" [Korea, Singapore, Hong Kong and Taiwan: The Middle Class are Rising], *Hangzhou Daxue Xuebao*, 2 (2006); Li Luqu: "Dongya de zhongchan jeiji, shimin shehui yu zhengzhi zhuanxing" [Transformation of East Asian Middle Class, Civil Society , and Politics], *Contemporary Asia-Pacific Studies*, 4 (2004); Du Wei and Tang Lilu: "Xi riben zhongchan jieji de xingchen yu shehui yingxiang"[Analyzing the Formation and Social Influence of Japan's Middle Class]", *Guizhou Shifan Daxue Xuebao*, 3 (2004); Guo Xuguang: "Qianxi xinjiapo zhongchan jieji" [A Brief Analysis of Singapore's Middle Class], *Dongnanya Yanjiu*, 3 (2000).

social class research on the middle class has gradually progressed from simplistic discourse to one based on real data analysis (from quantitative statistical surveys to qualitative interviews), while both collated and focused research is also conducted. This shift has made research on the middle class more specific, and has enriched peoples' understanding of the middle class. But at the same time, a lot of researchers have overly focused on estimating the numerical size of the middle class, mapping its social structure, and debating the practical implementation of definitions of the middle class (especially middle class income standards). These researchers have lost sight of the fundamental essence of the middle class question, which especially weakens their theoretical analysis and structure. Current middle class research lacks a systematic theoretical approach. Even though some researchers have used certain Western theoretical ideas in their specific research, generally speaking there is no framework for theoretical explanations from a middle class-perspective. Whether it is Neo-Marxist class theory, Neo-Weberist, Industralist, Post-Industrialist, Bourdieu's cultural division and consumption class theory, postmodern class theory, or orientalist theory, it is hard to determine the theoretical perspective of current research. How can these theoretical approaches be modified, integrated, and developed to be used for researching China's middle class? This is the question facing current Chinese middle class research. The simultaneous progression of theoretical and empirical research will help our deeper analysis of the phenomenon of the middle class, with its globalized characteristics, and of the uniqueness of the middle class in China.

References

Bourdieu, Pierre. *Distinction: A Social Critique of the Judgment of Taste*, Cambridge: Harvard University Press (1994).

Chen Xiaoya. *Zhongguo zhongchan jieji tuochu shuimian* [China's Middle Class Rises to the Surface], *Shangye Wenhua*, 2 (2002).

Fussell, Paul. *Class: Style and Status in the USA*. Translated by Liang Lizhen et al. Beijing: Zhongguo Shehui Kexue Chubanshe (1998).

He Jianzhang, "Woguo suoyouzhi jiegou de tiaozheng he shehui jieji jiegou de bianhua" [Changes to China's System and Social Class Structure], *Shehuixue Yanjiu*, 5 (1987).

He Jianzhang, "Woguo xianjieduan de jieji jiegou" [Class Structure in China's Current Stage], *Shehuixue Yanjiu*, 5 (1988).

He Jianzhang, "Lun 'Zhongchan jieji'"[Discussing the "Middle Class"], *Shehuixue Yanjiu*, 2 (1990).

He Ping, "Dangxia wenxue zhong de "xiaozi qingdiao" he "zhongnchan jieji quwei"" ['Petty-bourgeois sentiment" and "Middle class tastes" in Contemporary Literature], *Wenyi Pinglun*, 6 (2005).

Hisao, Hsin-Huang Michael, editor. *East Asian Middle Classes in Comparative Perspective*, Taipei: Institute of Ethnology, Academia Sinica (1999).

Hisao, Hsin-Huang Michael, editor. *Exploration of the Middle Classes in Southeast Asia*, Taipei: Academia Sinica (2001).

Hisao, Hsin-Huang Michael, editor. *The Changing Faces of the Middle Classes in Asia-Pacific*, Taipei: Institute of Ethnology, Academia Sinica (2006).

Li Chunling, "Zhongguo dangdai zhongchan jieceng de goucheng ji bilie" [The Formation and Proportion of China's Contemporary Middle Class], *Zhongguo Renkou Kexue*, 6 (2003).

Li Chunling, *Duanlie yu suipian: dangdai zhongguo shehui jieceng fenhua shizheng fenxi* [Fragmentation and Rupture: Empirical Analysis of Contemporary China's Social Class Stratification] Beijing: Shehui Kexue Wenxian Chubanshe (2005).

Li Chunling, *Shehui Fenceng Lilun* [Social Stratification Theory], Beijing: Zhongguo Shehui Kexue Chubanshe (2007, in print).

Li Qiang, *Guanyu zhongchan jieji he zhongjian jieceng* [On the Middle Class and the Mid-level Class], *Zhongguo Renmindaxue Xuebao*, 2 (2001).

Li Qiang and Chen Zhenhua, *20 Shiji xifang shehui jiegou yi ge genbenxing de bianhua – xi xifang guojia de zhongchan jieji* [Fundamental Change in 20th Century Western Social Structure – Analyzing the Middle Class in Western Countries], *Hongqi Wenzhai*, 11 (2003).

Lu Hanlong, *"Zhongchan jieji" yu xiao kang shehui* ["Middle Class" and *Xiao Kang* Society], *Shehui Guancha*, 1 (2005).

Lu Xueyi, editor. *Dangdai zhongguo shehui jieceng yanjiu baogao* [Contemporary China Social Class Research Report], Beijing: *Shehui Kexue Wenxian Chubanshe*(2002).

Xiao Wentao, *Zhongguo zhongjian jieceng de xianzhuang yu weilai fazhan* [The Current State and Future Development of China's Middle Class], *Shehuixue Yanjiu*, 3 (2001).

Xu Jiang, *Xin zhongchan jieji jueqi: zhongguo fuyu shidai de kaishi* [The Rise of the New Middle Class: The Beginning of China's Era of Wealth], *Jingmao Shijie*, 8 (2001).

Xiang Rong, *Xiangxiang de zhongchan jieji yu wenxue de zhongchanhua xiezuo* [The Imagined Middle Class and Middle Class-ified Works in Literature], *Wenyi Pinglun*, 3 (2006).

Zhang Qinghua, *Women shidai de zhognchan jieji quwei* [Middle Class Taste in Our Era], *Nanfang Wentan*, 2 (2006).

Zhou Xiaohong, *Zhongguo zhongchan jieji: xianshiyin huo huanxiang* [China's Middle Class: Reality or Fantasty], *Tianjin Shehui Kexue*, 2 (2006).

Zhou Xiaohong, *(Bailing)*, *zhongchan jieji yu zhongguo de wudu* [*White Collar*, Misreadings by China and the Middle Class], *Dushu*, 5 (2007).

Zhou Xiahong, editor. *Zhongguo zhongchan jieceng diaocha* [Survey of China's Middle Class], Beijing: Shehui Kexue Wenxian Chubanshe (2005).

Chapter 2

Political Crossroad, Social Representations
and Academic intervention:
The Formation of a Middle Class in China

JeanLouis Rocca

In his seminal book, Boltanski deals with which is often considered as the core of the French middle class: the persons occupying intermediary positions in private and public enterprises (Boltanski). For him, there are two ways of dealing with the issue of class in academic fields. The first one is to give a clear definition in using objective (income, jobs, wealth, etc.) and subjective (lifestyles) criteria. The second one aims at understanding what is lying behind the different definitions in terms of cultural representations, social and political conflicts and public policies and then at explaining the process of identification to the groups generated by the definitions. In other terms, the different definitions have to be considered as expressions of group interests, state policies, economic transformation etc. which contribute to give birth to new representations of society stratification and identification.

Boltanski advocates the second approach. He attempts "to account for the form taken by the group in questioning *the work of gathering*, of inclusion and exclusion" (Boltanski, p. 51). Actually, this *work of gathering* takes advantage of academic research. When scholars give preliminary definitions they intervene in the field of practices. Instead of this approach, we must "analyse the field of competing definitions of the socially used object and to aim first and foremost to record and to operate dialectically all the data (...) provided" (Boltanski, p. 300). To use this approach does not mean that scholars are constrained to negate the existence of a group. As a Bourdieu's follower, not only does Boltanski take into account the practices but he also emphasizes practices as the very basis of the understanding of the social reality. For him, it is possible "both to take into account the existence of the group and the difficulties nearly insurmountable against which the work of definition and the establishment of 'objective' criteria come up" (Boltanski, p. 49).

Here, I would like to use the same approach by focusing on "the work of gathering" which is at the core of the controversy about the Chinese middle class. In other terms, my hypothesis is that behind the different definitions and characteristics of the Chinese middle classes provided by discourses it is emerging major issues at stake in the Chinese society. Discourses on new classes or strata are nothing less than expressions of endless effort to reassess and reinterpret the deep change that China has undergone since the 1980s and to give voice to specific groups.

Using a method set up in a given time (from the 1920s to th 1970s) and space (France) to analyse a phenomenon which has taken place at so different a time (the 1990s and the 2000s) and space (China) can be perceived as a little bit odd. Nonetheless, if we consider that concepts and methods of social sciences have the ability to encompass a large range of phenomenon regardless the differences in terms of cultural, historical, social structures, there are no grounds to deny the interest of such an approach.

The attempt certainly involves a laboring effort for "translating" (in geometric meaning) the approach. This translation process has twofold. It is necessary to define both the original context and the context at stake in order to demonstrate the heuristic efficiency of the approach. Concepts and methods are context-born and must be systematically contextualise.

On which discourses it is possible to base our analysis? The social expression of knowledge of restructuration of the Chinese society takes place in various fields. In the academic field scholars are describing competing patterns of change. New classes and social categories are defined, inequalities are evaluated, relationships between strata are described. Official discourse is a second channel of perception and knowledge of social changes. Social stratification has become a major source of interests for government and Party officials as well as for scholars working in hybrid official/academic organs like Party schools. Media is another channel of discourse. Newspapers and magazines and above all "women magazines" contribute greatly to the production of "class awareness". The notion of "distinction" (Bourdieu, 1979) is here of a great help. The question at stake in media is how to eat, drink, love, buy, educate children, work, climb in the social ladder, enjoy life, etc. in accordance to ways that display a distinctive nature from the other groups and which can be easily identified as the lifestyle of a specific group of people. In addition, the conceptions expressed by the people who are supposed to belong to a social group or a class constitute a diffuse, fragmented and confused but by definition very efficient channels of influence on people's practices. If a group of people considers that they belong to the middle class and then if these people try, by all possible means, to look like middle class people, how to deny them this identity except in introducing the notion of false conscience which is quite a difficult notion to manipulate?

Generally speaking, by focusing on these various sources of knowledge, the approach adopted here assumes that there is no objective, statistical, scientific, positivist way of defining a class. This position is in tune with one of the main theoretical feature of the so-called critical sociology (Foucault, Elias, Bourdieu, etc.): the fact that apart from practices and consciences (or imaginary) there is no reality. No world behind the stage. In other words, discourses and the different means (including statistics) mobilised to support discourses are the expression of will to give grounds to groups and personal interests (including intellectual interests, moral based interests, etc.). And, unfortunately, we have no other materials to base on our analysis of social structures.

In this paper, I will focus on the numerous works written by scholars (particularly sociologists) on the hot issue of the Chinese middle class. I am far from neglecting the other sources of discourse. Not only do I take into account the attempts to explain and to justify public policies but I am also doing interviews of people who are supposed to belong to the so-called middle class in order to evaluate the change in lifestyles. In addition, I am collecting information acquired from a survey on "women magazines" whose development has been striking in recent times. The reason which justifies the focus on academic discourses has purely pragmatic grounds. Compared to the other ones, sources based on scholars' articles are quite easy to obtain and to interpret.

The contextualisation of controversies about middle class

The establishment of a new social order

In his book, Boltanski considers that the term "cadres" and the constitution of "cadres" "as a pressure group pretending to be recognised officially in the space of political struggle cannot be separated from attempts of takeover and of imposition of social order which are growing in number after the strikes of 1936" (Boltanski, p. 63). In the industrial sector, the technical progress and the change in production organisation have given birth to a new social category, a wage-owning bourgeoisie which is in charge of management at intermediary level. The spread of the wage-earning system is then the essential vector of the development of the middle class. Upper wage-earners can not rely on the valorisation of a capital or on ownership to survive but they play a prominent role in the decision-making process, they have a high level of technical and cultural knowledge and they can enjoy much higher incomes than workers and foremen. From which previous categories do these people come? At that time, the traditional petty bourgeoisie and a part of the bourgeoisie were on the decline. A large proportion of siblings of shopkeepers, small traders, craftsmen and small bosses were forced to become salary men. This is the beginning of a period in which the new social category as well as a part of the bourgeoisie try to redefine mentally the structure of the society and to impose a representation based on three classes : the bourgeoisie, the workers and the "middle class", which is supposed to represent the "healthy" and "stable" element of the "nation". In the 1920s and the 1930s this representation was politically embodied in right and extreme right groups which oppose both capitalism and socialism and defend a "third path", that is to say corporatism, fascism or personalism.

In the 1950s, a new representation of middle class prevailed. The core of the "middle class" has not changed of « objective characteristics », it remains a highly fragmented group of intermediate employers in terms of income and of hierarchical position but the environment has completely changed. The influence of American aid, the growth of the "middle class", "the increase in nominal and (....) of real wages, the growth of productivity, particularly in the most integrated sectors (...), the extension of working class consumption, the spreading of consumer durables, spreading of social patterns, especially urban social patterns, etc." (Boltanski, p. 63).

This "new middle class" is put in the same category as American middle class, a huge aggregation of various social categories characterised by a high standard of living and uniform moral values. they are incorporated in organisations but have very individualistic conceptions of life dominated by the importance of personal success and competition. This class is supposed to secure the stabilisation of the society in countries which are subjected to rapid and deep change (Bourdieu 1975). For Lipset, this new class stabilises the tensions between classes and support moderate parties and collective negotiations, contribute to productivity growth, they favor scientific approaches and expertise. For members of middle class, "achievement" must prevail on "ascription", universalism on particularism. They are the most representative social group of the postindustrial society whose model is in the USA (Lipset).

The controversy about the middle class, its composition and its role in economic modernisation is not only intellectual or purely sociological. It has a political impact. Groups want to be recognised by the state as legitimate representatives of the new class and to be considered as "social partners" in the same ways as the working class is by the employers. Moreover, the state is highly influenced by the supposed political characteristics of middle class. A country with a huge middle class is perceived as more stable than a country with a simple opposition between the elite and the masses. As such, the state has become a prominent actor in the sharing out of wealth among the different categories and the design of policies which aims at favoring the access of workers to middle strata.

In China, the context in which emerges a "middle class" is both very close and very far from the one which prevails in France. Post-socialist China is characterised by a high level of economic growth and dramatic change in economic structures and social stratification. The marketisation of economic has created opportunities for making money and for getting well paid jobs. A group of small businessmen and shopkeepers have appeared as well as independent workers (actors, lawyers). As physical labour is gradually replaced by intellectual labour, a new category of workers "using their brains" (*naoli laodong zhe*) enjoy high wages and prominent positions in management apparatus. New economic sectors (information, advertisement, media, etc.) and massive foreign investments attract a new generation of university graduates which are inventing new life styles. These people hold intermediate social status, neither belonging to elite (people with very good political connections) nor to the working class (*zhigong*) which are now constituting the lower strata among urban dwellers.

However, the conditions of the recognition of the new group are different from the French case. First of all, the "history" of the Chinese middle class is short and then quite complicated to analyse. There is only one phase of "constitution" of the group and we do not have the passing of the time to stand back the events and the phenomena. The second difference lays on the social origin of the members of the groups. They cannot be identified as wage-owners since everybody had already been in that position before the 1980s but as people who have successfully taken advantage of reforms. Most of "contemporary" middle class members are coming from the ranks of the class which was officially playing the role of "master of the country" (employees and workers of urban public enterprises and administration) or are the siblings of them. In reality they were having a position very close from the one of a middle class, between peasants and cadres.

The existence of a new middle class then is less a question of "emergence" than a question of "reproduction". The hypothesis is quite easy to prove by induction. Education and social capital are the main vectors to enter the rank of middle class, the access of these two factors is largely limited to urban dwellers, therefore urban dwellers have easy access to middle class. Besides, the dominating group is not a "bourgeoisie" or a class of "capital owners" but is composed of people occupying straddling position in administration and in business. Consequently, social capital, political capital and education capital are more important than economic capital in the struggle to ascend the social ladder and to avoid descending trajectory. The social conflict between the elite and the middle class cannot be but restricted to the fact that the access to higher positions depends on the access to political resources.

Finally, the conditions of expression of this new class is specific. No question of organisations, parties, associations, trade unions to represent the group or a part of it. The main discourse on middle class is produced by scholars and more marginally by officials. The media is another channel of expression but not in terms of reflexion on the nature and characters of the group. Media is one of the main institution in which the process of subjectivation of middle class has taken place: definition of lifestyles, of an ethic of life which cover a large range of aspects : food, drink, decoration, purchase, sex, etc. Nevertheless, the middle class is not absent from the political scene. Some kind of protests are perceived as typical expression of middle class discontent. For example, flat owners set up associations devoted to the defense of proprietors against the infringement of their rights perpetrated by the companies in charge of the management of compounds. The disputes are not strictly of "civil" nature as management companies have strong connexions with local political apparatus. Besides, as the State is supposed to protect propriety rights, middle class people are expecting political move on that matter.

Actually, the middle class is a political issue but not in term of public struggle for power and recognition of groups and people. The question at stake concerns the ways which have to be used to stabilise the society. Fragmentation of the society, high level of growth and marketisation of economy lead to a lack of regulations of status and conflicts. What is the most important to protect the general interest of the private interests ? Regarding private interests, which ones should prevail and what kinds of mechanisms are the most useful to manipulate ? Far from being broached in the framework of a "public sphere" or of a peaceful and rational confrontation of interests and rights, these questions are dealt within the framework of power struggle between sets of representations.

The symbol of modernisation of social relations

In France, being perceived as what we can call « the class of modernisation » and perceiving themselves as such, the middle class gather the social categories that takes the most advantages of the period of economic growth European countries underwent from the end of 1940 to the end of 1970s. They enjoyed high wages, high level of social protection, easy access to public goods. They contribute to the growth of consumption through the use of credit and saving and the role they play in the rapid change in fashion.

This new middle class advocates new conceptions of leadership based on a new ideology which "substitutes merit for heritage, skills based legitimacy for money based legitimacy, and authority of managers for power of owners" (Boltanski, p. 37). Nevertheless, since the group gathers people who have very different situation in terms of merit, heritage, skills, money, authority and ownership, it is then important for belongers to define "who is the 'real' middle class, the 'core' of the middle class". In other terms, a struggle for symbolic domination on the group is taking place. The winner, the group of *cadres*, which is defined by a specific status given to them by public and private entreprises. Being *cadres* means that not only do you belong to the managerial staff, but you are also entitled to pay contributions to specific social security funds which secure very good health and retiring benefits. In reality most *cadres* are people having education capital recognised by private and public big companies. They are *la crème de la crème*. A part of *cadres* can climb the ladder and reach this position without possessing the level of education required but they constitute a second rank groups of *cadres* trying to find out constantly and anxiously signs and symbols proving that they are belonging to this category.

The cadres constitute a "salient point of the social space" (Boltanski, p. 235).They are a force of attraction for the people perceiving themselves as members of the middle classes. They imitate their behaviours and their so-called life style and they are as anxious as self-taught *cadres* to live and work as the legitimate *cadres* and to be recognised as such.

The economic backwardness of France compared to the ideal (the USA) is not explained by technological inferiority but by the effect of the underdeveloped state of social relations. The *clichés* describing the life of *cadres* define what is a modern "subject". They have a hectic life, always busy, upset by the success, and mouthful of "management". They are competent and they refuse to be supported by kinship relations and money, they take good care of their bodies, practising sport and watching figure, they are supporting the empowerment of women and the liberation of sex behaviours. They are very interested in psychology and personal development skills. They are market oriented but they consider it essential to accept and support state regulations. They have ennemies: the small and conservative boss/owner, the nationalism, the colonialism, the fascism. All these forces are opposed to the homogeneisation of moral values systems and styles of behaviours which are very important tools of management integration in transnational companies. In brief, the persons who have decided to represent the leading group of the middle class promote a new economic subject, free from the past and full of desire of consumption and success. Of course, that does not mean that every *cadre* and every middle class member identify with all aspects of this new lifestyles, it means that these clichés are at the core of the social practices and identities.

Yet, since the 1980s, the discourse on the growing of the middle class has been gradually replaced by a discourse on the crisis of the middle class. The dramatic increase in the number of students and the postindustrial crisis have led a growing number of university graduates and postgraduates to the ranks of unemployed. Consequently, not only has the dream of workers' siblings to become middle class members turned to nightmare but numerous youngsters belonging to the middle class are confronted to serious difficulties to finding jobs. In other terms, the growing of the middle class as a tool of social integration and political pacification seems to have its effect.

In this area the similarities are numerous. The Chinese middle class is supposed to be the class of merit, talent, honesty and modernity. It opposes these values to the ones dominating in the elite or more precisely to the absence of moral valuers and virtues within the elite. Yet the members of the middle class have highly benefited from the reform policy but they are not perceived as having used tricky ways or political protection for that purpose. As such, this social category constitutes a sort of ideal social class, a third force beside the declining one and the dubious one. Here also, the backwardness of China is less supposed to be based on a technology gap with the western countries but on a deficit in terms of moral values and social customs. The "new middle class" is perceived as a notion which can only be understood through the appropriation of western historical experience. To be a middle class member is then not only the consequence of a spontaneous phenomenon but also something it is necessary to learn and to build up. As we will see below the American way of life and of behaviours is the main reference. Like in Mills, Miller or Lipset analysis, the middle class members are supposed to be dynamic and rational, spenders and savers, individual-oriented and perfect citizens, educated and honest, focusing in networks but opposed to string-pulling and corruption, etc.[6] In other terms, the image is perfectly fitting with the theories of modernisation and the theories of development which considers modernity as a radical change in terms of moral values and social customs. Modernity would need new kind of human beings.

As it appears in France, the rapid emergence of a middle class has given birth to tensions in labor market. The focus on intellectual capital have led to an increase in the number of university graduates, an increase apparently quicker than the increase in job opportunities. Consequently, graduates are meeting difficulties to get a job and Shanghai many middle class members complains about the poor conditions of white collars. On the

---

6 This tendency is partly at odds with the national/confucianist revival which is touching every circle of the society. Only partly, as in many interviews people refer to "Chinese way of being modern", mixing national (reinvented) tradition and foreign influence.

other hand, Chinese and Foreign companies laments the lack of good managers on the market which could be due to the inadaptation of education curriculum to the needs of enterprises. But, as Boltanski says regarding the French case, the argument is challenged by the fact by entreprises emphasise on adaptability as the main quality of a manager. Under such circumstances how to train future managers for specific duties ?

The modernising process of social relations reveal an element which makes the Chinese case very different from the French case. During thirty years, a system prevailed in China in which not only were discrepancies between social groups and within social groups limited but in which every attempt made by individuals to distinguish from others were repressed. The new middle class has no patterns of behaviours. The lifestyle of the previous generation is still very influenced by the ascetic way of life prevailing in the 1960s and 1970s which cannot be of any help in the present times. They have to imitate or invent modernised life styles.

Sociological investigation

In the process of "objectivation" of the middle class, that is to say the process of recognition of the group by the institutions (the state, the media, the trade-unions, etc.), the engineers have played a determinant role, notably from the 20s to the end of the 50s. These people have a lot in common. To be a proper engineer means to have studied in elite schools (*grandes eroles*) and then to belong to catholic practicing families. They are members of the same religious and professional organisations, they are working in the same branch (industry). They have the same educational and social background as company owners but they do not have enough economic capital to become "capitalist". Moreover, since they have very high technical skills they can pretend, unlike the "capitalists" by birth, to have an objective legitimacy to manage companies. The engineers, as a group which can cumulate every kind of legitimacy : social, religious, level of education, etc. display a high power of attraction towards surrounding groups. After the second world war and the setting up of the status of cadres, the engineers have kept playing an important role but they were not the only one. Besides, the cadres have set up their own organisations (trade unions, associations) which aim at gathering the maximum of people in order to be recognised as "social partner" by the State. Not only cadres have very different power status and ways of life according to their work, in big or small, private or public companies, in a plant or in the headquarter of the firm, etc. but representative organisations accept and the category attract people who are very far from belonging to the "core" of the category: technicians, employees, etc. Consequently, the group is trapped in a contradiction. Organisations must be opened to all categories to reinforce their power but at the same time along with the increase of members the group looses its cohesion.

It is only after the group has been accepted as a legitimate and objective group that the controversies about the definition of the group have started. In that matter, media and sociological investigation have taken the lead. At the beginning of the 1960s sociology have penetrated all circles of the society (university, government agencies, entreprises, etc.) and have gained a dominant position as an overall instrument of knowledge. The representations of the society and the classifications of groups, not only do they have become stakes and instruments in the competition between intellectuals and scholars, but they have become stakes and instruments in the political and social battlefield (Boltanski, pp. 245248).

Which group deserves to represent the new middle class in China ? There is no social category as *Les cadres* which is, at the same time, a legal category and a group displaying a great power of attraction. From this point of view, the Chinese case is far more confused than the French one. However, as in France in the 1960s the sociologists are at the first place in the controversies concerning the new structuration of Chinese society. In the recent years, Sociology has gained great influence. Not only in academic fields but also in official circles. The new generation of leaders who succeeded to Jiang Zemin at the head of the State had no choice but to deal with social problems which were challenging social and political stability. Hence, the development of a middle class appeared as an official and clear solution to this problem.

Therefore, the Chinese situation is very specific. The controversies do not concern a group which is objectively existing but to define a group which must exist and to find solutions for increasing the number of its members. The building of a middle class society has become a national duty. In such a context, sociologists are not only supposed to define the middle class but also to define policies able to strive the emergence of an olive shaped society in which most people would have average conditions of life.

In search of the middle class

The analysis is based on the reading of nearly seventy papers and several books dealing with social stratification and middle class. Compared to the number of papers published on this subject my sample is then limited. The figure I concerning a unique data base reveals the huge number of articles published from 1979 to 2006, and containing the most common translation of "middle class", be as keyword or in the title of the article. However many articles aims only at making scientific works accessible to general or a specific public. It is obviously trendy to deal with the middle class and many works lack of originality and deep analysis. The chosen articles are the most representative and the most comprehensive of the dominant perceptions of the issue.

Table 1   Statistics of keywords and titles used by books and articles about middle class

Words / Years	Middle property class (Zhongchan Jieji)		Middle property stratum (Zhongchan Jiecen)		Middle stratum (Zhongjian Jiecen)	
	Keyword	title	Keyword	title	Keyword	title
1979	6	0	0	0	0	0
1980	1	1	3	1	4	1
1981	7	0	1	0	4	1
1982	5	0	1	0	2	1
1983	6	1	0	0	2	0
1984	7	0	0	0	1	1
1985	5	0	0	0	2	0
1986	8	2	0	0	4	0
1987	9	0	0	0	4	2
1988	5	1	2	1	5	1
1989	14	6	4	1	4	0
1990	19	10	1	0	1	0
1991	15	5	2	1	8	0
1992	11	3	3	0	6	2
1993	8	2	4	1	6	3
1994	21	6	7	2	12	3
1995	26	7	14	0	12	4
1996	14	6	6	0	13	2
1997	14	5	17	0	15	1
1998	27	3	8	3	13	3
1999	25	5	21	3	35	7
2000	28	20	50	11	48	6
2001	37	13	47	5	48	6
2002	53	20	50	11	48	6
2003	60	19	82	17	71	16
2004	62	37	111	20	92	20
2005	106	42	99	31	83	22
2006	248	44	119	27	73	18
Total	858	256	631	128	566	118

The sample respects the fact that the number of studies devoted to Chinese middle class have gradually increased over the years. Most of the materials is composed of articles and books published from 1998 to 2004.

Why has a middle class emerged in China?

There is a general agreement among Chinese researchers on the fact that a middle class

emerged in the 1990s. Until then, the Chinese society was considered as not having undergone a dramatic change. At the beginning of the 1990s, Deng Xiaoping, in giving a new impulse to reform policy, allowed economic development which has led to two different phenomena. The first one is the marketisation of economy: marketisation of goods, then of labour force, and finally of credit and finance which transforms hierarchy of income and status. Before the 1990s, workers and employees of public enterprises were still enjoying very good status in terms of income and social protection, and very close from the one of the first group of the contemporary China middle class, people who left their jobs to jump into the sea of private economy *(xiahai)* and people working in foreign companies. But, in the 1990s, everything changed: the class of workers and employees were on decline while new middle class has considerably increased its income and social position (Li Qiang 1999). In other terms, the fact that, according to Deng Xiaoping's words, it is allowed to become rich before the others *(xianfuqilai)* has caused discrepancies within the urban population (Tan Ying 2001, Liao and Tan 2005). The State does not exert anymore a total *(zongti)* control on society and particularly on economy (Huang Xianghuai, 2003). The consequence of the marketisation of the economy (Luo Biliang, 2002), the middle class is also the symbol of the modernisation of the society and of the increase in the level of education of Chinese people. The non-manual work, the brainwork *(naoli laodong)* replaces the manual work, giving birth to a new category of workers, white collars *(bailing)* people who have a high level of education but who do not belong to the elite (Qing Lianwu, 2001, Li Dezheng, 2001, RMRB, 16 January 2003, Lin Yuming, 2003, Lu Dan, 2004). In brief, the economic change has created a group of people "in the middle" between the elite and lower strata *(xiaceng)*. However, this new category has not popped out from nowhere. It emerges from the redeployment of a part of the old (socialist) middle class who takes advantage of their urban status (social capital and education capital) to monopolize new positions. As such, many papers develop ambiguous analysis on that point. The gap between reform and prereform policy, between "traditional" and modernizing society, does not appear so wide (Li Qiang 1999, Zhou and Zhao, 2003).

There is also a broad consensus on the normality and legitimacy of the phenomenon. In every country, economic development has produced a middle class which became the core, the subject (*zhuti*) of society (Xiao Wentao, 2001, Shen and Li, 2003, Zhao and Zhang, 2003, Zhang, Li and Gao, 2004). According to different researchers, in developed countries, the proportion of the middle class reach from 60% to 80% (Chen Xiaoya, 2002, Wen Jing 2003). China is far from this proportion, yet the emergence of a middle class is the sign that China is on the right path to development. In other words, if the middle class is a consequence of economic development it is also a condition to economic development. Economy, politics and society need a stabilising class. This is one of the biggest difference between China and Russia. In Russia the middle class has no firm "roots" (*wugenxing*). As a consequence, the economic growth is weak and the development of the society "winding" (*quzhe*) (Zhao and Zhao, 2003).

Most researchers devote a lot of energy to connect the appearance of middle class to official discourse. Apart from Deng Xiaoping' slogan (*xianfuqilai*), papers refer to Jiang Zemin's speech delivered on the 1 July 2001 for the anniversary of the foundation of the Party. In this speech, Jiang justifies the demands of middle class to see their income and status correctly appreciated: "leading officials should care for and trust people of talent and do their best to create good working conditions for these people. It is necessary to expedite the establishment of an income distribution mechanism which is designed to keep the talented and bring out the best in them so as to put in place a system which guarantees that their rewards are commensurate with their endeavors and contributions"[7]. The concept of *xiaokang* (small well-off) is often quoted as advocating the growth of middle class and the improvement of its status. In his 8 November's speech (16th Congress) called "Build a Well-off Society in an All-round Way and Create a New Situation in Building Socialism with Chinese Characteristics", Jiang clearly expresses the necessity to build up in 2020 a (small) well-off society in which the great majority of the population would enjoy middle range income (Lu Xiaowen, 2003, Yu Jianping, 2003, Zhang Xing, 2003). Less attention seems to be given to new leaders' speech but it is probably because there is not a need anymore to prove the correctness of the issue. Talking of the necessity of the development of a Chinese middle class has become a standard.

Besides, some researchers try to link the issue to the Marxist theory. Most recognise that Marx was wrong when he says that the middle class is completely waning the further capitalism advances. The petty bourgeoisie (old middle class) disappeared but a new

---

7 Translation from China.org.cn.

middle class has emerged. Capitalism needs consumers and then needs to integrate workers in the rank of middle range wage owners (Liang and Yu, 2003 Li Qiang, interview). However, they remark that Marx referred time to time to the growing importance of "intelligence" in the future development of capitalism and that, to a certain extent, he has predicted the importance of brainwork (Li Qiang, interview). Papers insist also on the fact that in China the old middle class is not replaced by the new one, the two growing hand by hand (Qing Lianwu, 2001, Guan Renting, 2003, Zhou and Zhao, 2003, Wen Jing, 2003). The phenomenon discredits marxist theory and modernisation theory since both consider old middle class as doomed to decline.

However, except in the end of 1990s, papers give more importance to new middle class than to old one in the meaning given it in Western countries. Although a part of the middle class is composed of uneducated people who have succeeded thanks to new opportunities provided by the marketisation (Li Dezheng, 2001), the future of the category is not depending on them. Economic development and social stability need the emergence of a well educated, modern, white collars class of people. As we will see below, the middle class has a political and social mission. To achieve this mission, China does not need people who are only able to make money (shopkeepers, small businessmen, etc.) but also people who have the ability to behave as conscious citizens. Two kinds of people seem to fit perfectly the profile. Firstly, technicians and managers working in foreign (Lu Xiaowen, 2003) and more specifically transnational companies (Bi and Zhu, 1999) and secondly the "intellectuals" (RMRB, 16 January 2003, Lu Xiaowen, 2003) people with very high level of education, the talented people (*rencai*). The two categories adding up partly.

Is the emergence and development of middle class a spontaneous phenomenon or are public

policies needed ? The answers are pretty blurred. On the one hand, the phenomenon seems to be unavoidable and then out of hands. On the other hand, nearly every piece insists on the necessity of adopting new regulations to alleviate obstacles. On this point, chronology plays a determinant role. At the beginning, studies tries to analyse the mechanisms of emergence and to explain what kind of advantage it can provide for Chinese society. Gradually, the legitimisation of the social fragmentation and the recognising of the importance of contributions of middle range wagers have led to more policy oriented arguments. "The three represents", "the xiaokang society", the "harmonious society",etc. clearly support the idea of the creation of a middle stratum of "small well-off" people. While the number of articles published by Party school's professors reveal the officialisation of the issue. Consequently, scholars' duty is now to give advices to reach this objective. In western countries, the phenomenon would be spontaneous. In China, obstacles would be so numerous and strong that public intervention are unavoidable.

Definition of the middle class

The definitions given by scholars are trapped in a tension between two tendencies. The first one aims at gathering a maximum of people under the label and then to limit criteria. In that case the income takes a dominant role since it is the only universal and objective criterion. The second tendency is to specify the different categories which are legitimate to belong to the class. Here, authors use multiple criteria: job, level of education but also lifestyles and moral values and then contribute to create a very limited image of the group. These two contradictory positions can be often found in the same paper.

According to an author the Chinese middle class is composed of people working in transnational firms (*kuaguo gongsi*) at medium and lower levels (Bi and Zhu, 1999). They have no property rights on means of production but they have control on them. However, other ways to enter the middle class exist. For example, middle strata employees on the monopolistic sector, that is to say what is remaining from the public sector in banking, energy, transport, etc. Their wages are 50% to 120% higher than average wage. Likewise, the bosses of private and countryside companies as well as doctors and lawyers can be considered as middle class members. Finally, in Shanghai, engineers (*gongchengshi*) technicians (*jishu renyuan*) and managers (*guanli renyuan*) have enough money to take part (Bi and Zhu, 1999). Others analysis defines similar groups: bosses of private enterprises, individual entrepreneurs, intellectuals, workers of monopolistic firms and employees of foreign companies (Li Dezheng 2001, Chen and Wang, 2003, Zhang Xing, 3003, Zhao and Zhang, 2003,). Zhou Xiaohong defines different groups belonging to middle class: 1)bosses of private and countryside enterprises (*siying qiyejia. xiangzhen qiyejia*) and middle class investors (6,22 millions in 2002), 2)small bosses, small traders and bosses of individual enterprises (*getihu*), their number reaching 47,42 million 3)people who have close relations with the Party and the government organs, that is to say officials and intellectuals, as well as leaders of SOEs, 4)white collars working in foreign firms such as high tech workers and managers (7,2 million), 5)managers of social organisations and enterprises, people with a MBA, MPA or law degree, 6)people having high technical level and working in the new economy, lawyers, architects, accounters, real estate and stock exchange agents, movie technicians, all of them having studied abroad (Zhou Xiaohong 2005). As we can see profession and education level is perceived as highly connected. Actually a lot of people insist on the fact that middle class success is mainly based on education (Zhou Xiaohang,

2005). For Lu Xieyi, middle class members have a "knowledge capital", they work with their brain and have expectations concerning job "qualities". They earn money from wages and have execution power in labour organisation (Lu Xueyi, 2002). For Zhu, the definition is simple: middle stratum members use their brain and are working as white collars (Zhu Guang, 1998). Middle class members are talented people (RMRB, 16 January 2003), brain workers and educated people (Huang Xianghuai, 2003, Sheng and Li, 2003). The age is a also a determinant element: the data reveals that 2030 years old group is the wealthiest group in China (Li Qiang 1999). Sometimes, the definition is based on economic sectors (monopolistic sectors, bosses of private and countryside enterprises and independant workers) the localities (coastal provinces and particularly Guangdong and Shanghai) (Xiao Wentao, 2003).

For another researcher, since we lack of quantitative data, we have to base analysis on qualitative criterion. The middle class is composed of people « who have middle range incomes, accumulated medium size properties (*caichan*), who have a middle range standard of living and who have modern behaviours and conceptions of life» They have opposite positions to wenbao (literally dress warmly and eat one's fill) stratum and to fuyou (rich) stratum. In terms of jobs, they are bosses, technicians, medium range officials, doctors, lawyers, etc. In cities, they have urbanised lifestyles, a big flat, money in bank, and a small proportion has a small car. They like concurrence, to plan actions, focus on rational decision making and efficiency, they have a clear conscience of citizenship and law based conceptions. They focus also on individuals' rights and freedom. They oppose to people who have subject (of rulers) conscience. The author talks also of white collars and includes officials but finally he considers that we can not put all these categories under the same hat (Ma Deyong, 1999).

In that discussion, we can oppose, to a certain extent, the definition advocated by Lu Xueyi based on a collection of social ressources: job, education, lifestyle (Lu Xueyi, 2002, Gong Weibin, 2003, Chen and Wang, 2003, Qi and Wei 2003) and the conceptions of people like Ma Deyong (1995) or Li Qiang who are mainly focusing on income and properties. An example can be found in Xu Sihe's paper according to whom the criterion of income is first and foremost considered as determinant (Xu Sihe, 2001). Concerning the first approach we can quote a very complex definition using seven criteria: job status, work conditions, employment capacity, employment rights, income and properties, mode of consuming and lifestyle and influence on society (Zhang, Li and Gao, 2004). The problem is that articles give very few insights on the ways to define and to use lifestyle, influence on society, conscience of rights and citizenship, moral values as distinctive criteria. On that matter, we have very few data, if any, to give grounds to statements on the specificities of the so-called Chinese middle class.

Difficulties exist also in the second approach. The income or properties based classifications are largely arbitrary and have to move regarding the change in standards of living according to time and places (Li Chunling, 2003). Moreover, the type of consumption evolves from time to time and very quickly in contemporary China. To buy a car was not a criterion of belonging to the middle class in 1999 (Ma Deyong, 1999). Nowadays, it has become a distinctive element (Liu Huihao, 2004).

Nonetheless, the general impression given by all these papers is that Chinese middle class is a collection of groups having very few in common. Differences between old and new middle class (Li Qiang 1999, Yang Suyun, 2003, Xu Yong, 2003), between officials and bosses of private enterprises, between intellectuals (researchers and professors of university) and individual entrepreneurs, between independent workers and technicians working in foreign firms are so great that it is difficult to put them all in a unique category. And the differences certainly increase when we are using moral values, lifestyle or modes of consumption as determinant elements of classification. A survey made by researchers from the department of sociology of CASS reveals that the classification changes greatly according to criteria. The occupation based classification leads to call middle class members people who would have not been included if income based or life style based approached were used (Li Chunling, 2003). When Li Qiang advocates that splitting tendencies (*fenlie*) are stronger than uniting tendencies (*tongyi*), we cannot but agree (Li Qiang, 2005 and interview).

Under such a context it is not surprising to see the lack of interest for taxinomy. The researchers use a wide range of expression to talk about middle class, but very few attempts are made to clarify their contents. The problem is easily solved in remarking that in English, class and stratum have now very close meanings. Much attention are paid to the focus on the core middle class, the category which is supposed to represent the very nature of the class : intellectuals, employees of foreign countries, white collars. It is of course depending on the nature of functions attributed to the category.

Functions

On this point the consensus is nearly complete. Since the end of the 1990s, the new middle class is an ideal class perfectly matching modernity and economic development. Moreover, the expanding of middle range wageowners will generate an olive shape society (Zheng Guoxia, 1998, *Renmin Ribao*, 27 October 2004) which guarantees political stability and happiness for the great majority of the society.

In 1998, an article describes the category as searching for stability and dreading disorder (*qiuwen paluan*), doing one's best to go up (*liqiu shangjin*), supporting the poor and helping the needies (*fupin jiukun*), stimulating the process of democratisation (*tuijin minzhuhua jincheng*) (Zheng Guoxia, 1998). Afterwards, the characteristics have been more precisely designed. Firstly, the middle class stimulates economic development (Chen Xiaoya, 2002, Xiao Wentao, 2001, Guan Renting, 2003, Wen Jing, 2003, Chen Xiong, 2004, Liu Huihao, 2004). They have money, less than rich people, but they are much more numerous and much more keen on spending money on domestic goods than the upper class. They buy flats and cars and the extension of leisure time makes them open to new activities and spendings. The growth of financial and stock markets depends on this type of consumers. They have a rational way of consuming and banks do not hesitate to lend them money and to give them access to credit cards. In other terms not only do they personify the appearance of hedonism in China but they also introduce a reasonable approach of consumerism. As such, their attitude to consumption is considered as "modern" and should play a role as model for other classes (Kang Xiaoguang, 2002). Secondly as a new class they can easily cope with change. They have a high degree of ability to adapt themselves to new situations (Ma Deyong, 19994, 19999). Thirdly, face to social conflicts or political problems, they defend a "conservative and moderate ideology" (*wenhede, baoshoude yishi xingtai*), they support social stability (*shehui wending*), they try to find rational solutions and they do not like extreme solutions (*jiduan*) (for example Ma Deyong, 19994, Li Dezheng, 2001, Xiao Wentao, 2001, Wen Jing, 2003, Chen Xiong, 2004). Fourthly, they have very strict and positive moral values and set of behaviors. They display modern set of values. They rely on education and work to succeed and refuse to use political connections or illegal tricks. They are polite and have civilised manners (*wenming*) (Li Dezheng, 2001, Xiao Wentao, 2001, Guan Renting, 2003, Chen Xiong, 2004). They do not steal money from the pockets of the poor and they are not as greedy as the rich are. Fifthly, they advocate pluralism and democracy because they are rational and wants to defend their rights. As we have already seen they have a citizenship conscience (Ma Deyong, 1999-4, Zhang Xing, 2004). Lastly, some researchers emphasis on more precise elements. Middle class people are supposed to focus less on structure oriented social relations and more on network oriented one, paying contribution to Castells' theory. More specifically the people working in foreign firms represent the bridge between Western and Chinese cultures, and allow this one to assimilate external influence (Li Dezheng, 2001).

In brief, the Chinese middle class has four functions. First of all they have to strive economic growth. Not only is it the main consuming group but the goods they consume are high valueadded ones. As such it is playing a strategic role. A growing number of scholars advocate the development of a domestic market so as to avoid the Chinese economy to be too dependent on the international economy. Without an important middle class they have no chance to see this goal achieved. Middle class members have also a great role to play in the struggle against the way China is polarised between rich and poor (*liangjihua*). Every paper mentions the fact that the gap between poor and rich has dramatically widened. A big middle class would integrate ascending categories (part of workers and migrants) and descending categories. That would be the main instrument of social mobility and then of political stability. The contesting groups which so far has been unable to climb in the social ladder would now find a channel of satisfaction for their demands and would avoid to resort to violent means of expression. The middle class is an airlock between tradition and modernity. In becoming middle class members, "workers" (urban and migrant) would have less reasons to contest and would adopt negotiation and rationality based ways of protest. Middle class cushion (*huanchong*) social conflicts.

Moreover, as a group whose success is only due to effort, education, and talent, middle class proves the fact that it is possible to be rich (reasonably) in remaining honest. It is then the class of the reconciliation between money and moral values. No need of privilege (tequan) to reach small well-off. Using Bourdieu's analysis, Zhou's book emphasises the importance of "distinction" in middle stratum behaviours. Middle stratum members would have a tendency to work more than other groups, to strive continuously to climb the social and professional ladders. They have more social relations, they read more than lower strata members (Zhou Xiaohong, 2005). They have resources (*ziyuan*) and capacities (*nengli*). More important, in Zhou's book it is given an ideal picture of middle stratum. The success of its members would only be based on their effort, on accumulation of education capital and not on "relations" or corruption. As such, the emergence and the growing of middle stratum appears as fully legitimate: "the success of the middle stratum and its change of its social position is able to constitute an example for common people, not only because the means they used are rational and then cannot create a feeling of injustice but also because everybody can see that this success is based on education"(Zhou Xiaohong, 2005). This statement opposes the common views which considers that success is the simple result of relations and corruption.

Finally, the middle class is the class of the democratisation. Because they want to defend their rights, the members of the middle class are supposed to be democrats. But reasonable democrats. Not only because they are rational and moderate by nature but because they benefit a lot from the reform policy. They have revolutionary spirit (*gemingxing*) in political matters but with Reason (*lixing*). They do not want to make trouble but just make the society more open, more democratic, more pluralistic in civilising political mores (Guan Renting, Sun Chang, 2004, Liu Huihao, 2004, Liao and Tan, 2005). These statements are indirect criticisms both of supposed lack of interest of lower classes in politics and exclusively moneyoriented behaviours of the new rich (Zhou Xiaohong, 2005). Sometimes, the criticisms are direct: the middle class is a democratic and legal bastion against both the revolutionary and violent tendencies prevailing in lower strata and the privilege and arbitrary run political system dominated by upper classes. The middle stratum can play a go-between role. Its members "can not be dominated by another group and they can not dominate freely other groups" (Zhang Wei, 2005). In other terms they possess a quite important degree of autonomy; an autonomy that we can see in lifestyle and as well in work attitudes.

In describing middle class, Chinese scholars are designing an ideal society. Nearly every piece of article opposes two shapes of society, the olive (ganlanxing) or rugby ball (*ganlanqiu*) one and the pyramid one and every piece of paper voices the first one as the most desirable. At the same time, scholars build up an ideal "people": consuming but in planned manner, changing the society but trying to solve contradictions through rational means, successful but honest. However, the problem is that except concerning consumption, very little is provided to justify the existence of this "people". It is obvious that economic development needs middle range wage-owners to absorb mass production goods. But on the other points, the rare surveys tend to show more discrepancies than identities between the different groups. Actually, all the argumentation is based on the commonplaces developed by the American creators of the concept of middle class who were viewing it as the perfect class. But, nobody seems to be keen on having more critical approach of the notion. Consequently, we have neither empirical date nor theoretical framework which could justify the existence of the ideal people and of the nature of the historical duty of the Chinese middle class.

Examples of involvement in social movements are very few. Zhang talks of homeowners protest movements, and he seems to consider that these movements which protest against infringements to their rights are a good example of political modernisation[8]. These people are supposed not defend an ideology but their interests and rights, they try to get the support of the media and of governments leaders. They behave rationally. In that

---

8   The fact is that 45,2% of urban dwellers have bought their flat, (Zhang Wei, 2005).

case, protest movements evolve from "reaction" to autonomy, from ideological claims to "modern political concept" (i.e. interest-based), from unique-type of protest to several types protest, from mass participation to interest group participation (Zhang Wei, 2005). However, this analysis is at stake with the social origin of middle stratum members that everybody recognises. How could a stratum, which is a result of the reform policy handled by the regime, and also the main winner of the new game be able to question this regime? Most of these people succeeded because of their connections with political field as a whole. Goodman has shown that in Jiangxi most of "The new Middle Class" is largely connected with power-holders (Li Lulu, 1998, Goodman, 1999, Li and Niu, 2003). Lu Chunling explains that political cadres and intellectuals who have improved their position are those who had the ability to transform political resources in economic resources (Lu Chunling, 2003). Others papers insist on the fact that a large portion od the middle class is composed of people coming from the "core of power" (*quanli zhongxin*) with whom they have affinities (*qinheli*) (Xiao Wentao, 2001, Liu Guofeng, 2002). Therefore there is a contradiction between the economic dynamism of the middle stratum members which enables them to climb the social ladder and political conservatism which follows from the fact that their success is largely due to political connections. Besides, we have also to take into account that once having entered the ranks of middle class, there is no reason they should keep the door open for other people. Through the interviews of high level white collars university graduates working in foreign and in/or high tech firms) what emerges is an image of people less interested in struggling for a legal system protecting the whole society (Huang Xianghua, 2003) than in using laws and regulations to protect their own interests. Under such a context it is then difficult to make a difference between the elite who, according to most scholars, have monopolised all position of prestige (economic, social, cultural) and the middle class who could be considered, to a certain extent, to "small monopolisers".

To get out from this contradiction, researchers try to distinguish vanguard groups from the mainstream of middle stratum. The first distinction to be made is between old middle stratum (*lao zhongjian jieceng*) and new middle stratum (*xin zhongjian jieceng*). The former is the result of industrialisation and is considered as quite conservative and routineminded. The latter, a byproduct of postindustrialisation, is defined as more openminded and politically active. A parallel distinction is proposed by Zhou' book between the rearguard middle stratum (*zhongjian jieceng houwei*), characterised by a high degree of connection with political apparatus (for example SOEs leaders) and vanguard middle stratum (*zhongjian jieceng qianwei*), composed by high professionals, etc.) who would show more independence. Finally it is also possible to distinguish between people "within the system" and people "outside the system", the latter having entered the middle stratum thanks to the "market". In the different cases, what is viewed at stake is the ability of the groups to accumulate wealth, legitimacy and power outside political apparatus.

Statistical evaluations

Two positions dominate the controversies. Some scholars consider that China is already a middle class society or that it will become one in the very near future, most focus on its weak number and on the fact that without public policies in favour of middle class, the olive shape society would remain a dream. Generally speaking, scholars are less and less optimistic about the dimension of the group.

Referring to the National Bureau of Statistics the great majority of the Chinese population belongs to the middle class in terms of income and property (Zheng Guoxia, 1998). According to Chinese Academy of Social Sciences, the group has represented 15% of the total population in 1999, 19% in 2003 (48,5% of urban population) and will reach 40% in 2020 Xinhuanet, (26 March 2004). Xiao Wentao considers that 2025% of the families earn from 10,000 to 100,000 yuan a year and whose property is worth between 30,000 and 100,000 yuan (Xiao Wentao, 2001). In Shanghai, 71% of the population would have reached the level of small well-off (Chen Xiaoya, 2002, RMRB, 16 January 2003). 48,5% of the urban population would have middle range properties in 2002 (Luo Biliang, 2002). According to an official from Shenzhen, 200 millions are to enter middle class rank from 2002 to 2008 (Huang Xianghuai, 2003). According to a survey even in Hefei a quite undeveloped big city, one tier of the population has a middle class profession Chen and Wang, 2003). According to the National Bureau of Statistics which did a survey concerning 300,000 persons, the middle stratum represents 5% of the total population but the figure will reach 45% in 2020 (*China Daily*, 20th January 2005). A newspaper states that from 2001 on 200 million people will enter middle class within 5 years (*Xinxi shibao*, 21 July 2001).

Yet, most evaluations are far less optimistic. An author refuses to talk of Chinese middle class since no required criterion has been fulfilled in China. A middle class society needs an urbanization rate of 70%, a number of white collars superior to the one of blue collars, a low level of discrepancies between the poor and the rich and an average of 12 years education (Ma and Huang, 2004). The people who own a flat and have an income between 30,000 to 50,000 were 18% of the population at the beginning of the century and will count for 35% in 2020 et 50% in 2050 (Shen Liren, 2004). 18% of the Chinese families have an average annual income comprised between 8,000 and 10,000 Ma and Huang, 2004. Lu Xieyi estimates the real figure at 80 million people for the beginning of the 21st century (Lu Xueyi, 2002). In the province of Jilin, the middle class represents 10% of the population and will count for 25% in 2010. In 2004, only between 78 million and 95 million of people have an average annual income between 25,000 and 125,000 (Liu Huihao, 2004). According to a professor of the Party school of Hubei, the lower strata represents 80% of the entire population (Guan Renting, 2003). Lin Yuming estimates the proportion of middle class as 18% (Lin Yuming, 2003).

Obviously, the determinant factor which can explain the discrepancies concerns the criteria used. As life style, moral values, etc. that is to say where subjective criterion cannot be used, evaluations are based on income and more marginally professions. Actually, the essential question concerns the income thresholds of the stratum. Down threshold but also upper threshold: from 10,000 to 100,000 yuan (Xiao Wentao, 2001), 60,000 to 500,000 yuan per household (*China Daily*, 20th January 2005), more than 5,000 yuan per month (*Zhongguo qingnian bao*, 2 september 2005)? And how to use a threshold for the entire country whereas the difference in standard of living are so huge from place to place?

Once again the survey of the department of CASS presented by Li Chunling is particularly fruitful for shedding light to difficulties met by scholars. According to the survey, if one takes into account all criterion; type of profession, income, consumption, lifestyle, etc. the number of middle class numbers represent only 4,1% of the total 16 to 70 years old population and 2,8% of the entire population, then something like 40 million people. Actually the difference between figures roughly from 40 million to 300 million-depends not only on the level of the criteria but also on the way categories are added together or not. For example, half of white collars have middle class income and half of middle class income owners are middle class consumers (Li Chunling, 2003).

In search of policies

Most papers consider that although the emergence of the middle class is spontaneous, further developments need political intervention through laws, regulations and policies. Explicitly (Ma Deyong, 1999-9) or implicitly, China is facing a choice between different sorts of society. To go back to equalitarism (*pingjunzhuyi*)? A system that very few Chinese are willing to support. A two classes the rich and the poor-system which could lead to disorder and violence ? A middle class society whose structures can guarantee development and stability?

What kind of public policies does China need to build up this ideal society. Here also a few positions coexist which can be roughly gathered into two camps. The first one focuses on the blossoming of the middle class upper strata: bosses of private enterprises, employees of foreign firms, white collars, ?intellectuals ? etc. The second camp emphasizes on the necessity to integrate portions of urban and migrant workers. In that case, the notions of justice, opportunities equality, redistribution, etc takes a dominant role. Under such a context, the most striking is that the same policy or the same instrument (laws and regulations for example) is supposed to reach completely opposed objectives depending of scholars' political position. That tends to prove the role of politics in the debate.

Everybody considers or supposes the pursuit of economic development is the main prerequisite (Xiao Wentao 2002, Shen Liren, 2004). When the fact is not mentioned it appears implicitly in the analysis. According to some papers, the expanding of services sector (Zhang Xing, 2004), then the decrease in the number of blue collars (*lanling*) (Ma and Huang, 2004) and the flourishing of innovation (*chuanxin*) (Chen Xiong, 2004) is a determinant element. In the same way, the improvement of education (Xiao Wentao, 2002, Chen Xiong, 2004) is emphasized but very important differences. Sometimes, the education in countryside (Zhou and Zhao, 2003) and the vulgarisation of knowledge (Wen Jing, 2003) is viewed as the keypoint. Sometimes the stress is put on university education (Zhang Xing, 2003, Yin and Song, 2004, Zhang Xing, 2004). Another quite consensual point concerns the urbanisation, everybody considering that the process is too slow. (Yin and Song, 2004, Zhang Xing, 2004 and 2003). No real middle class society without 70% of urban population. China would be at 30% (Mao and Huang, 2004).

For many scholars, the main point lays on the necessity to guarantee economic and social concurrence, but here also with significant discrepancies. We should develop marketisation to avoid the monopolisation of economy by people who use political connections to do business (Zheng Guoxia, 1998, Zhou and Zhao, 2003, Qi and Xiao, 2003, Wen Jing, 2003). China must eliminate barriers which impede new forces to enter the market (Zhang Xing, 2004). Corruption and use of illegal means are sometimes clearly mentioned (Mao and Huang, 2004). Therefore, the most market is not perceived as spontaneously functioning, even by the most marketoriented people. It needs state intervention and public policies struggling against "capital" (*ziben*) and "power" (*quanli*) (Gong Weibin, 2003). On this point, the modernisation theory is explicitly challenged. The opposition between "state" (or "political system") and market have no sense. It is impossible to imagine a stratum whose autonomy is based on "market" since the "market" has become a core element of the strategy of the Chinese leaders (Mengin and Rocca).

In a quite different manner, the monopolisation is politically addressed: we must "avoid some interest groups to penetrate and to control the political realm, and to become a force of opposition to China political democratization" (*bimian zhexie liyijituan shentou bing kongzhi zhenzhi lingyu, chengwei zhongguo zhengzhi minzhuhua de fandui liliang*). Democratisation must be reasonable and needs control though non violent.

Other scholars (and sometimes the same ones) focus on justice and redistribution. Fiscal reform is needed in order to change the present situation in which high income owners pay little or no taxes whereas poor people or peasants pay a lot (Zheng Guoxia, 1998, Xiao Wentao, 2001, Zhang Xing, 2003). It is not a question of equality but a question of justice (*gongping*) (Shen Liren, 2004) to allow the middle class to grow from the bottom and to limit the privileges of wealthy people. Taxation of high wages should be raised (Ma and Huang 2004). Similarly, many scholars stress on social protection. It is also a question of justice (Xiao Wentao, 2001, Liu Guofeng, 2002). Only the wealthy people have the ability to protect themselves. It is necessary to help and to protect needy groups (*kunan qunti*), including migrants (Gong Weibin, 2003, Qi and Xiao, 2003), Wen Jing, 2003) to include some of them in the middle class. One article advices to make workers shareholder of their company to increase their income (Gong Weibin, 2003). Peasants' incomes should be raised, and according to professors from a Party school the peasants must be organised to improve their fate (Yin and Song, 2004).

The role of laws and regulations must be raised but who must enjoy rights and which kind of rights? Some authors view property rights as an essential mean to assure the position of bosses of private entreprises (Zhou and Zhao, 2003) others to protect peasants' rights (Gong Weibin, 2003). Lastly, the marketisation of labour market is largely emphasised (Guan Renting, 2003, Shen Liren, 2004, Yin and Song, 2004). The objective is to make the market more flexible ((Gong Weibin, 2003), to put migrants in an equal position with urban workers (Zhou and Zhao, 2003) and to increase their income.

Conclusion

Social classes are entities which should not be seen from a supposed objective point of view but through the analysis of the social process of their construction. Objective facts do not exist per se but thanks to their *mise-en scène*. This *mise-en scène* is not less real than the reality as it determines behaviours and representations. Concerning the middle class, everything taking place on the stage has a political impact since it is generally perceived as the result of modernisation and the driving force of the modernisation.

In the Chinese case, the discourses and the controversies about the nature of the middle class reveal the same kind of feature. But since the Chinese political scene is not characterised by the existence of a democratic (but conflictual) process of representation of interests, the forms and the contents of definition of the middle class cannot but be the same than as in democratic countries. That does not mean that the issue is neither pluralism nor politics in China. The pluralism exists and scholars express positions and representations of social groups (Rocca, 2006). But the channels of expression are not institutionalised through a downtop process but through a topdown process. Some people are entitled to represent the opinions of a group (urban workers, needy people, peasants, migrant workers, middle class) but without any designation process. Often, the representative is not even belonging to the group. But the pluralism of expression is a reality. Similarly, the issue of the middle class is highly political. China is facing a challenge: to solve what Robert Castel calls a "social question", the existence of groups of people society is unable to integrate. From this starting point, scholars elaborate social imaginaries a "good society" and then to define a "good class" to convince power-holders to adopt new political guidelines. Notions of justice, of equality, of rules, etc. are deeply reassessed.

Controversies and arguments are largely maintained within the circles of the political and academic elite. Discourses must respect the dogma. However, scholars criticise marxist theories and the official discourse is used and manipulated to advocate arguments and opinions.

Apart from the consensus concerning the origin and the positive effect of the middle class, there are alot of differences between analyses. What is the emblematic group of the middle class? Is its most important function: to integrate lower strata or to extend the number of brainworkers? Must the state protect migrant workers or bosses of private enterprises?

References

Bai Yang, "Shehui fenceng lilun yu zhongguo chengshi de lei zhongjian jieceng", *Dongfang luntan*, 2002-3, pp. 47~52.

Bi Qiuzhu, Zhu Gehui, "Kuaguogongsi yu zhongguozhongchanjieceng de xingcheng yu fazhan", *Guanli shijie*, 4-1999, pp. 171~175.

Boltanski, Luc, *Les cadres. La formation d'un groupe social*, Paris, Les éditions de minuit, 1982.

Bourdieu, Pierre, "Structures sociales et structures de perception du monde social", *Actes de la Recherche en sciences sociales*, (2), mars 1975.

Bourdieu, Pierre, *La distinction.Critique sociale du jugement*, Paris, Les Editions de Minuit, 1979.

Castel, Robert, *From Manual Workers to Wage Laborers: Transformations of the Social Question*, Transaction Publishers, 2002.

Chen Shiyong, Wang Huabin, "Hefeishi zhongjian jieceng xianzhuang fenxin", *Anhui nongye daxue Xuebao (shehui kexue ban)*, Vol. 12, n.3, May 2003, pp. 91~94.

Chen Xiaoya, "'zhongchanjieceng' yunyu er sheng", *Jinri zhongguo*, 2002-2, pp. 40~41.

Du Jiangnan, "Jinqi zhongchan jieceng we,ti yanjiuguandian zongshu", *Dang zheng ganbu xuekan*, 2004-2, pp. 23 and 26.

Chen Xiong, "Kuoda zhongchan jieceng ying chengwei jianshe quanmian xiaokang shehui de zhongyao zhengce quxiang", *Guihai luntan*, 2004, 20 (4), août 2004, pp. 57.

China Daily, 20th January 2005.

Gong Weibin, "Tiaozheng shehui zhengce, peiyu zhongjian jieceng", *Zhonggong fujia weidangxiao xuebao*, 2003, n. 4, (10 February 2003), pp. 59.

Goodman, David, "The New Middle Class", in Merle Goldman and Roderick Mac Farquahr (ed.), *The Paradox of China's Post-Mao Reforms*, London, Harvard University Press, 1999.

Guan renting, "Zhongjian yu shehui wending", *Hubeisheng shehuizhuyi xueyuan xuebao*, 2003-4, pp.33~35.

Chapter 3

Globalization, Social Transformation and Construction of the Chinese Middle Classes

Zhou Xiaohong and Qin Chen[*]

Globalization and social transformation are two basic issues in the discussion about emergence and growth of the Chinese middle classes. The two issues are interwoven firstly because they both denote social transition that took place after the 1980s. Globalization signifies a synchronic social transition in which transnational and cross-regional flow of capital, technology, commodity, service and labor either spreads or popularizes throughout the world production modes, life styles and cultural representations from the US and other Western capitalist countries. Social transformation, as a diachronic transition, was initiated by market transition and has thereafter ushered in great changes in various aspects of the Chinese society. Social transformation may be regarded as the fruit of globalization, or rather, it is the social transformation in China and former socialist countries of Eastern Europe and Soviet Union that has paved the way for "globalization" in the real sense. Further, as far as the topic in discussion is concerned, the social transformation, more than anything else, has contributed to changes of class relations and social structure within a socialist country like China; these domestic changes are also inevitably being influenced by global variations in industrial structure, vocational structure, labor market and consumer goods market. In this sense, the emergence and growth of the Chinese middle classes, as the result of changes in class relations and social structure, cannot be comprehensively and accurately interpreted unless against the background of globalization and social transformation.

Globalization: How Have the Middle Classes Become a Topic of International Discussion?

Ever since the Industrial Revolution and the French Revolution, the middle classes in

---

*   Zhou Xiaohong, Ph.D., Dean of School of Social and Behavioral Sciences, Nanjing University(xhzhou@nju.edu.cn); Qin Chen, Lecture of the School of Humanities, Hehai University(joyqinchen@gmail.com).

modern sense have been existing for centuries. [9] Nevertheless, it had never been a topic of global importance until the 1970s and 1980s. Besides, the early middle classes were confined in the US and traditional capitalist countries in Europe; even in these countries, the middle classes were not a mainstream social being. Take France in the 18th century for instance. As is widely known, early form of the French middle classes stemmed from the Third Estate, which played an active role in the 1789 French Revolution. Compared with the so called "First Estate" (the Clergy) and "Second Estate" (the aristocracy), the Third Estate, which constituted 97% of French population, was an immense group of people. However, only 10~15% of it was made up of the "middle classes" in the accurate sense, or what the French meant by "petty bourgeoisie", which included small farmers, small entrepreneurs, small shop owners as well as a small number of government employees and professionals such as writers, doctors and scholars. It is such a social structure that has made insightful Karl Marx, who actually has been the first author to use the concept "middle classes" in its modern sense, divide Western society into two rival groups, namely the proletariat and the bourgeoisie—despite that he admits existence of the middle classes (Marx & Engels, 1972: 250).

The growth of middle classes has been promoted by two major factors. One is the transformation of Western capitalist societies from the industrial to the post-industrial; the other is the spread of Western-style industrialization throughout the world, termed as globalization.

The first transition has not only enlarged the scale of middle classes in Western developed countries but also changed its components: small farmers, small entrepreneurs and small business owners, termed as the "old middle class" by American sociologist C. Wright Mills, gradually gave way to the "new middle class", those engaged in mental work for big businesses or government organizations (Mills, 1951: 63~65). The new middle class drew attention firstly in German at the beginning of the 20th century, when industrialization progressed rapidly. Social Democrat Eduard Bernstein, citing Gustav Schmoller, adopts the concept of "new middle class" to designate salary earners such as civil servants, technical employees, managers, office workers and salespeople. Bernstein also modifies Marxian theory of class polarization and argues that, in modern capitalist societies, petty bourgeoisie, or the middle class, is not a diminishing class, but "one whose number is increasing both relatively and absolutely" (Bernstein, 1961:48). This

---

9   According to American historian John Smail, the middle classes and their culture originated in the 18th century, shortly after the beginning of the Industrial Revolution (Smail, 1994:12).

somewhat bold assumption soon becomes a new theme in writings on the middle classes by Mills and other authors. Later, in the post-industrial wave proposed by Daniel Bell, the assumption turns into reality (Bell, 1999:17).

Compared with the first transition, the second one is obviously of more importance to birth and growth of the middle classes out of Western developed countries. Although the Four Asian Tigers, Mainland China, India, former Soviet Union and socialist countries in Eastern Europe differ from one another in driving forces and progress phases of economic boom as well as in development degree of capital and market, changes they witnessed in the last few decades of the 20th century were more or less the aftermath of ever-stronger power of economic globalization. Further, the reshaping of class formation and birth of the middle classes within these countries and regions have also been linked with world-wide spread of Western capitalism.

Inevitably, growth of the middle classes has been influenced by globalization; yet these influences may have varied implications for different countries and regions. Globalization has shaped development of the middle classes in the following ways: it has directly caused changes in world industrial structure and corresponding vocational structure; moreover, global economic activities have resulted in a global labor market, which in turn has reshaped income distribution throughout the world; it has also ushered in a global consumer goods market and relevant consumption and life styles (Zhou [Xiao-hong], 2007). It would be pointless to discuss in general whether the influences of globalization are positive or negative, for any such influence is virtually a double-edged sword to every nation and the growth of its middle classes. For example, due to globalization, the Four Asian Tigers, and later Mainland China and India, have witnessed radical development of low-tech manufacturing industries in past few decades. In this process, losses such as over-consumption of energy, ecologic disturbance and social disorganization have paralleled gains such as employment and income increase enjoyed by more members of the populace, thanks to the realization of preliminary industrialization. The double-edged sword proposition can also find evidence in the US and European capitalist countries. Globalization has enabled their radical exploitation of resources, environment and labor force of developing countries, hence their accelerating accumulation of wealth. [10]Moreover, they are not only dumping surplus products to developing countries but also instilling their

---

10 According to UNDP (United Nations Development Program) statistics, annual per capita income gap between developed countries and developing countries increased from $5,700 of 1960 to $15,000 of 1993, more than tripled in over three decades (UNDP, 1996: 2~3).

own values and ideologies—termed by Joseph Nye as "soft power" (Nye, 1990)— to the latter. Meanwhile, developed countries are paying price for what they have gained. For instance, in spite of easy and quick money made by technological elites like Bill Gates, the middle class people in many developed countries, faced with competition and challenge presented by migrant labor market, are undergoing unprecedented shock against their living conditions. Although their average annual work time in the last two decades of the 20th century increased by over 10%, from 3,020 hours of year 1979 to 3,335 hours of 1997, their average annual income increased barely by 1% (Hutton & Giddens, 2003:140). In addition, things keep deteriorating for the middle classes in developed countries because of the financial crisis that is presently sweeping the whole world.

The Chinese Road: Power of Social Transformation

Based on European and American history, the middle classes have been a fruit of industrialization. Firstly, because the Industrial Revolution initiated in the 18th century dismantled feudal guilds in the city and manor economy in the countryside, the emergence of large-scale modern industries was accompanied by the establishment of market-centered capitalist system. Secondly, the Industrial Revolution also triggered the process of urbanization. Densely-populated cities boasted free, unrestrained economic life and complex, pluralistic social network; city residents enjoyed an abundance of modern public spaces such as banks, offices, hotels, clubs, cinemas, museums, restaurants, cafes, luxury apartments, conference centers, plazas, horse-racetracks and churches. City life largely contributed to formation of the civil society, which was of critical importance to growth of the middle classes (Taylor, 1999). Thirdly, the Industrial Revolution, and the preceding technological revolution, made it possible for the average family to accumulate economic and cultural capital. After the 1930s, especially after World War II, with increase in the number of salary earners, also known as the "new middle class", an "olive-shaped" social structure soon appeared in the Western world.

At present, growth of the middle classes is being unfolded against the background of globalization. However, Chinese stories typically follow their own logic.

In Mainland China, large-scale industrialization was not initiated until after 1949. To be exact, it was initiated by implementation of the first Five Year Plan (1953~1957) of national economic development. From 1949 to 1978, the year marked by the beginning of Reform and Opening-Up, in spite of many trials and tribulations, the three decades saw China's worldly-recognized achievements in industrialization, with average annual growth amounting to 6.1%. Through ups and downs, by the time Mao Ze-dong passed away, a fairly comprehensive industrial system had been virtually established in Mainland China. Nevertheless, industrialization development during the three decades did not have a considerable bearing on the reshaping of Chinese class structure, let alone give birth to the middle classes.

Unlike its counterparts in the West, China's industrialization process from 1949 to 1978 failed to mould middle classes because China was following a unique political and economic way. From the political perspective, social stratification and class structure in Maoist China had always been affecting by two seemingly contradictory policies: (1) After overthrowing rule by former landlords and bourgeoisie, a "symbolic" exploitation class was created confronting peasants and workers. This symbolic class had been maintained for as long as three decades in Mainland China firstly in order to support Mao's assumption of "long-term existence of classes and class struggle" with reality evidence and secondly in order to endow the Chinese people with a psychological comfort of "being boss". Under guidance of the "class struggle" ideology, not only suppressed landlords and bureaucrat-comprador bourgeoisie were regarded as rival classes, but also all classes other than workers and peasants were excluded. So far as the theme in discussion is concerned, old middle classes, labeled either as "national bourgeoisie" or as "petty bourgeoisie", had always been the object of socialist rehabilitation of industries, businesses, and thoughts. Meanwhile, intellectuals and professionals were also grouped as "petty bourgeoisie". With their grey identities, throughout the three decades, they had been the main target of varied thought rehabilitations, also known as *xizao*[11](Yang, 2004). Under such situation, further class differentiation was checked not only politically, but also culturally and psychologically. (2) Within the circle of so-called "people" (*renmin*), egalitarian distribution policies were implemented, which led to a radical destratification structure after 1966. According to research on these egalitarian policies by William L. Parish, in the 1960s, even among socialist countries, China was the most egalitarian one. High-income people earned only 2.2 to 2.3 times what's earned by those with low income, and China boasted a Gini coefficient as low as 0.20 to 0.21. Such an egalitarian and destratified social structure was built on varied economic and political cornerstones: an egalitarian salary system,[12] measures to bridge salary gaps,[13] abolishment of military ranking

---

11 In Yang Jiang's book, *xizao* literally means "body washing" in Chinese. However, it is actually a figurative expression of "brainwashing". English translation of the book is entitled *"Baptism"*, though.

12 Even this virtually egalitarian wage system was condemned and challenged during the Cultural Revolution. For instance, in 1975, one year before Mao's death, he attacked so-called "eight-level wages" implemented among workers, calling it "bourgeois concept of the right".

13 Together with others, Mao himself also contributed to bridging salary gaps. For instance, when the "salary system" (*xinjinzhi*) was put into effect in 1956, Mao degraded his own salary from level I to level II, remarking sentimentally, "level I should be granted to the people; me, level II."

system (which had been effective for no more than one decade in the Maoist era), allotment of everyday consumer goods and housing distribution system, to name only a few of them. During the Cultural Revolution, piecework wage system and bonus system were condemned and later invalidated. After 1966, the year when the Cultural Revolution broke out, a series of extreme policies further dragged the moderately egalitarian social structure of earlier years to the prevailingly egalitarian structure of the Cultural Revolution decade. In the situation of destratification, personal efforts, such as the raise of educational level (which, in the West, is the principal means of becoming a member of the middle classes), typically degraded one's vocational status instead of improving it (Parish, 1984).

Looking from the economic perspective, there had also been different reasons why Chinese society failed to produce middle classes that could have been proportionate to its industrialization process. In particular, affected by the economic pattern of former Soviet Union, China's industrialization had been preconditioned by the priority of heavy industries (including military industry). Therefore, the development of light industries and service industries, which are highly relevant with daily consumption, lagged far behind Chinese people's need for the improvement of life quality. According to statistics, in GDP of year 1950, percentages of the three sectors of economy were respectively 29, 29 and 42; in 1980 GDP they were 12.6, 57.8 and 20.6. Meanwhile, in 1980, other developing countries witnessed an average proportion of 24, 34 and 42 (cited in Zhou [Tian-yong], 2008). The above statistics are adequate evidence that in Maoist China, while industrialization was advancing fast, development of the tertiary sector of economy was greatly held back. Moreover, in the domain of agriculture, after 1958, establishment of the People's Commune, "grain production as the key" principle and state monopoly for grain trading caused serious shortage of agricultural consumer goods including grain (the great variety of coupons and certificates was the best footnote of such shortage). As far as foreign affairs were concerned, due to China's successive military confrontations with the US, India and former Soviet Union, defense expenses had been consuming a considerable part of national revenue. All these factors deprived the populace of substantial income increase throughout 1952 to 1980.[14] Combined with political restraints on social stratification, they made birth and growth of the Chinese middle classes nothing but a fairytale.

---

14   According to statistics in *Chinese Agriculture Yearbook (1980)* and *Chinese Statistic Yearbook (1981)*, the average annual salary of state-run-organization employees was 446 *yuan* in 1952 and 529 *yuan* in 1980, with a gross increase of 18.6% throughout 28 years. In the countryside, under the collectivistic system, in 1953 (after collectivization was completed), the average income per capita was 38.8 *yuan* and in 1975 (one year before Mao's death) the amount was 54.4 *yuan*, with a gross increase of 40.2% throughout 22 years (cited in MacFarquhar & Fairbank, 1992: 517).

However, in the following three decades, it has been a different story. After 1978, the year when the Third Plenary Session of the Eleventh Central Committee of the Chinese Communist Party was held, a massive movement, known as the "Reform and Opening-Up" (*gaige kaifang*) was unfolded. Sprouting in the countryside from the household contract responsibility system (*lianchan chengbao zerenzhi*), the movement extended into many economic domains in cities. From then on, China has been drawing global attention with its economic achievements. During the three decades, China boasted an increase of Gross Domestic Product (GDP) from 364.5 billion *yuan (renminbi)* of year 1978 to 24,953 billion *yuan (renminbi)* of 2007, the annual growth averaging 9.88%. China became the third economic power in the world, ranking only next to the US and Japan. While the economic boom has set solid material foundation to better Chinese people's living conditions, the post-1978 social transformation has been directly and tightly linked with birth and growth of the Chinese middle classes. Initiated by conversion from mandatory planned economy (or redistribution economy) to modern market economy, this originally economic transformation soon became a driving force of comprehensive social transformation, including the changing in class relations and social structure.

Although in a fundamental sense, this social transformation have been caused by the market transition, the loosening of class relations and social structure, which had been frozen for almost thirty years in Maoist China, was in the first place triggered by policy modification. In 1979, the Central Committee of the Chinese Communist Party declared to delabel landlords, rich peasants (*difu*) and their children and to replace the so called "class-struggle-centered principle" with the "economic-development- centered principle". This policy change, together with other transitions in social life, especially vocational differentiation, has caused the criteria of social stratification to convert from "symbolic" class standards to vocational standards, which serves as precondition for emergence of the middle classes.

Once the dam of political stratification collapsed, power of market, which became ever stronger after 1978, began to have its irresistible bearing on the shaping of a different social structure. When class backgrounds ceased to be stratification criteria, new criteria were introduced based on the amount of wealth people earned with their social, economic and cultural capital. Considering its influence on formation of the Chinese middle classes, China's social transformation can be divided into two phases: (1) The fifteen years from 1978 to 1992 constituted the first phase. During this period, thanks to the liberation of privately-run enterprises and advance of the policy of "allowing some people to get rich earlier than others" (*yunxu yibufen ren xian fu qilai*), two groups of people took the initiative in becoming the Chinese middle classes. One group was made up of early adventurers of market economy in both urban and rural China. Having risen from grass roots, they amassed various capital mainly through their keen economic awareness and industriousness. In this sense, they resembled those people depicted by Szelényi who were engaged in the "second economy" during early stage of the Hungarian reform (Szelényi, 1978). The other group that became prosperous in the first phase were offsprings of cadres (*ganbu*, a Chinese word for "government official"). Benefited from their parents' power and the dual pricing policy (*shuangguizhi*), they traded the political and social capital from their parents for their own economic capital. Actually it was partly their misconduct that triggered the Tiananmen Square turmoil in 1989. (2) The second phase has spanned from 1993 to the present. With the full-scale switch from redistribution economy to market economy and advance of housing reform (*fanggai*) and other policies, cadres and professionals, who had previously enjoyed privileges in the redistribution economy, now either resorted to their political capital, which guided the transformation, or took advantage of their cultural capital, which was also of vital importance to the transformation. Soon they became main components of the Chinese middle classes. In good accordance with what Szelényi wrote about Eastern Europe (Szelényi & Kostello, 1996), those poorly-educated Chinese who had been the first to rush into the market were now marginalized. At the beginning of the reform, people used to remark that "missile makers earn less than egg sellers" and "scalpel holders (meaning 'surgeon') earn less than razor holders (meaning 'barber')", but now such complaints were nowhere to be heard. In the labor market of China today, one's educational level has become a determinant of employment, re-employment and income (Maurer-Fazio, 1999; Liu, 2006), hence an essential factor influencing social stratification and growth of the middle classes.

Path of Construction of the Chinese Middle Classes

So far, it has been analyzed from perspectives of politics and economy why the three decades beginning from 1949 did not witness development of middle classes parallel to China's industrialization process during that period. Admittedly, the political and economic policies of the Chinese Communist Party (CCP) in these three decades played a vital role in eradicating class inequality. However, implementation of these policies had been dependent upon the planned economy, or redistribution economy. While the deprivation of private ownership of means of production had put an end to the unequal stratification system, which had existed before the Chinese Revolution, the elimination of market economy had made class differentiation totally impossible. The redistribution system based on planned economy had deprived the Chinese people of opportunities of amassing wealth and capital through free market exchange and had thus prevented the Chinese society from possible differentiation based on economic inequality. As proposed by Szelényi, inequality of socialist societies is typically represented by distribution of public products, to which power and political loyalty are of critical importance (Szelényi, 1987).

Now our narrative path is winding towards the macro, or institutional construction of the Chinese middle classes. On this level, rebirth of the Chinese middle classes after 1978 has been undoubtedly interwoven with the market-oriented reform and transformation. Before 1978, China was dominated by what is termed by Polanyi as "redistribution" economy (Polanyi, 1944/1957), in which the horizontal relation between producers and consumers was cut. Resource transference and income distribution were realized through a vertical multi-stratum bureaucratic system running from the "central" to local governments. In post-1978 era, the previous redistribution system gave way to market pricing system, which demanded users of production factors to reward their providers according to the factors' market prices or their contributions to ultimate distributional products. It was through this rewarding mode that the policy of "allowing some people to get rich earlier than others" became a reality. Victor Nee has insightfully argued that "since the transformation from redistribution system to market system incorporates changes in resource transference and distribution modes, chances are that this transformation will reshape the ranking of social stratification." (Nee, 1989). Accompanied by the GDP boom in three post-1978 decades, the direct drives of changes in social stratification and emergence of the middle classes have been the following market-inclined distribution modes. (1) The practice of paying rewards based on market pricing has inevitable widened income gap between different groups and different individuals of the same group, as is evidenced by rise of the Gini coefficient from 0.21 of the 1960s, to 0.33 of the 1980s, and finally to the present figure of 0.458. It is the widening of income gap that has laid a foundation for emergence of the middle classes. (2) The transformation from redistribution system to market system has changed the resource-gripping capacity of two basic powers, namely the state and the market. The interest structure has been rebuilt, which in turn has reshaped structure of the Chinese middle classes. In interpretation of such structural change, there have always been two confrontational views. A holder of the first view is Victor Nee, who emphasizes the power of market and reform. He argues that market transition, while lowering the economic reward of political privileges, will raise the economic reward of human capital (Nee, 1989). The supporters of the other view include Rona-Tas, Yan-jie Bian and Logan, who emphasize the variation and maintenance of power. They either propose that political privileges can be transformed to economic advantages (Rona-Tas, 1994), or argue that the reward of redistribution power is increased, not decreased, in the process of reform (Bian & Logan, 1996). The fact is, Chinese market economy has been cultivated in the presence of previous political powers. Therefore, state power and market power are not necessarily incompatible, instead, they might function in parallel or interwoven patterns. For instance, among the three major components of the middle classes in present China, while the group of civil servants and those in charge of social organizations are considerably dependent on state power, managers and professionals have achieved their middle-class status mainly as the fruit of marketization. (3) Along with the advance of marketization, the tax reform and housing reform have somewhat restrained the widening of income gap and facilitated growth of the middle classes. Take the tax system as an example. It is widely known that the validation of personal income tax policy in 1980 was a result of marketization reform. With its progressive taxing practice and preferential measures for areas in central and western China, this policy has contributed to bridging the income gap between individuals and regions (Koichi Utsunomiya, 2009). Such tax policies have prevented wealth from unrestrained flow to the rich, moreover, the deduction standard of personal income tax has been constantly raised, both of which have helped enlarge the scale of the middle classes.

As far as emergence of the Chinese middle classes is concerned, the market-oriented reform discussed above has constituted its macro or institutional background. Following will be exposition of their consumption patterns, which embody change of life style and therefore constitute the micro or psychological mechanics of their constructing self-identity or winning social recognition. Considering that, in past three decades, the Chinese people have been endowed with their desire and capacity of consumption by nothing but market transition, a link or interaction between the macro background and micro mechanics concerning birth of the middle classes may well be noticed in China.

To the Chinese middle classes, there have been various historical, economic and social determinants to make consumption their principal means of constructing self-identity and seeking social recognition. Historically, ever since introduction of the English term "*middle class*" into China, its Chinese translation has remained *zhongchan jieji* (meaning "the class with medium amount of property"), which emphasizes its "mediocrity" in possession and consumption. As is stated earlier, after 1949, Maoist Revolution put an end to private ownership of not only production means but also life necessities. Under the redistribution system, even a major life necessity like housing was allotted by the government; how could any Chinese possess a private car? While in pre-1978 China, one's position in social strata was a function of his or her share of power in redistribution, after the reform of 1978, stratification of the Chinese society has followed different logic, thanks to the cultivation of market economy as well as the legitimization of accumulating private property. A significant aspect of the transition is, people begin to define their own and others' status according to amount of wealth and level of consumption, the latter determined by the former. Meanwhile, in order to erase the political implication of the middle classes, half unintentionally yet half-deliberately, state authorities have been designating them as "the group with medium income" (*zhongdeng shouru qunti*), which has strengthened the inclination of stratification based on personal income and consumption. Both Li Chun-lin's research and ours have unveiled the fact that the middle classes are eagerly seeking their identities through consumption (Li, 2005; Zhou [Xiao-hong], 2005a). Despite that our survey in 2005 has collected varied answers to the amount of wealth supposedly possessed by the middle class family (among all subjects, 21.2% have proposed 500, 000 and above; for 19.3%, 1,000,000 and above; yet 30.6% of them have been unable to pin it down), all of those that responded to the survey have agreed unanimously that the basic criterion of being a member of the middle classes should be "private ownership of housing and car" (*youfang, youche*).

Looking from the economic perspective, consumption has become a major means of self identification by the Chinese middle classes because the economic status of these classes has not only been established by the GDP boom in three decades of Reform and Opening-Up, but also been pushed by the above-mentioned market-oriented transition. These two factors have constantly lifted the income of urban residents. Annual income of the average Chinese worker in 1978 was no more than 615 *yuan*, however, this figure has been continually updated: 1,148 *yuan* in 1985, 2,140 *yuan* in 1990; 5,500 *yuan* in 1995; 9,371 *yuan* in 2000; and 18,364 in 2005 (National Bureau of Statistics of China, the stated years), doubling almost every five years. Meanwhile, consumption has been encouraged by the government out of different motives in different eras. Before 1997, a series of policies, including salary raise, industrial restructuring and lowering the rate of accumulation, were carried out in order to eradicate the disastrous aftereffects of Maoist Revolution, improve people's living conditions and "overcome the legitimacy crisis" (Wang, 2009: 235). After 1997, consumption was promoted because the Asian Financial Crisis, combined with insufficiency of domestic need, had been a bottleneck in further development of Chinese economy. Aimed at solving this problem, the CCP and the Central Government proposed strategically that "new consumption highlights such as housing should be created; residence construction should be made a key industry; and consumption of telecommunication, tourism, culture, entertainment, health care and other tertiary industries should be encouraged" (Zhu, 2001:1174). Urged by a variety of government policies, the Chinese middle classes have been updating their consumption items from consumer durables like televisions, washing machines and refrigerators to private houses, apartments and cars, which are considered better manifestations of their status. In less than one decade since beginning of the new millennium, housing prices in China have averagely been doubled; coastal areas have witnessed their increase by as much as several times and numerous people have suddenly become rich through investing in housing. Meanwhile, on China's entering WTO in 2001, private cars were driven into Chinese households. In the following six years, the production and selling of domestically manufactured cars boomed by annual increase of more than 10%, from 820,000 cars in 2001 to 5,320,000 in 2007 (Li [An-ding], 2008). What's more, to the Chinese middle classes, the private housing and car mean not only consumer goods that help them build self-identity and win social recognition, but also practice fields for moulding new consumption notions.[15]

Encouraged by the CCP and government, the Chinese middle classes have accelerated their consumption. Besides, this consumption promotion has more significant social implications. Under the background of globalization, which becomes ever more sweeping after the 1990s, consumeristic values and life styles are evolving among the Chinese people, especially the newly rich power and wealthy elite, and the ever growing population of the middle classes. This trend is contributing greatly to identity construction of the middle classes. As is widely known, the ideological propaganda of Maoist era used to portrait consumption as representation of the "capitalist life style"; to a certain degree it was regarded as an equivalent of extravagance, luxury and moral degeneration. However, after the beginning of Reform and Opening-Up, especially after the 1990s, the mainstream discourse has "transformed" the notion of consumption because the government is better aware of the role consumption can play in advancing national economy. Meanwhile, the state will is bolstered by the market desire for consumption, which has ushered in a great variety of advertising that aimed at stimulating consumption. Moreover, the appeal of Chinese advertising is beginning to transfer from functional value to symbolic value of consumption (Chen [Sheng], 2003). All these changes of public interpretational frames for consumption have helped legitimize the improvement of living conditions by the newly

---

15   Take HP(hire purchase) as an example. The Chinese used to show disapproval of such payment mode, calling it "eating corn in the blade" (*yinchimaoliang*). In 2002, the proportion of housing loan balance to the total of Chinese financial institutions was below 2%. However, in only one year, housing loan balance soared to 1,200 billion, 10% of the total loan balance of Chinese financial institutions.

rich, including the middle classes, and their distinction from the grass roots. A good evidence of this is housing advertisements that prevail in China in past decade: in such advertising, houses and apartments appeal to consumers not because they are comfortable, but because they guarantee to manifest and promote the owners' social status (Fraser, 2000). Chinese housing advertisements are abundant with slogans like "birds of a feather flock together", "buy a new house and become a real boss" and "the unanimous choice of professors, entrepreneurs and bankers". Boldly linking housing purchase with one's social stratum and status, these advertisements are strongly favored by the housing market, which can be viewed as another proof of how important consumption is to identity of the Chinese middle classes.

Globalization, Social Transformation and Duality of the Middle Classes

The high relevance between consumption and the Chinese middle classes is supplementary to the widely-known proposition by American sociologist Wright C. Mills. Earlier than half a century ago, in his research on the American middle classes, Mills depicted them as "the rearguards of politics" (Mills, 1951:423~354). Nevertheless, the Chinese middle classes present themselves as both "the rearguards of politics" and "the vanguards of consumption". Not only their values, but also their life attitudes and behavior patterns are directly shaped by this status. Through a comparative study on development of middle classes in different countries, it can be revealed that the contradictory dual characters of the Chinese middle classes have been cultivated by two eventful trends during their formative years: globalization and social transformation.

Although Mills depicted the American new middle classes, who emerged after the Second World War, as the rearguards of politics, it is widely recognized that the middle classes have not been born with such an image. Earlier history of the European middle classes had witnessed their radical anti-feudalism stand. Having fought as vanguards of politics, the European middle classes won private ownership of property, freedom of market economy and participation in public issues. Besides, their efforts resulted in the European tradition of civil society, including the institution of elected congress and freedom of press. In more recent years, this tradition played an important role in the social transformation of Hungary and other Central European countries (Eyal, Szelenyi, & Townsley, 2008: 5). Even in those emerging capitalist countries in other parts of the world, the middle classes have inherited the traits of political vanguards from their European predecessors. Take the Korean middle class as an example. Despite their unsteady political stands (Koo, 1993),   during all the social protest movements that spanned from the 1960s to the 1980s, they never stood as onlookers. Instead, they took a very active part in the democratic reform, which by itself was "a fruit of political democratization." (Han, 2009: 427) In the comparison of development of middle classes in various capitalist countries running market economy, the US turns out to be the only exception. Blessed by the absence of autocratic tradition and the presence of free economy and free media, which cushion the effects of political conflicts, the US has produced middle classes that are political rearguards. As is contended by Mills, "there have never been any clear-cut middle class movements on American political stage" (Mills, 1951: 351).

Just as the French Revolution bestowed European middle classes with the radicalism traits typical of that era, the parallelism between the rise of Chinese middle classes and the expansion of globalization has bestowed this group of people various characters typical of the globalization age, among which the most distinct is consumerism. As a matter of fact, this character is also shared by the Indian middle class, who rose on large scale at roughly the same time as their Chinese counterparts (Varma, 1998:26; Rajaram, 2009; Bose, 2009). It is frequently heard that the Chinese middle classes can only develop in the dimension of consumption due to the given political environment of China. However, this interprets only half of the story. The other side of the coin is, although China and India differ considerably in political institutions, there are many commonalities in consumption by the middle classes in these two countries because both are deeply involved in the trend of globalization. It is noteworthy that, on the one hand, globalization is expanding capitalist production worldwide and prospering manufacturing industries and service trades in developing countries such as China and India; on the other hand, globalization is also cultivating an international consumer market and corresponding values, life attitudes and behavior patterns based on consumerism. In the age of globalization, despite that the middle classes in countries like China and India vary in origins, political statuses, occupations, religious beliefs and even races, they resemble each other surprisingly in constructing self-identity via means of consumption. They both emphasize the importance of consumption and life styles to one's class categorization and social status. Therefore, in a more fundamental sense, both in China and in India, inaction of the middle classes in political and social matters has been caused by the fact that such public concerns are compatible neither with consumerism, which is being promoted by globalization, nor with the notion of personal success, which is being defined by consumption.

Undeniably, besides the factor of globalization, it is also because of China's unique social transformation after 1978 that the Chinese middle classes have become vanguards in consumption and rearguards in politics. In comparison between China, former Soviet Union and former socialist countries in Eastern Europe, although all of them have witnessed market-oriented transition, China has followed a completely different path from the rest. As is the case in Russia, radical privatization was initiated after the disintegration of the former Soviet Union at the end of the 1980s. In less than one decade, the ruling class, consisted of bureaucrats and economic oligarchs, finished their primitive accumulation of capital, which would have taken decades, even a whole century, in Western countries (Lian, 2005: 310). The speed of accumulation of private wealth far exceeded the speed of establishment of market system. Finally this process brought about what were termed by Eyal, Szelenyi and Townsley as "capitalists without capitalism". Meanwhile, the Russian middle class that had formed at the beginning of privatization reform was degraded into a poverty-stricken stratum. As is the case in Hungary and other Central European countries, thanks to the civil society tradition, the post-communism era saw market system established faster than private wealth accumulated, hence the "capitalism without capitalists"(Eyal, Szelenyi, & Townsley, 2009: 6). Moreover, during this process, the middle class intellectuals, namely the well-educated group with abundant cultural capital, "especially those who have been trained in engineering and economics" (Eyal, Szelenyi, & Townsley, 2009: 42), were made beneficiaries of the social transformation.

Compared with the case in Soviet Union and Eastern European countries, transformation of the Chinese society has been showing its own characteristics. On the one hand, the reform in China has not undermined its fundamental political institution or the ruling status of the CCP; on the other hand, the reform has in the first place provided adequate space for the development of private economy; what's more, it has been pushing the market transition at full speed after 1995. Through the interaction of state and market, the Chinese reform fruited in a typical twofold process: while the socialist state and its agents are actively advancing the market economy,   mature market and adequate capital owners [16] in turn are equipping the former with ever stronger capability to adjust market and grip resources (In the present financial crisis, the Chinese government has invested at one stroke as much as 4,000 billion *yuan*, which plainly manifests the raise of its economic capacity). Consequently, in both the state and market, in other words, both inside and outside the institution, a large population of the middle classes has been developed. In this sense, the Chinese middle classes have kept a profile of the political rearguard out of two reasons. One is that the state has not let go its political grip and the present political structure has

---

16   As far as market is concerned, echoing the "capitalists without capitalism" of Russia and the "capitalism without capitalists" of Central Europe, China may be figured as a country "with both capitalists and capitalism".

left the middle classes little room for action; [17] the other is that the state, through its advancement of market economy, has guaranteed economic benefits of the middle classes in and outside the institution, which has considerably undermined their motive for interest demands through political activities.

Discussion about Future Development of the Chinese Middle Classes

One of the most frequently discussed issues concerning the Chinese middle classes has been their future development and will of political participation (Li [Chun-lin], 2009). The discussion has been dominated in past decade by the opinion that the development of such classes can function as a social stabilizer. This remark may also be paraphrased as the Chinese middle classes are "the vanguards of consumption and the rearguards of politics" (Goldman, 1999; Zhou, 2002). This opinion was under attack recently, though (Zhang, 2009). Considering the dishonorable role played by the German middle classes in the rise of Fascist Germany, it is undeniable that the middle classes cannot be a social stabilizer unless under certain conditions (Zhou, 2005b: 9~10). However, at least till now, the Chinese middle classes have not shown any signs of political radicalism. On the contrary, it has been interacting with the state in a desirably active way.

As is demonstrated above, the Chinese middle classes are characterized by the consumption vanguard and the political rearguard, the former being a result of consumerism, which has been reinforced by globalization, while the latter being an aftermath of the particular social transformation of China. This transformation has been showing two distinct traits. Firstly, it has not shaken the status of the CCP as a ruling party or undermined the original political institution (although it has brought some changes to the institution). Such a transformation pattern has enabled the intra-institution elite and their descendants to reproduce their privileged status. Secondly, as for the extra-institution elite, market orientation of this transformation has bestowed upon them opportunities of prosperity via economic and educational efforts. As a matter of fact, the dual system of economy has also driven stratum reproduction along the same dual track, which has guaranteed China political stability throughout the three decades of social transformation.

Therefore, no prospect of large-scale conflicts between the state and the middle classes can be seen in Chinese social transformation. However, problems do exist, only

---

17 In today's China, organizational actions of the middle classes seldom target on fundamental problems in politics and social life, but on issues of group interest concerning specific actors. (A common example of such issues is the housing quality issue while a very special example of them is the Xianmen Paraxylene (PX) Project, which could have been a potential source of pollution. See Chen [Ying-fang], 2006).

increasingly between the state, the interest groups and the grassroots. Admittedly, the three-decade economic reform has brought China great economic achievements, but it remains doubtful whether these achievements can be duly shared by the populace. Due to unfairness of existing distributional policies, absence of social security system and inadequacy of government regulation and adjustment, recent years have witnessed many mass events, which were mostly triggered by interest demands of the lower classes (migrant workers, landless peasants, laid-off workers and demolished-home owners). To name only a few of such events, there have been rubber farmer clash of *Menglian* (a county in *Yunnan* Province), taxi strike of *Chongqing* (a city in Southwest China) and demolished-home owner riot of *Longnan* (a city in *Gansu* Province). The *Wengan* Turmoil of 2008 and the *Tonghua* Steel Company Atrocity of 2009 are among the most shocking. [18] Although these clashes had broken out between the lower classes and those representing capital or local governments, hostility and resentment of the populace are typically unleashed on the middle class members such as civil servants, law implementers, managers and professionals (doctors, judges and teachers). In China, conflicts keep rising between the populace and local governments as well as between the populace and capital groups. Now that the middle classes are besieged by all these conflicts, whether they can stay unaffected is practically at stake. Therefore, for the Chinese middle classes, it may well be concluded that both their future development and the exercise of their political potential will be influenced by the seriousness of social conflicts, such as the above mentioned, and measures taken to solve them. In this sense, chances are that the Chinese middle classes have now been brought to some political crossroads.

References

Bain, Yanjie and John Logan, 1996, "Market Transition and the Persistence of Power: The Changing Stratification

---

18 On June 28, 2008, in Wengan, a county in Guizhou Province, a turmoil was triggered by the drowning of a middle school girl student named Li Shu-fen. Over 20,000 people were involved in the turmoil, known as the Wengan Turmoil, setting on fire several local public buildings including those housed the county government, the public security bureau, the civil administration bureau and the financial bureau. It is observed that, the drowning of Li was nothing but a superficial cause of the turmoil. The real cause of the event was much more complex and fundamental: with the local underworld dominant in the contention for mineral resources, the populace had been deprived not only of their economic interests but also of their sense of security (Liu [Zi-fu], 2009).

On July 24, 2009, in Tonghua, a city in Jilin Province, a demonstration involving about 10,000 steel workers broke out because of conflicts emerging in the process of enterprise restructuring. Feeling their own interests at stake and losing their confidence in the government representatives, workers of Tonghua Steel Company initiated a mass protest, during which they battered to death a man named Chen Guo-jun, the new general manager designated from a privately-run enterprise by the government.

System in Urban China", *American Sociological Review*, 61: 738~758.

Bell, Daniel, 1999, *The Coming of Post-Industrial Society*, New York: Basic Books.

Bernstein, Eduard, 1961, *Evolutionary Socialism*, New York: Schocken Books.

Bose, Pradip Kumar, 2009, "Rise of the Middle Classes in India and China", in Li Chun-lin (ed.), *Bijiao Shiye Xia De Zhongchan Jieji Xingcheng* [Formation of Middle Classes in Comparative Perspective], Beijing: Shehui Kexue Wenxian Chubanshe [Social Sciences Academic Press].

Chen, Sheng, 2003, "The Channel of Desires: A Content Analysis of Advertisements Published on Yangcheng Wanbao [*Yangcheng Evening News*] in Past Two Decades", unpublished thesis for master degree, Guangzhou: Zhongshan University.

Chen, Ying-fang, 2006, "Ability of Action and System Restrict: Middle Class in the Urban Movement", *Shehuixue Yanjiu* [*Sociological Studies*], 4.

Eyal, Szelenyi, & Townsley, (Chinese Language Edition Translated by Lu Peng, etc.), 2008, *Wuxu Zibenjia Dazao Ziben Zhuyi* [Making Capitalism without Capitalists]. Beijing: Shehui Kexue Wenxian Chubanshe [Social Sciences Academic Press].

Fraser, David, 2000, "Inventing Oasis, Luxury Housing Advertisements and Reconfiguring Domestic Space in Shanghai", in Deborah Davis (ed.), *The Consumer Revolution in Urban China*, Berkeley: University of California Press.

Goldman, David, 1999, "The New Middle Class", in Merle Goldman & Roderick MacFarquhar (ed.), *The Paradox of China's Post-Mao Reform*, Cambridge, Mass.: Harvard University Press.

Han, Xiang-zhen, 2009, "Political Trends of the South Korean Middle Classes", in Li Chun-lin (ed.), *Bijiao Shiye Xia De Zhongchan Jieji Xingcheng* [Formation of Middle Classes in Comparative Perspective], Beijing: Shehui Kexue Wenxian Chubanshe [Social Sciences Academic Press].

Hutton, Will & Anthony Giddens, 2003, *On the Edge: Living with Global Capitalism*, Beijing: Sanlian Press.

Joseph Nye, 1990, *Bound To Lead: The Changing Nature Of American Power*, New York: Basic Books.

Koo, Hagen,1993, "The Social and Political Character of the Korean Middle Class", in Hsiao, Hisn-Huang Michael (ed.), *Discovering of The Middle Classes in East Asia*, Taipei, Taiwan: Institute of Ethnology, Academic Sinica.

Li, Anding, 2008, "Three Decades of Reform and Opening-Up: Millions of Private Cars Driven into Chinese Households", *Jingji Cankao Bao* [Economic Information Daily], Oct. 3.

Li, Chun-lin, 2005, *Duanlie Yu Suipian: Dangdai Zhongguo Shehui Jieceng Fenhua Shizheng Fenxi* [Cleavage and Fragment: An Empirical Analysis on the Social Stratification of the Contemporary China], Beijing: Shehui Kexue Wenxian Chubanshe [Social Sciences Academic Press].

Li, Chun-lin, 2009, "Change in Theoretical Orientation and Concerns of Studies on the Chinese Middle Classes", in Li Chun-lin (ed.), *Bijiao Shiye Xia De Zhongchan Jieji Xingcheng* [Formation of Middle Classes in Comparative Perspective], Beijing: Shehui Kexue Wenxian Chubanshe [Social Sciences Academic Press].

Lian, Lian, 2005, "The Russian Middle Class under Transition", in Zhou Xiao-hong (ed.), *Quanqiu Zhongchan Jieji Baogao*, [Report of Middle Classes in the World], Beijing: Shehui Kexue Wenxian Chubanshe [Social Sciences Academic Press].

Liu, Jing-ming, 2006, "Expansion of Higher Education in China and Inequality in Entrance Opportunities: 1978~2003", *Shehui* [Society], 3.

Liu, Zi-fu, 2009, *Xin Qunti Shijian Guan* [New Point of View of Mass Events], Beijing: *Xinhua Chubanshe* [Xinhua Publishing House].

MacFarquhar, Roderick, & Fairbank, John K (ed.), 1992, *Jianqiao Zhonghua Renmin Gongheguo Shi: Zhongguo Geming Neibu De Geming* [The Cambridge History of China: Revolution within the Chinese Revolution], Beijing: Zhongguo Shehui Kexue Chubanshe [China Social Sciences Press].

Marx, Karl, & Engels, Friedrich, 1972, *Makesi Engesi Xuanji* [Selected Works of Marx and Engels], (Vol. 1),

Beijing: *Renmin Chubanshe* [People's Publishing House].

Maurer-Fazio, Margaret, 1999, Earnings and Education in China's Transition to a Market Economy, *China Economic Review*,Vol. 10, Issue 1.

Mills, C. Wright, 1951, *White Collar, The American Middle Classes*, London: Oxford University Press.

Mills, Wright C., 1951, *White Collar, The American Middle Classes*, London: Oxford University Press.

National Bureau of Statistics of China, 1978; 1985; 1990; 1995; 2000; 2005, *Zhongguo Tongji Nianjian* [*China Statistical Yearbook*], Beijing: China Statistical Press.

Nee, Victor, 1989, A Theory of Market Transition: From Redistribution to Market in State Socialism, *American Sociological Review*, 54: 663~681.

Polanyi, Karl, 1957, *The Great Transformation: the Political and Economic Origins of Our Time*, Boston: Mss.: Beacon.

Rajaram, N., 2009, "The Middle Classes of India and China: Problems and Concerns", In Li Chun-lin (ed.), *Bijiao Shiye Xia De Zhongchan Jieji Xingcheng* [Formation of Middle Classes in Comparative Perspective], Beijing: Shehui Kexue Wenxian Chubanshe [Social Sciences Academic Press].

Rona-Tas, Akos, 1994, "The First Shall Be Last? Entrepreneurship and Communist Cadre in the Transition from Socialism", *American Journal of Sociology*, 100: 40~69.

Smail, John, 1994, *The Origins of Middle-Class Culture: Halifax, Yorkshire, 1660-1780*, Cornell University Press.

Szelényi, Ivan & Eric Kostello, 1996, The Market Transition Debate: Toward a Synthesis? *American Journal of Sociology*, 101(4): 1082~96.

Szelényi, Ivan, 1978, "Social Inequalities in State Socialist Redistributive Economies", *International Journal of Comparative Sociology*, 19:63~68.

Taylor, Charles, 1991, "Models of Civil Society", *Public Culture*, 3(1): 95~118.

Thompson, E.P., (Chinese Language Edition Translated by Qian Sheng-dan), 2001, *Yingguo Gongren Jieji De Xingchen* [The Making of the English Working Class] (Two Volumes), Nanjing: *Yilin Chubanshe* [Yilin Press].

United Nations Development Program, 1996, *Human Development Report*, New York: Oxford University Press.

Utsunomiya, Koichi, 2009, "The Income Adjustment Function of China's Personal Income Tax and Its Problems", in Zhou Xiao-hong, & Xie Shuguang (ed.), *Zhongguo Yanjiu* [China Studies], the Spring Issue (Vol. 9), Beijing: Shehui Kexue Wenxian Chubanshe [Social Sciences Academic Press].

Varma, Pavan K., 1998, *The Great Indian Middle Class*, New Delhi: Viking.

Wang, Ning, 2009, *Cong Kuxingzhe Dao Xiaofeizhe Shehui* [From the Ascetic Society to the Consumer Society], Beijing: Shehui Kexue Wenxian Chubanshe [Social Sciences Academic Press].

Yang, Jiang, 2004, *Xizao* [Baptism], Beijing: Renmin Wenxue Chubanshe [The People's Literature Press].

Zhang, YI, 2009, "Are Middle Classes a Stabilizer of the Society?" in Chunlin Li (ed.), *Bijiao Shiye Xia De Zhongchan Jieji Xingcheng* [Formation of Middle Classes in Comparative Perspective: Process, Influence and Socioeconomic Consequences], Beijing: Shehui Kexue Wenxian Chubanshe [Social Sciences Academic Press].

Zhou, Tian-yong, 2008, "Why Did We Choose to Reform and Open up Three Decades ago", *Xuexi Shibao* [Study Times], Aug. 26.

Zhou, Xiao-hong (ed.), 2005a, *Zhongguo Zhongchan Jieji Diaocha* [Survey of the Chinese Middle Classes], Beijing: Shehui Kexue Wenxian Chubanshe [Social Sciences Academic Press].

Zhou, Xiao-hong (ed.), 2005b, *Quanqiu Zhongchan Jieji Baogao*, [Report of Middle Classes in the World], Beijing: Shehui Kexue Wenxian Chubanshe [Social Sciences Academic Press].

Zhou, Xiao-hong, 2007, "Globalization and Making of the Middle Classes: Theories and Realities", *Tianjin Shehui Kexue* [Tianjin Social Sciences] (4).

Zhou, Xiao-hong, 2008, "Identity Theory: An Analyzing Method of Sociology and Psychology", *Shehui Kexue* [Journal of Social Sciences] (4).

Zhu, Rong-ji, 2001, *Zhengfu Gongzuo Baogao* [Report on the Work of the Government, presented in the Third Session of the Ninth National People's Congress (NPC) on March 5, 2000], in Zhonggong Zhongyang Wenxian Yanjiushi [Party Literature Research Center of the CCP Central Committee] (ed.), *Shiwuda Yilai Zhongyao Wenxian Xuanbian* [A Selection of Important Documents since the 15th National Congress of the CCP] (Vol. 2), Beijing: *Renmin Chubanshe* [People's Publishing House].

Chapter 4

The Transformation and Power of "Middle Class" Language in Chinese Media Publications

He Jin

The rise of China's middle class has already become a widely watched social phenomenon, and a hot topic of research in the academic world (Chou Liping, Gu Hui 2007). And it is hard to ignore the unique role public media has played in this historic process. In related research outside of China, the relationship between the middle class and public media possibly shows a constant "strengthening", even a "re-creation", of the middle class image by public media. Likewise, public media also created the widespread "political apathy" of the middle class (Mills, 1951); possibly through specially targeted media products such as middle class magazines. These media products, which appeal to the specific social status and significance of middle class consumers, construct the self-identity of this class (Ohmann, 1996; Liechty, 2003). What form this takes in China has yet to be explored, but in the last decade an "intimate" relationship between public media and the "middle class" is quite apparent.

Starting in the mid- to late-1990's, the heating up of "middle class" language in Chinese media gripped the nation – media clearly advocated concepts of "white collar", "middle class", and all its linguistic iterations, spreading hot debate on the subject. The image and livelihood of people from this class became a focal point of public media content. Middle class (white collar) people also became the target audience of some media outlets, thus creating a fiercely competitive divided market. Much like how some academics have said: "As an inverted process, in order to strengthen itself, (media) is attempting to 'nurture' and construct China's middle class" (Dai Jinhua, 1999: 37).

The results of this 'nurturing' are already starting to appear. On the one hand, over more than a decade of the cumulative, percolating effects of media images and the constructing of the middle class, combined with the defining of a "middle class" concept, public media has already successfully turned "middle class" into a social rallying cry.

"Regarding the yearning for status of the middle class, it has already become the most significant, and irreversible, trend of our era" (Meng Fanhua, 2004: 216). From the level of social goals, there are also people who think that "middle class" has become the "*xiao kang*" (small comforts) livelihood standard after the "*wen bao*" (food and shelter) of earlier (Li Zhengdong, 204).[19] On the other hand, by raising shared issues, middle class-focused media products (such as *White Collar Magazine*) have gradually become culturally-defining and a vehicle for middle class self-identification (Sun Liping, 2003). As a result, sociologist Zhang Wanli, long-time observer of middle class research in China, perceptively realized that this "possibly has created a unique question in research on the middle class in contemporary China; 'The relationship between Chinese media and the middle class'" (Zhang Wanli, 2004). Within this research question, some foundational questions might be: As a censored topic in Chinese political language, how did the concept of the "middle class" emerge publicly in the body of Chinese media discourse in the 1990's? In the early formation of China's middle class, with such a small number of people, how did the middle class receive such a heated "following" from Chinese media? These questions are ones that this research should strive to explore.

As a social class structure clearly taking reference from the West, the experience of China's middle class has grown within a different linguistic context from that of the West. From globalization, to the era of public media, and the rise of China as a superpower, all these unique factors of the times influenced China's middle class, and they have all received much media attention. Looking at the unique role public media has played to the middle class, is to understand an important aspect of the growth of the middle class in China.

1. Media's Construction of Chinese Middle Class Language

Of the many forms of media, periodicals represent the most important role in constructing middle class language. Periodical media mainly uses two forms and three major channels to establish middle class language in China. Namely, the discourse was developed by utilizing the social agenda- and status-forming function of media products, through the defining and emergence of the middle class imaginary, and by establishing common middle class "issues".

First, the clear raising of the concept of the "middle class" opened debate in Chinese

---

19 Translator's Note: *wen bao* refers to providing basic food an d shelter needs for particularly rural Chinese, while *xiao kang* refers to the change in policy under Deng Xiaoping to pursuing more middle class comforts.

periodicals, which brought the concept into the public imaginary as a social class. More formal, focused reports on the middle class started to appear at the end of 2000 in *China Youth Daily* under the special series "Searching for Urban Middle-level People". This special series of reports gave a definition of the middle class, and began early descriptions of the appearance, work, and lifestyle characteristics of this class. It particularly emphasized the role of the middle class as a "tool for social stability". In July, 2001, China Central Committee Secretary Jiang Zemin published his "July 1st Talk", in which he pointed out that, "Since China's Opening and Reform, China's social structure has experienced new changes; private science and technology businesses, entrepreneurs, specialized professionals, foreign-owned business employees, small business owners, private corporate leaders, middle-group professionals, and freelance professionals have emerged in the social structure. Furthermore, people have been moving and prospering under different forms of ownership, in different careers, and in different fields, and people's careers and status often change. These kinds of changes will continue. Middle-group professionals, freelance professionals, and other social classes are special builders of China's socialist enterprise." This talk confirmed the existence of these newly-emerged classes. At the end of 2001, the China Academy of Social Science *Contemporary China Social Class Research Report* clearly affirmed the existence of the "middle class" in contemporary China, as well as its important social role. Media responded rapidly. The *Economic Observer*, *New Weekly*, *Newsweek*, *Lifeweek*, *China Business Times*, *Nan Feng Chuang Magazine*, and *Nan Fang Zhoukan* , to name a few, media outlets successively followed suit, publishing articles or special reports discussing China's "middle class". Middle class-related concepts frequently appeared, becoming "vogue" vocabulary in publications.

Second, through media forms such as special reports, personal columns, and advertisements, the phenomenon, appearance, and worldview of the middle class group was put on show. Through such character portraits, the image of the middle class was constructed.

Aside from starting initial discussion of the middle class concept, media products outlined the "collective image" of contemporary China's middle class in terms of aspects such as lifestyle, attitude, values, personality characteristics, and social function. *New Weekly*'s "Six Middle Class Criteria" article is a representative piece that comprehensively lays out the lifestyle of contemporary China's middle class. The criteria it raises are the "New Qifu Village" housing standard, the "SHINING" brand name home interior standard, the "T8 Bar" nightlife standard, the "M on the Bund" dining standard, the "United Family

Healthcare" medical standard, and the *"Economic Observer* and *21st Century Business Herald"* reading standard.[20] *Lifeweek, Capital China,* and *Newsweek,* among others, also described China's middle class collective image through special report-style articles.

Moreover, through outlining the individual meaning of the middle class through character portraits, media used this accumulated self-imaging to construct a holistic picture of the middle class. For example, *Trends - Cosmopolitan*'s "3F Woman" and "Unusual Conversation", and *Trends - Esquire*'s "Fashionable Personalities" portraits, all take wealthy and middle class people as their object, comprehensively showing the state of their work, lives, marriages, and emotions. *New Weekly*'s "Personalities" portraits also focus on the newly-emerged urban middle class. Advertisements in middle class periodicals appeal even more to the sense of status of the middle class phenomenon.

During this time, a flood of periodicals emerged, all of them either declaring their middle class association, or else considered by all as middle class-tinted. For example vogue lifestyle publications like *Lifestyle, Shanghai Times, Elle China, Rayli, New Weekly*; financial publications like *China Business Journal* (established in 1985, and which by 1996 was made the standard of comparison for new periodicals), *Economic Observer, 21st Century Business Times, Financial Times,* and *New Financial Times*; current affairs publications, such as *Lifeweek, China Newsweek, Xin Min Weekly,* and *Oriental Outlook.* The three waves of middle class periodicals – lifestyle, financial, and current affairs – have successively established the social existence of the middle class in terms of lifestyle, economic status, and political appeals. They further began to take on the role of cultural vehicle for this social group, and also showed potential to grow into a discursive space for the middle class.

Periodical media publications clearly raised and discussed the role of founding issues in a public forum in defining a concept of the "middle class", and bringing a new social class concept into the public imaginary. They also discussed at length the status of media products in bringing attention and status to people and their image. Furthermore, they also provided certain topics to establish issues for the middle class, in order to construct a discursive space. In a manner of speaking, media was fully aware of their creating a forceful middle class discourse.

2. The Dynamic System of Media-Constructed Middle Class Language

The media's active construction of "middle class" language originates in the profound

---

20 Translators note: *New Qifu Village, SHINING., T8 Bar, M on the Bund,* etc. are all high-end brand names or locations found in Shanghai and   Beijing.

social changes of 1980's China. China's interior society has endured three external forces, and has also been driven by its own structure. The three external forces are: from middle-class self-structuring, from national discourse validating the middle class, and from ideas from public intellectuals on this class. From the point of view of media, the realization of this construction is an objective response to global changes, and comes from the proactive actions from tension within media organizations. At the same time, looking at China as a whole system, it is hard to overlook forces from outside this system, meaning the advance of globalization in China acting as a "midwife" to the middle class's birth.

i) The practical foundation of media's focus on the "middle class" is the historically significant rise of China's middle class.

The rise of the middle class is an important change in the social structure of post-Reform China. It is a kind of new social phenomenon, one where "white collar workers" represent a middle class, which is a contemporary class of global significance to sociology. The image of this new social phenomenon and social class necessarily finds itself projected in public media. Simultaneously, as a newly-risen, upper social class, middle class needs for a discursive space and a position to self-identify with are conducive to the emergence of related media forms and content.

Even though scholars have differing opinions on the formation, size, and social function of the middle class, but after 2000, whether China has a middle class was no longer an academic debate. The awareness formed was that a middle class had already emerged in China. The middle class received prominent presence in media language, mainly because of the change in Chinese government language (He Jing, 2008). The vagueness of the middle class was recognized to be because of the relatively strong political meaning of the class, and because the class had touched the sensitive nerves of people who had experienced China's unique era, so naturally the middle class would incite fevered media responses, domestically and abroad. As a result, the fervent constructing of middle class language by media primarily is a projection of the rise of this class. In terms of Ge Lanxi's theory, this is a conscious cultural process: when any social class takes the stage, it will demand a discursive space that fits its needs. E.P. Thompson's study of the formation of England's working class (Thompson, 2001 [1966]), and Koo Hagen's research on the developmental history of Korea's working class (Koo, 2001), both show that working class culture is an important force in constructing the working class. Within this, working class periodicals are an important part of forming working class culture, as working class people use periodicals to express their opinions and bring together their needs. Thompson also found in his investigation of the formation of England's working class, that the formation of the radical "middle class" during the industrial revolution also followed this path.

While the middle class is a relatively relaxed social structure, it is different from that of the working class, but if Thompson's ideas on class formation are used to understand class concepts, it is likely his explanations of working class behavior can help illuminate understanding of middle class needs. "When we talk about class, we are talking about a group of people within a loose definition, who have common interests, social experience, traditions, and values, and have an awareness of class action and of difference with other classes. Through their actions and awareness, they define class preferences" (Thompson, 2001: 357). More importantly, "the working class does not rise up at predetermined times like the Sun, but emerges in its self-formation" (Thompson, 2001: 1). From Thompson and Koo's discoveries researching the working class, when a group of people with common interests, social experience, and values appears, there is a definite need for a common discursive space. As a newly-risen, highly-educated, democratically-oriented social group, China's middle class objectively has expectations for such a discursive space, especially following the strengthening of the group's economic weight. The middle class will strive to express their opinions and hopes regarding politics, economy, and culture. For example they will pay close attention to important issues of the social system, and appeal to issues such as limiting government, democratic governance, free economics, and social equality, and advocate values such as rationality, constructiveness, and peace and stability. Similarly, media such as *Newsweek*, and *Oriental Outlook* say that on some level they conform to these expectations.

To the middle class, aside from needing a space for discussion, it also needs to complete self-identification through some form of cultural vehicle. Mills thinks that America's middle class acknowledges and affirms its status through credit card applications and subscriptions to magazines such as *The New Yorker* (Mills, 1951). While researching the rise of American public culture at the turn of the 20th Century, Ohmann also established the connection between the then-forming managerial and professional class (the new middle class) and magazines of a certain orientation. He thinks that "the central need of the readership of *Cosmopolitan*, the *Ladies' Home Journal*, and other similar magazines, is to steady their place in a rapidly moving society, which is beneficial to their social status. Upon entering a household, such magazines establish and proclaim their social status, and provide certain information and points of interest. This information can become topics which connect readers in similar social circles, culturally organizing a social group with a similar way of thinking, on the national scale (Ohmann, 1996: 220).

As a result, the construction of the middle class by current media language has primarily appeared due to the middle class's role as a growing, newly-arisen social structure.

ii) The historic national transition from censoring and avoiding the middle class to affirming and nurturing it, is the basis of political legitimacy for media focus on the "middle class".

Marxist theory of class struggle is the steering thought behind the Chinese Communist Party's taking political power. During the era of peacefully building socialist China, especially during the "Anti-Rightist" and "Cultural Revolution" eras, class struggle was increasingly simplified and propagated, creating a lot of artificial class conflict. Class became a sensitive word in Chinese political life. The "middle class" became equivalent with "bourgeois" in Maoist discourse, a class status mutually exclusive with the socialist system. These kinds of definitions have continued until today, and the *Modern Chinese Dictionary* defines "middle class" as: "mid-level bourgeoisie; bourgeoisie in China".[21] Because of this historical inertia, "class/middle class" expressions are all forbidden in political language, and even amongst the public there remains a taboo on such concepts. Furthermore, how post-Reform emerging social groups will be defined is also a politically sensitive subject. Thus while media's construction of the middle class might have been in response to emerging objective changes in society, at the outset it did so with a sense of swallowing much of its words. Around 2001, following the loosening of national ideology, Chinese media opened a debate on the middle class that gripped the nation. At this time the "middle class" – using the term most favored by the media – properly took the stage, and this evolved into a dynamic and spectacular formative movement for the middle class. Beyond this exterior, this phenomenon depended heavily on the recognition given to the middle class by the state, as well as new policies aimed at further cultivating the middle class.

Following the rapid economic development since China's Reform and Opening, the emergent increase in inequality, and insufficient purchasing power in Chinese consumer

---

21 Wang Tongyi, editor. *Xiandai Hanyu Cidian* [Modern Chinese Dictionary], Hainan Chubanshe (1992): 1811. Of course, in *Cihai*, published in 1999, two explanations are provided for "middle class": "1) Shortened term for 'Middle-level bourgeoisie', namely China's bourgeoisie; 2) in contemporary Western society primarily refers to white collar class workers with relatively high income, including public servants, business managers, upper-middle level specialized workers, journalists, doctors, teachers, etc." (Cihai pianji weiyuanhui: *Cihai*, first published 1999, Shanghai: Shanghai Cishu Chubanshe (2002):4751. But clearly in the Chinese language, middle class corresponds with the national bourgeoisie.

markets to sustain healthy development, threaten political stability, and led the government to make cultivating the middle class a top priority.

At the beginning of Reform, in order to defeat the doctrine of absolute equality and improve efficiency, the government adopted the "allowing and encouraging some areas and some people to first get wealthy, through hard work and legal enterprise" policy. This policy played an important role in stimulating and spreading reform. After more than two decades of development, and the increase in gross national wealth, new interest structures gradually emerged, inequality gradually increased, class stratification became clear, and social polarization grew as each day passed, jeopardizing social stability and economic development. In sociologist Sun Liping's 2002 report, *New Trends in the Evolution of China's Social Structure since the Mid-1990's*, a key concept is put forward: that Chinese society after the mid-90's is a new phenomenon, vastly different from that of the 1980's. In sum, the 1980's was an era of distributing resources, where almost every member of society was a beneficiary, creating a brief period of equalization. By contrast, the 1990's generally was an era of renewed accumulation of resources, with clear polarization of interests. A key manifestation of this is the increase of income and resource inequality between groups. In a report by the World Bank in 1997, China's GINI coefficient was 0.28 in the 1980's, while in the 1990's it rose to 0.38, and then rose to 0.458 by 2000. The results of several research projects generally all show this conclusion, and these figures are all far in excess of national warning levels (safety guidelines).[22] The report says that no nation has achieved such rapid income inequality in a mere fifteen years (Sun Liping, 2004). According to the China Academy of Social Science Economic Research Institute's statistics, in 2002 6.1% of China's GNP was earned by the 1.0% highest income proportion of the population, a 0.5% increase since 1995. Those people in the top 5.0% income bracket earned 20.0% of national income, or a 1.1% increase since 1995, while those in the highest 10.0% income bracket earned 32.0% of national income, a 1.2% increase. [23] The increase in income inequality is one of the major sources of social conflict in today's era. Back in 1993, Deng Xiaoping said, "With so much owned by so few, and so many with nothing – continued development this way will create problems one day" (Leng Rong, Wang Zuoling,

---

22 According to common international standards, the best average condition is GINI coefficient of less than 0.3, 0.3~0.4 is a normal condition, over 0.4 enters the warning condition, and over 0.6 indicates a dangerous condition of potential random chaos and crisis.

23 "Shei zu'ai le zhongguo furen chengwei zishanjia"[Who stopped China's rich from becoming philanthropists], *21 Shiji Jingji Baodao*, 2004(03-01). The data provided in this report shows a certain bias which needs to be examined, but the continuing entrenchment of inequality is beyond a doubt.

2004: 136). Given these conditions, cultivating a middle class majority between the extremely wealthy and impoverished classes to play a cushioning role has become the top priority of national policies. "The connection between the middle class and social stability is quite like that between wealth and stability; a large middle class is just like widespread wealth, and is a sobering political force" (Guo Yandun, 1991: 251). Sixteen reports on "the importance of enlarging the middle-income group" are to a certain degree responses to this reality.

Additionally, in terms of the need to sustain economic development, due to the existence in the differentiated consumer class structure of the law of descending consumer limits following growth in income, excessive income inequality and overabundance of low-income people lead to lacking domestic demand and consumption, and struggling and stagnating consumer markets.[24] Continued years of weak consumption and China's lack of a large middle class are closely related. Thus fostering a middle class is a necessary measure for ensuring healthy economic growth.

China's cry to "raise the proportion of the middle-income group" is a result of waking up to and recognizing this reality. The political significance of the newly-risen middle class has been recognized, and "raising the proportion of the middle-income group" was written into National Congress reports, signifying the acceptance of the middle class by Party and National Government as an important force for continuing modernization, and political resolve to cultivate this future mainstream social group.[25] Thus the middle class is already protected and nurtured by mainstream ideology. Within this context, public media took the lead in the process of giving the middle class a "proper name".[26] National ideology decided the middle class's historical orientation, and its legitimacy in media language.

---

24 Li Peilin: "Quanmian jianshe xiaokang shehui de ji ge guanjian wenti" [several key issues in comprehensively building a *xiao kang* society]. *People's Daily*, 2003(05-23).

25 "Middle-income group" and "middle class" are two different concepts. The former only considers "income" as a criterion to define class meaning, while the latter takes income, employment, education, etc. to holistically define class difference, extending also to multi-factored concepts such as lifestyle, values, and employment characteristics. The middle-income group can only explain a certain class situated in the middle of society in terms of income, and is unable to explain class employment, education, social status, lifestyle, values, political stance, or any other characteristics. The "middle-income group" concept used in the sixteen important reports emphasizes "income" criteria, and certainly does not use the complete sociological meaning of the "middle class". But looking at the newly-risen middle class recognized politically in Jiang Zemin's July 1st Talk connected with the sixteen reports, combined with a firm grasp on contemporary Chinese society's fundamental development trends, explanations of the official recognition of academia and media and new policies nurturing the middle class were able to be accepted.

26 Translator's note: giving a "proper name" is an ancient concept related to finding one's correct social position and function.

iii) The endogenous impetus of public media's construction of middle class language.

As the undertakers of the construction of middle class language, the source of impetus behind public media is complicated. This phenomenon is refracted by the sudden and profound transformation of Chinese media since 1978. As a relatively independent language-producing structure, media's construction of the middle class phenomenon and issues is a reproduction and projection of objectively-occurring changes beyond China, and also stems from proactive behavior driven to a certain degree from within. Of the forces driving media to fervently "construct" China's middle class, market factors is one extremely clear, and powerful, structure. Under the marketizing conditions of media, as high-end consumers, the middle class is an important target audience. At the same time, some media outlets aspire to become influential, in particular, in an intensely competitive environment, traditional mainstream media outlets maintained and increased pressure to wield social influence, and so pushed forward the constructing of the middle class as "mainstream readership" as the media's identity. Aside from this, media professionals recognize society's mission to further professionalization, have expectations of influencing broader society through the middle class, and they agree with the middle class on social expectations and ethics. As members of the broadening middle class structure themselves, media professionals bear a naturally close relationship with this class, and make media strive to construct common issues and a self-identity for the middle class.

First was the drive of market forces under the new wave of news media reform. From 1978, news reform had two major periods: the information wave, and the post-1992 marketization wave (Ji Aijun, 2005:31). After the 1980's media transition from "political mouthpiece" to "information provider", Deng Xiaoping's Southern Tour talks and Fourteen Points called for "founding a socialist market economy" as a starting point. China's public media entered a momentous era of market-based development. In the early 1990's, weekend papers took off, in the mid-90's it was evening papers, and at the end of the 1990's urban media took off, again starting an era of popular commercial newspapers. At the same time, television broadcasts constantly increased film, fashion, sport, and financial programs and broadcasts.[27] Commercial media took great leaps into the market, expanding quantity of information rapidly, and diversifying media products daily. This led to the first peak in commercial media development. As the end of the 1990's approached, competition was fierce, and homogenization began to appear. Key considerations in the ambitions of the

---

27   In the above section reviewing the history of news media reform, Li Liangrong's *Li Liangrong zixuanji—Xinwen gaige de tansuo* [Li Liangrong's Personal Anthology – Exploring News Reform] was the primary source.

media market were how to diversify while improving broadcast quality and avoiding low-quality, repetitive competition. China's news reform entered a new stage of seeking to improve quality, due to the growth of information broadcast quantity, and the concept of dividing audiences took off. In this wave of dividing audiences, the mainstream group/middle class became the red-hot object of attention.

The basic economic flow of secondary distributor media, and the commercial rules of its client base, make the middle class the most specifically attractive audience. Because the middle class is not only able to pay for higher-priced media products (applicable to primary distributors), but, most importantly, because their consumption power allows them to also buy the high-end products advertised (applicable to secondary distributors) they are extremely important to advertisers. China's *New Weekly* director Feng Xincheng puts it clearly: "We will only ever choose the top of the pyramid, which is the middle class. You can call it *"Vanity Fair"*, as this group is exclusive". Furthermore, middle class consumer magazines take advantage of the inner aspirations for upward mobility in comparatively lower class people, meaning middle class periodical publications can draw in readers from beyond the middle class, helping publication and advertising income. "By mastering the use of 'middle class' consumer taste, not only do you have the middle class wrapped around your finger, but is also enough to draw in the so-called 'middle- and lower-class blue collar workers', making them aspire towards and emulate the projected 'identity' of upper classes. In terms of rational strategy, this is the lowest-risk, highest-return kind of appeal" (Ye Qizheng, 1989:117). Aside from this, connecting with the middle class also has the advantage of establishing a high-end periodical market phenomenon, and helps media draw in resources from within and beyond the industry. As a result, in terms of marketizing commercial media, the purchasing power of the middle class, and the resulting economic returns, has produced a strong internal drive in media to build up this class.

Secondly, strong media also fully exploits that the pushing forward of middle class audiences originates in influential Party-strengthening language. Since the 1980's, following the amelioration of government subsidies and rapid marketization, periodicals sprang up, and Party publications were gradually marginalized. A prominent question became how to ensure that the Party and Government retained its leadership in guiding public opinion in the new media environment. Traditional mainstream media necessarily must reform and change, so one way of thinking was to target "mainstream readers" and influence influential people. So-called mainstream readership, from a social structure perspective, is the primarily middle class audience group. As the *Nan Fang Daily* puts it, "our mainstream readership is public servants, managers, researchers, and intellectuals".

The *Da Zhong Daily*'s key readers are "different levels of Party cadres, scientists, intellectuals, and business managers." Xin Hua Publishing and Liao Wang Weekly Publishing's *Oriental Outlook* weekly's readership is "a newly risen social class. They are in the middle, consist of commercial science and technology business entrepreneurs, foreign-backed corporate employees, small business owners, private company managers, and mid-level and freelance professionals. They especially are rational individuals with myriad individual opinions, and hopes of creating wealth, mastering knowledge, pursuing future dreams, and of escaping the old, restrictive system." This "mainstream" social group is essentially the middle class as understood by sociologists, and some mainstream media directly acknowledges this point. For instance *News Weekly*'s target readership is the "growing middle class". It is thus evident that mastering, guiding, and serving the "influential" social group – mainly the middle class – was a key technique, within the context of market transformation of the media industry, in improving a media outlet's economic gains. It is also the measure taken by Party publications in the current media environment to maintain and strengthen the Party and Government's role at leading and influencing public opinion.

Aside from the role of external market and Party forces, the "middle class-ification" of periodical media also comes from the traditional idealism of China's professionals in news and journalism – pursuing a high-quality readership, to influence society as a whole through influential people. The ethical tradition of China's intellectuals of "taking on the world's ills as their responsibility", also still has a deep influence on today's news professionals. This tradition urges Chinese media professionals to pursue a professional influence on society,[28] and one of the ways to realize this social influence is by "influencing those in positions of influence". *Nan Fang Weekly* journalist Li Minpeng puts it, "I believe elites can influence the nation. These elites are not the popular heroes you hear of occasionally, but everyday intellectuals and entrepreneurs in society, but which have a voice in society, and the authority to make suggestions. By making their voice heard, they can influence the public, and the power of the people will then influence the whole nation" (Zhang Zhi'an, 2007:201). Furthermore, following the daily appearance of social class division in China today, "people with influence" – those with voice, political clout, and

---

28 For the majority of news professionals, choosing a career in news is most often based on a yearning to take on the burden of media's social moral responsibility in broadcasting to the public, and also often on personal interest. As far as seeking fame and fortune goes, it is certainly not a major factor in choosing to work in media. Zhang Zhi'an. *Jizhe ruhe zhuanye: Shendu baodao jingying de zhiye yishi yu baodao celue* [How Journalists are Professional: Work Ideology and Reporting Strategy of Journlist Elites] Foreword. Guangzhou: Nanfang Ribao Chubanshe, 2007.

economic status – that vague group has been gradually formed into the united body of the "middle class".

Moreover, in terms of ethical and spiritual understanding, media professionals and their middle class audience also have a natural closeness as members of the same class. They have corresponding views on democracy, free market economics, cultural diversity, and a rational, objective worldview. It is not hard to understand why public media would show a fervent interest in the middle class.

iv) The unique role of public intellectuals.

While creating a public space for middle class expression, public intellectual language took on what became an almost foundational role. In a large number of important public issues during the formation of middle class periodicals, public intellectuals provided guiding advice. They began rational criticism, reflection, and suggestions on the national political, economic, cultural, and civil systems, embodying the spirit of rationality, justice, and equality. Public intellectuals and middle class periodicals together constructed a middle class discursive space. From the mid- to late-1990's, public intellectuals and middle class periodicals worked closely together, mainly due to the following reasons:

First, the insistent need of public intellectuals through the 1990's for a discursive space.

In recent decades, China's public intellectuals have taken the historic stage on a large scale twice. The first time was at the turn of the 20th Century, particularly in the two to three decades after the Sino-Japanese War of 1895. In that era, intellectuals made a stand for new media, new schools, and new teaching, started debates on key issues in Chinese politics, and advocated new thinking to the public. The second time was in the 1980's, during a time when civil culture and life made great strides. Having come through the post-1949 difficulties, especially the "nightmare" of the Cultural Revolution, the language of these intellectuals passionately surged. In the liberation of thought movement of the late-70's and early-80's, and the "new enlightenment movement" of the mid- to late-80's, a wave of well-known, widely-read public intellectuals emerged, creating great progress in civil life, and creating a civil space, [29] or public intellectual space. [30] At the end of the 1980's, external factors scattered the many public intellectuals and magazines of this era, and the public space that had been formed disappeared. During this period, public

---

29   Xu Jilin. *Zhongguo Zhishifenzi shilun* [Chinese Intellectual Debates]. Fudan Daxue Chubanshe, 2003.

30   Xin Gu, *The structural transformation of the intellectual public sphere in Communist China: 1979-1989*, Leiden: Bibliothek der Rijks Universiteit, 1997.

intellectuals implemented "rational reflection-based strategic retreat", turning from the public forum back to the academy to carry out "professional" self-cultivation.[31] As a result, public intellectual and the public forum they created and participated in faded away. Yet at the same time, in the early 1990's the widespread development of China's commercial media seemed also to be a vast public space. On the one hand, the public forum space already created by public intellectuals had been reduced, but on the other hand, the process of marketizing public media had greatly expanded this forum. The natural need for expression of China's intellectuals would naturally not be put down easily, and they used this new discursive space to convey their opinions of civil society and the holding up of ethics and justice.

Entering the 1990's, the demands placed on media by China's intellectuals came from a different level of pressure, namely that public intellectuals, mainly in humanities, had been increasingly "marginalized" in the era of market economics. They hoped to regain their weakened social value through the space created by public media. Furthermore, intellectuals also approached media due to practical economic practicalities. Following the combined political and cultural marginalization of humanities intellectuals, in terms of income they experienced a rapid decline, even faster than most, and improving their income became a practical necessity.[32] The practical benefits in writing for media for humanities intellectuals lie not only in the public forum created by public media, but also in terms of material gains and real income.

Meanwhile, public media also provided the ideal audience for public intellectuals – the middle class. "Compared to politicians, down-to-earth writers, politically-active movie stars, or everyday news journalists, public intellectuals target the highest-educated audience."[33] The works public intellectuals wrote for the public during the May 4th Movement were different; today's public intellectuals are much more willing to propagate their ideas through smaller publications. (Their voice on television and the internet is

---

31 At first glance this seems like the situation described by Yagebi in the United States in the 1960's, namely that universities and other research institutions called back public intellectuals, and by providing stability and social securities, the "enticing", "academist" intellectuals became absorbed in academia and no longer concerned themselves with civil society. But clearly this is completely different from the "strategic retreat" of intellectuals back to the academy in 1990's China.

32 *Beijing Ribao*, 5/16/1999, "News Observations" No. 6, adapted from Pei Yiran, *Zhongguo Xiandai zhishifenzi yanjiu yu sikao — xing er shang zhi jiazhi xuqiu*[Research and Thoughts on China's Modern Intellectuals -- Metaphysical Value Demands], *Shanghai Caijing Daxue Xuebao*, 2001: 61.

33 Posner, Richard A. . *Public Intellectuals: Investigating Their Decline*. Translated by Xu Xinyi. Zhongguo Zhengfa Daxue Chubanshe, 2002.

something else altogether, this paper looks mainly at periodical publication media forms.) Their intellectual discourse, based on a deeply cultivated professional quality, mainly focuses on public affairs and highly-educated people able to understand and engage with public intellectuals on a spiritual level. In contemporary China the group most like this "ideal audience" is the newly-forming middle class.

The middle class is mainly comprised of people born in the 1960's and 70's, who grew up after society's transformation in the 1980's, and who have grown up with the language of democracy, market economics, and cultural diversity. These are also the basic appeals of public intellectuals since Opening and Reform. As a social group that grew up in and benefitted from Opening and Reform, the middle class closely watches the many changes occurring in China's political, economic, and cultural systems in this era of transformation, as these changes are closely tied to their own interests. From this level, they hold the same set of issues as public intellectuals. Spiritually, a spirit of rationality, (constructive) criticism, and public concern makes up part of their values, resulting in reasonable dialogue between intellectuals and the middle class. The essence of the modern middle class will always be intellectual in nature, and have characteristics of individual struggle, earning social benefits through hard work. During social transformation, this social group's interests will gradually suffer from political corruption and unfair regulations, and so it will feel growing dissatisfaction with the unjustness of the political and economic system. The middle class hopes that their legitimate interests will be protected through gradual political reform and building a new system. Even though public intellectuals and the middle class come from different points of origin – the middle class expresses criticism based on their own interests – concepts of rationality and "constructive criticism" are common to both groups.

Yet, as an audience, part of the middle class has a natural closeness with the language of public intellectuals. The new middle class is generally highly educated, and according to the definition of a wide range of intellectuals, they are members of the intellectual group. According to class belonging, intellectuals and the middle class are also one. Gouldner considers those with cultural capital, such as humanities intellectuals and specialized intellectuals, to be the "new class" in world social and economic class orders, and this new class is becoming the main subject of middle classes in many societies – China is no exception. In terms of this meaning, public intellectuals are still included as part of the middle class. Within this class, public intellectuals are the elites that go beyond personal professionalism to focus on public issues, and fervently express their opinions. As a result, the language of public intellectuals is actually constantly constructing the self-expression of the middle class.

v) The global expansion of transnational companies created an early wave of modern white collar workers in China,[34] and in the shaping of middle class media language, globalization also played an indispensable role.

Transnational companies created China's foreign-employed white collar workers, who are also the "archetypal" middle class in media publications.

The birth of China's middle class followed two paths: first, an endogenous one as a result of industrial revolution and marketization; second, the Western-style path, namely after Western transnational companies entered China and hired and trained managerial and personnel talent. These people are the modern "white collar class" of the early Opening and Reform era. "At the same time as transnational capital constructed China's socially-divided labor market, it also influenced the reforming of China's social structure, creating a new class–the middle class" (Tong Xin, 2008:1). In media language, this group of foreign-company white collar workers was China's first generation of white collar workers, and in the early period foreign-company white collar workers was generally the word for the white collar class in China. Not only did this group become the earliest "white collar class" (middle class) in the media, but the image of these personnel became the source of early images of the middle class, and also became the standard structure of the middle class in media language.

Most importantly, transnational companies pushed forward consumer culture, building the characteristic status of the middle class as consumers, and establishing the acknowledged status image of the middle class as connected to specific consumer symbols. The vehicle of the media forcefully created this "middle class".

The global spreading of consumer culture stems from the developing of markets on a global scale by late-stage capitalism, pursuing the need for profits. At its core is the encouragement of and imperative for consumption. "The expansion created by capitalism, particularly the wide acceptance of scientific management and 'Fordism' at the turn of the century, has constructed new markets, 'nurturing' the public into becoming consumers through advertising and other media promotions, and making it a necessity" (Featherstone, 2000:19). When international capital entered China's development, how to effectively nurture consumers and strategically construct a consumer model were of key importance. Regardless of perspective, China's middle class is the most ideal subject for nurturing

---

34 "White Collar" in other related discourse usually refers to China's modern white collar class that appeared post-Reform, and does not include pre-Reform middle class, such as 1930's Shanghai early white collar class.

consumerism. In terms of the significance of this body, the middle class is the nucleus of China's future society, as it is an ideal market subject with its relatively strong consumer power. In terms of its symbolic meaning, the middle class is a model class with a domino effect on society; as a kind of representative voice on lifestyle, it steers consumerism, and can make society follow, opening up markets. Therefore, international capital strives to build China's "middle class", the main consumer body.

The "middle class" symbol constructed by international capital, mainly through building up a consumer status for the "middle class", and defining consumer products and behavior, took on two main kinds of action. One action again followed two different paths – one was an advertising offensive. International advertising company products had clear focus: they carved out a "middle class" group in the consumer market, and strove to manifest the uniqueness and superiority of this group. They did this by rapidly creating ubiquitous advertisements that formed this group into an eye-catching mainstream social group. Meanwhile, international advertising companies provided high-quality advertising products, which packaged the connection between middle class status and products established on the middle class meaning and condition. Through the cumulative effects of constant advertising, these companies constructed a middle class status image defined by special consumer products or lifestyle factors, in this way appealing for recognition from China's middle class, and also for recognition and emulation from non-middle class Chinese.

The other way in which transnational companies constructed China's middle class is through international copyright cooperation, directly entering China's middle class media industry. In particular the production of consumer fashion media content was directed at nurturing the lifestyle, opinions, and values of China's middle class, and of note are those nurturing middle class consumer patterns. These fashion symbols became factors in the construction of the status and image of the middle class, and, whether intentionally or not, permeated media language describing the middle class.

The third aspect of globalization's nurturing of the middle class is that in the global circulation of media products, the image of the Western middle class has entered China, becoming the point of reference for the Chinese middle class. Similarly, Western media also attempts to influence the construction of China's middle class issues.

Looking at primarily middle class, developed Western societies like the United States, their media content also makes the middle class their focus. Therefore, at the level of public culture and daily life, the lifestyle, tastes, and pursuits of the U.S. middle class are spread across the globe.[35] Due to long-term Western advertising, and the embellishments of film and television programs, in the eyes of Chinese people the Western middle class came to represent a lifestyle for which people yearned. In terms of the rapid upward mobility of that phase, and the growth of China's middle class, this yearning transformed into a real contrast and construction—contrast with the West, and construction of the self. This awareness profoundly entered media language, which can also be partly explained as those middle class media images with a particularly Westernized influence.

The spreading of Western media products not only provided real images for China's middle class to observe, but, most importantly, also entered the process of building the middle class's discursive space. One aspect is that Western media was attempting to construct Chinese middle class issues. Taking the periodical publication market as an example, in recent years some foreign-produced periodicals have sought hard to enter the Chinese market. *Elle, Vogue, Rayli,* and other fashion magazines, and *Fortune, Business Week (China), Life Week,* and other political-economic magazines, have all entered China, showing the effort Western media goes to in constructing a discursive space for China's middle class. Another aspect is that Chinese middle class media have based themselves on mature Western middle class media development directions, and this reality has led to the permeation of Western media concepts. For instance, *Newsweek* and *Life Week* compete with American *Time* magazine, and *21st Century Business Herald* competes with China's *Wall Street Journal.* In this process of pursuit, not only do Chinese publications use Western middle class media formatting, report models, and writing styles, most importantly, Western media also play a role in that their middle class values silently transform Chinese media language regarding the nurturing and building up of China's middle class.

Therefore, as a kind foreign-sourced power, globalization's unique approach has played a role in the growth of China's middle class, giving prominent place to the construction of the image and discursive space of the middle class, and displaying strong, active awareness in doing so.

3. Conclusion

Superficially, public media's exerted construction of middle class language is a media phenomenon. But in fact, this media phenomenon stems from the profound social changes in 1980's China. This is an act of "collusion" between the middle class, state, public intellectuals, and media, within a continuing social context of the force of globalization, all

---

35   Schiller, Herbert. *Mass Communications and American Empire. (2nd edition).* Routledge,1992.

participating together in the social construction of the middle class.

Since Opening and Reform, China's economy has continued to rapidly develop, democratization has speeded up, and changes in the socio-cultural environment have all influenced the growth of the middle class. While this new life force has been quietly growing, it has also been looking for a way to express itself and its existence. In another sector, reform of China's mass media industry has likewise been progressing. The continued breaking down of "(class conflict) political tool discourse", "political voice discourse", and "information-ism" in media has also given birth to huge reforms. In 1992, China's Central Government established the socialist market economy system, and China's social reform entered an important transition period. During this time, the newly-arisen middle class continued to grow, and China's media industry reform began to show comprehensive "marketization". The marketization of media finally brought the media to actively, fiercely even, construct the fervent desires of high-end consumers as the new middle class. Since *Shishang* magazine began in 1993, *China Business Times* in 1996, and *News Weekly* (China) in 2000 as regular, authoritative magazines, Chinese periodical media have continued to manifest recognition for the status of China's middle class in terms of lifestyle, wealth and status, and political appeals. Similarly, media has also carried out comprehensive construction of the middle class from its image to its expressive space. Since the 1990's, the fervent construction of the middle class by media language is a historic trend, and is also a common need for expression at different levels of society. At the national level, the social influence of the middle class is gradually growing, extreme inequality and social conflict are also apparent, and domestic demand and consumption is insufficient – these factors all combine to make affirming and nurturing the middle class a necessary policy direction. At the public level, plans for a future prosperous society and the entry of international capital since the 1990's have led to media cultivating "middle class" symbols, already leading to "middle class" imagery becoming the quintessential structure of prosperous society. Public "middle class" expectations act as one of the driving forces behind the media's development and construction of this phenomenon. From the perspective of the constructed subject, as media reflects the newest changes in society, and faces the market pressure of their high-end consumer subject, media looks favorably on the middle class. Public intellectuals have a broad forum for expression through the media market, and the middle class are the ideal audience. Following its own growth, the middle class feels a gradually imminent need for public expression of its values and beliefs. Meanwhile, globalization is another constant force that helps give birth to and push forward the middle class, from its initial presence to its own discursive space. The demands of different levels of society accumulate and appear in media, together urging forward the media's comprehensive construction of the middle class from image to issues.

References

Chou Liping and Gu Hui. *Shehui jiegou yu jieji de shengchan jiegou jinzhang yu fencing yanjiu de jieji zhanxiang* [Tensions in the Social Structure and Class Structure of Production and Stages of Transformation in Class Research]. *Shehui*, 2007(2).

Dai Jinhua. *Dazhong wenhua de yinxing zhengzhixue* [The Hidden Politics of Mass Culture]. *Tianya*, 1999(2).

Featherstone, Mike. *Consumer Culture and Postmodernism*. Translated by Liu Jingming. Nanjing: Yilin Chubanshe, 2000.

He Jing. *Woguo meijie wenben dui 'zhongchan jieceng' de xingxiang jiangou guocheng fenxi—yizhong 'huwenxing' fenxi de shijiao* [An Analysis of the Process of Constructing the 'Middle Class' Phenomenon by Chinese Media Products—A kind of 'interrelated text' analytical perspective]. *Guoji Xinwenjie*, 2008(2).

Huntington, Samuel. *Political Systems in Changing Societies*. Translated by Wang Guanhua. Beijing: Sanlian Shudian, 1991.

Leng Rong and Wang Zuoling, editors. *Deng Xiaoping Nianpu* [Deng Xiaoping Through the Years], Beijing: Zhongyang Wenxian Chubanshe, 2004.

Li Chunling. *Zhongguo dangdai zhongchan jieceng de goucheng ji bili* [The Structure and Proportion of China's Contemporary Middle Class]. *Zhongguo Renkou Kexue*, 2003(6).

Li Zhengdong. *Shilun zhongguo zhongchan jieceng—dangqian zhongguo shehui zhuanxing jincheng zhong shehui jiegou zhenghe de dongtai tansuo* [At Attempt to Discuss China's Middle Class — Dynamic Investigation of the Comprehensive Social Structure in Current China's Transforming Society]. *Guandong Shehui Kexue*, 2001(2).

Liechty, Mark. *Suitably Modern: Making Middle-Class Culture in a New Consumer Society*. Princeton, N.J.: Princeton University Press, 2003.

Meng Fanhua. *Chuanmei yu wenhua lingdaoquan: dangdai zhongguo de wenhua shengchan yu wenhua renting* [Media and Cultural Power: Contemporary China's Cultural Production and Cultural Self- identification]. Jinan: Shandong Jiaoyu Chubanshe, 2004.

Mills, C. Wright. *White Collar: the American Middle Class*. N.Y.: Oxford University Press, 1951.

Ohmann, Richard. *Selling Culture: Magazines, Markets, and Class at the Turn of the Century*. London, New York: Verso, 1996.

Qi Aijun. *Xinshiqi xinwen zhoukan de shengcun yu fazhan* [The Survival and Development of Periodical News in the New Era]. Jinan: Shandong Renmin Chubanshe, 2005.

Sun Liping. *Duanlie — 20 Shiji 90 niandai yilai de zhongguo shehui* [Rupture–Chinese Society Since The 1990's]. Beijing: Shehui Kexue Wenxian Chubanshe, 2003.

Sun Liping. *Zhuanxing yu duanlie* [Transformation and Rupture]. Beijing: Qinghua Daxue Chubanshe, 2004.

Thompson, E. P.. *The Formation of England's Working Class*. Translated by Qian Chengdan et al. Nanjing: Yilin Chubanshe, 2001.

Teng Xin. *Kuaguo ziben yu zhongguo zhongchan jieji de shengchan: yi zaihua kuaguo gongsi zhongfang gaoduan laodongli wei li* [Trans-national Capital and the Production of China's Middle Class: Talented Personnel in Trans-national Companies in China as an Example]. *Shehui*, 2008(4).

Xiao Wentao. *Zhongguo zhongchan jieji de xianzhuang yu weilai fazhan* [The Current Condition and Future Development of China's Middle Class]. *Shehuixue Yanjiu*, 2001(3).

Ye Qizheng. *Taiwan "Zhongchan jieji" de wenhua misi* [Misconceptions of Taiwanese 'Middle Class' Culture]. From Xiao Xinhuang, editor. *Bianqian zhong Taiwan shehui de zhongchan jieji* [The Changing Middle Class in Taiwanese Society]. Taibei: Juliu Chubanshe, 1989.

Zhang Wanli. *Zhongjian jieceng de jueqi yu shehui fencing* [The Rise of the Middle Class and Social Stratification]. From Deng Hangsheng, editor. *Zhongguo shehui jiegou bianhua qushi yanjiu* [Studies on Trends in China's Changing Social Structure]. Beijing: Zhongguo Renmindaxue Chubanshe, 2004.

Zhang Zhi'an. *Jizhe ruhe zhuanye: shendu baodao jingying de zhiye yishi yu baodao celue* [How Journalists are Professional: Work Ideology and Reporting Strategy of Journalist Elites] Guangzhou: Nanfang Ribao Chubanshe, 2007.

Author Information:

He Jing: Female, PhD, China Youth Politics Research Academy News and Radio Department, Assistant Professor.

Contact Address: Beijing Xi Sanhuan Beilu No. 25, 100089.

Email Address: jing.he@live.cn

Part II   Definition, Component and Size of China's Middle Class

Chapter 5

Profile of China's Middle Class

Li Chunling

Since the beginning of this century a social group with higher levels of income and educational and occupational prestige has been emerging in Chinese cities. In the popular media it is known as the middle class. Even though people dispute the exact definition of the term middle class, there is no doubt that this group exists in China and is expanding quickly.

The group has attracted increasing attention from the public, business leaders, and policymakers, as well as from researchers in sociology, economics, and politics. Sociologists especially have had a long-standing interest in the group and have discussed many aspects of it. However, because this middle class is newly emerging and its boundaries and attributes are unclear, these discussions provide very different, sometimes contradictory, descriptions of China's middle class. This chapter, based on data from several national surveys, attempts to present a general profile of China's middle class by elucidating the competing Chinese definitions and assessments of the middle class.

Based on a general description of China's middle class, the chapter deals with two important issues concerning the Chinese middle class. The first is definitional. The existing literature on the Chinese middle class contains various definitions of middle class, which provide very different pictures.[1] These disparate understandings of China's middle class reflect the uncertain condition and ambiguous boundary of this newly emerging group. Further, this definitional confusion has seriously disrupted research into China's middle class. The chapter distinguishes the various definitions, illustrates their exact meanings, and proposes a sociological concept of the middle class that can be accepted by a consensus of Chinese sociologists.

The second issue involves a sociological debate over the Chinese middle class. Is the Chinese middle class only a statistical category based on certain criteria such as income, education, and occupation? Or is it a real class in the sociological sense with sociopolitical homogeneities? This would mean that its members have developed a coherent identity, a class culture, and sociopolitical attitudes and values and have prob-ably taken some class action. By defining the components of the Chinese middle class and describing its characteristics, this chapter examines the homogeneities or heterogeneities of the alleged middle class so as to assess the possibility of the formation of a true class.

This study is based on data from a variety of sources, including the national census (1982, 1990, and 2000) and a 1 percent population survey (2005) conducted by the National Bureau of Statistics; a household income survey of Chinese cities (1988, 1995, and 2002) conducted by the Institute of Economics at the Chinese Academy of Social Sciences; a national survey on social structure change (2001); the China General Social Survey (2006); and the Beijing Middle Class Survey (2007) carried out by the Institute of Sociology at the Chinese Academy of Social Sciences.[2]

Emergence of the Middle Class

Discussion of the middle class in the Chinese academic community first began in the mid-1980s, but few people considered it to be a truly existing entity until the beginning of this century.[3] Only over the last decade have most Chinese people begun to recognize the emergence of a middle class, owing to the cumulative effects of the fast socioeconomic develop-ment of recent decades.

Economic and Income Growth

Stable and fast economic growth over the last few decades provided a foundation for the emergence of China's middle class. Figure 1 illustrates China's GDP growth and

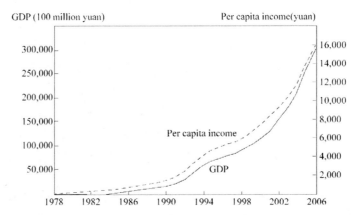

Source: Statistics Bureau of China, ZhongguoTongji Nianjian [China statistical yearbook] (Beijing: China Statistics Press, 2009), p.53.

Figure 1   GDP and Family Income, China, 1978~2006

income growth in recent decades. In 1978 China's GDP was only 364.5 billion Chinese yuan, but it reached 21,087.1 billion yuan by 2006, nearly fifty-eight times the 1978 figure. The average annual economic growth over these twenty-eight years was more than 13 percent. Alongside this fast economic growth, per capita family income also increased significantly. In 1978 per capita family income for urban areas was only 342.4 yuan, but by 2006 it had increased to 11,759.5 yuan, a thirty-four-fold increase.

Urbanization

Urban expansion and an increase in the urban population afforded favorable conditions for the emergence of a middle class in China. In 1978 there were only 193 cities in China. By 2007 the number had increased to 651. The urban population increased steadily during this period, as shown in Figure 2. It increased from 173 million in 1978 to 594 million in 2007. However, the rural population in China still remains very large. Today about 55 percent of the population lives in rural areas. Most of them have low incomes, low educational levels, and disadvantageous living conditions. Because of such a huge rural population, the middle class is still a small proportion of China's national population despite growing very quickly in cities.

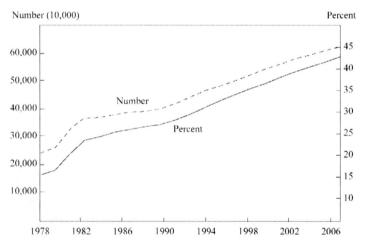

Source: Bureau of China,ZhongguoTongjiNianjian [China statistical yearbook] (Beijing: China Statistics Press, 2009), p. 95.

Figure 2   Urbanization of China, 1978~2007

Higher Education and White-Collar Jobs

The expansion of higher education and the growth in white-collar jobs have also stimulated the rise of the middle class in China. Figure 3 shows the trend of expansion of higher education in China between 1990 and 2007. Since 1999, when the government announced a policy to vastly expand higher education enrollment, the number of the college students and the opportunities to pursue higher education have increased sharply. Over the five years following 1999, the number of college stu-dents increased four times, and the opportunity to pursue higher educa-tion almost doubled.

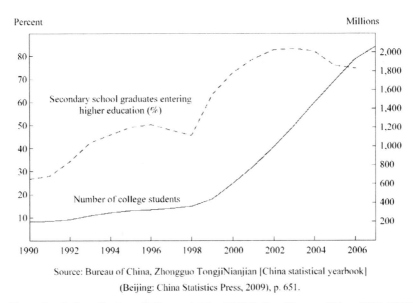

Source: Bureau of China, Zhongguo TongjiNianjian [China statistical yearbook]
(Beijing: China Statistics Press, 2009), p. 651.

Figure 3   College Students Before and After 1999 Policy Change, China, 1990–2007

At the same time, the number of persons with higher education among the population has been increasing significantly. In the 1980s, among the population over eighteen years old, only about 1 percent nation-wide and 11 percent in cities had received higher education. In 2005 the percentages had increased to 7 percent and 17 percent, respectively. Moreover, China has witnessed a corresponding increase in the num-ber of white-collar employees. In 1982 about 7 percent of the national population over eighteen years old held white-collar jobs. By 2005 this percentage had increased to 12 percent. Figure 4 shows the increase of the population with white-collar jobs and higher education. These people constitute the major part of the new middle class, and expansion of this group implies an enlargement of the middle class.

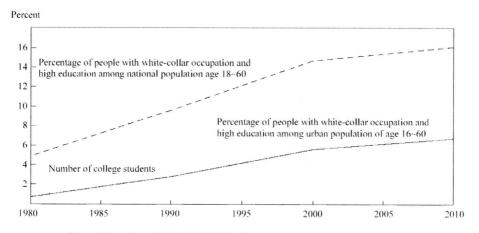

Percent

Source: Census data of 1982, 1990, 2000; 1 Percent Population Sample Survey of 2005.

Figure 4   Number of Persons with White-Collar Occupations and Higher Education,
China, 1980–2010

Definitions of Middle Class

Who makes up the middle class? What is the actual definition of middle class? These are highly controversial questions in China. There are many different and conflicting definitions. Usually four criteria are used to define the middle class in China. The first is income. A member of the middle class should be a person with relatively high and stable income. The second criterion is occupation. A member of the middle class should be a person holding a professional or managerial job. The third criterion is education. A middle-class person should have received a higher education. The fourth criterion is consumption. A member of the middle class should be able to afford a comfortable lifestyle and should enjoy a relatively high standard of living.

At present, there are at least three major perspectives of the middle class in China: the public image of the middle class, the government's official description of the middle class, and sociologists' definition of the middle class. Each version highlights one or two of the criteria men-tioned above. Different concepts of middle class can denote quite diverse social groups. In addition, there is large disparity in the size of China's middle class depending on the definition.

Public Image of the Middle Class

The public image of the middle class was initially derived from advertisements for real estate, automobiles, and other expensive com-modities.[4] These advertisements, printed in newspapers and maga-zines, featured beautiful pictures of these commodities and the people enjoying them. Expensive commodities thereby became a symbol of the middle class. TV dramas, novels, and other mass culture phenom-ena further elaborated and enriched this image of the middle class predicated upon the consumer behaviors and lifestyles of the rich.[5] It contributed to a Chinese impression of the middle class consisting of business people, managers, and intellectual elites with very high incomes and consumer habits.

By this definition, consumption is the decisive criterion to distinguish the middle class from other classes. The middle class is expected to be able to afford large houses, luxurious cars, and other expensive goods. They wear name-brand suits, work in modern office buildings, go abroad for holidays, invest in the stock market, and send their children to study abroad. This image of middle class created by the public media and business people has become the dominant definition of middle class in China.

It is very different from the concept of middle class in Western societ-ies, where middle class usually means regular people in the middle of the socioeconomic hierarchy. In China, however, the middle class is considered by the public to be a special group with quite high socioeconomic status. By the sociological definition, discussed below, these people belong the upper class or upper-middle class. According to the public definition, the size of China's middle class is very small, usually thought to be less than 8 percent of the total population.

Government's Definition of the Middle Class

China's authorities have long disliked the term middle class for political reasons. The term was almost prohibited from formal publications during 1990s. This was because the term had acquired political connota-tions when it was referenced by liberal scholars during the 1980s. At the time, middle class mainly denoted private entrepreneurs, a newly emerging social group in the 1980s, which developed quickly in the 1990s. Liberal intellectuals thought the growth of this social group would bring about political changes, such as political democratization. Accordingly, authorities have continued to deem the middle class a threat to the exist-ing political system.[6]

In the late 1990s a few influential sociologists argued that a large middle class was one of the general characteristics of modern societies and could be a stable force, not an unstable force, for society.[7] These sociological arguments have become more prevalent since the late 1990s and seem to have gradually convinced Chinese policymakers that a rising middle class could be a positive element in maintaining political stability. These sociologists especially stressed that the growth of the middle class would help to reduce the income gap, which the state considered to be one of Chinese society's most serious problems, one that could even trigger political unrest.

Although political leaders seemed to partly accept this view, they have remained distrustful of the middle class. They continue to prefer the term middle-income stratum to the term middle class. In November 2002, Jiang Zemin, then secretary general of the Chinese Communist Party (CCP), stated in his report to the Sixteenth National Party Congress that "expanding the middle-level-income group" was one of the policy targets of the government. Some analysts considered this statement to be a signal that the government would make an effort to develop the middle class, or middle stratum, as defined by the income criterion. But the question arose, how much income makes a person a member of middle class? It is difficult to reach a consensus view. Some believe that if a person has an annual income of $5,000 or higher he is a member of the middle class. But others think $30,000 should be the baseline. This is clearly a huge difference. Large disparities of income between urban and rural areas and among regions have made it impossible to arrive at a nationwide standard of income to define the middle class.

Sociological Concept of the Middle Class

Chinese sociologists tend to favor a definition of middle class different from the public and government definitions. They think the public's image of the middle class only describes the upper stratum of the middle class. Ordinary members of the middle class in China do not have high incomes and costly consumption habits; they cannot afford luxurious cars and large houses. Sociologists think that the concept of a middle stratum defined by income alone differs essentially from the concept of a middle class. They point out that such an income group includes diverse people, for whom it is impossible to develop a shared class identity, class consciousness, or class culture.

Thus sociologists usually define the middle class based on occupa-tional classification and employment status. Following the traditional class theories of neo-Marxism and neo-Weberism, sociologists tend to highlight the divisions between employers and employees, as well as those between manual labor and mental labor.[8] The distinction between white-collar workers and blue-collar workers is believed to be a critical division between the middle class and the working class.[9]

Property ownership is another important criterion to divide the middle class from the upper, capitalist, class. Large owners fall in the upper class. Midsized or small property owners and self-employed people are middle class. The problem for sociologists is that if all white-collar work-ers are members of middle class then the size of China's middle class should be very large. Indeed, it would encompass up to 30 percent of the total national population. Obviously, nobody believes the Chinese middle class is this large. Furthermore, most white-collar workers deny that they belong to the middle class because they feel they are far from experiencing the socioeconomic conditions a member of middle class should enjoy.

To solve this problem, sociologists propose adding another crite-rion-such as education, income, or consumption-to the definition of the middle class. However, different criteria adopted by different sociologists result in huge disparities in the estimated size of the middle class, which range from 4 percent to 25 percent. Corresponding percentages of the urban middle class range from 8 percent to 50 percent.[10]

Composition of the Middle Class

Although Chinese sociologists have not arrived at a consistent definition of the middle class, most of them think that it includes various subclasses. They find the subclasses of the middle class to have differ-ing economic conditions, living standards, and sociopolitical attitudes. Some sociologists prefer the plural, middle classes, to the singular, middle class. They argue that distinguishing different middle classes is as important as distinguishing the middle class from the working class or from the upper class. When talking about the economic conditions and sociopolitical characteristics of the middle class, we should be mindful of these differences. A framework outlining the heterogeneous composition of the Chinese middle class will help to clarify its characteristics.

Four Subclasses of the Middle Class

There are four social groups that most Chinese sociologists consider to be the major components of China's middle class.[11] One group is pri-vate entrepreneurs, whom some refer to as the capitalist class.[12] Another group consists of professionals, managers, and government officials; it is sometimes called the new middle class. A third group, known as the old middle class, is composed of small employers, small business owners, and the self-employed. The fourth group, or the marginal middle class, consists of low-wage white-collar and other workers.

This classification of the middle classes is derived from John H. Goldthorpe's class scheme, one of the most popular classifications of contemporary societies.[13] Table 1 illustrates the similarities between Goldthorpe's class scheme and that of the author.

Table 1   Four Subclasses of the Middle Class, Two Classification Methods

Goldthorpe's middle-class subclasses	Author's middle-class subclasses for China
I Higher grade professionals	1. Capitalist (employers with 20 or more employees)
II Lower grade professionals	2. New middle class
IVa Small employers with employees	3. Old middle class
IVb Small employers without employees	
IIIa Routine nonmanual employees	4. Marginal middle class
IIIb Personal service workers	
V Technicians and supervisors	Addendum
VIa Skilled workers	Working class
VIIa Semiskilled and nonskilled workers	
IVc Farmers	Farmers/farm labor

Source: John H. Goldthorpe, Social Mobility and Class Structure in Modern Britain (Oxford: Clarendon Press, 1987); also see Hsin-Huang Michael Hsiao, ed., East Asian Middle Classes in Comparative Perspective (Taipei Institute of Ethnology Academia Sinica, 1999).

The new middle class is the subclass of the middle class that might have the most significant influence on the direction of sociopolitical change in China. Its members occupy important positions in the social, political, and economic fields. Their institutional affiliations provide them with access to policymakers and elite groups. However, the insti-tutional segmentation between the public and private sectors continues to divide the new middle class into two parts. One part is the group of officials, professionals, and managers in the public sector, including state-owned enterprises, governmental organizations, and institutions funded or controlled by the government. Another part are professionals and managers in the private sector. The public sector group differs from its counterpart in the private sector in terms of its social, economic, and political characteristics.

Private entrepreneurs, or the capitalist class, is an active actor in the economic field and might become a politically actor in the future. Actu-ally, this group has been increasing in its political influence, especially at the local level. But its influence has been restrained by the central govern-ment, because top CCP leaders remain suspicious of this group's political loyalty. Both sociologists and the public consider the new middle class and the capitalist class to be typical of China's middle class.

As for the other two subclasses-old middle class and the marginal middle class-although most of the public does not think they count as middle class, sociologists deem them to exist between the working class and the typical middle class. Although the socioeconomic status of these two groups appears to be lower than that of the new middle class and the capitalist class, some of their members will probably join the new middle class or the capitalist class in the future. The marginal middle class is considered to be younger than other middle-class subclasses and to have higher educational attainment, more democratic consciousness, and greater capacity for political participation. This subclass has lately gained a high profile in the media, mass culture, and on the Internet. They are the most active participants in grassroots social movements and display much more political liberalism than the new middle class. Some analysts imply that China's middle-class mainstream, a relatively politically conservative group, might change when these young people become more dominant.

Growth of the Middle Class

Table 2 lists the percentages of the urban population aged sixteen to sixty composing the four subclasses of the middle class- the capital-ist class, the new middle class, the old middle class, and the marginal middle class-over the period 1982 to 2006. Even though the different methods of classification used across these various data sets means that one cannot reach a perfectly precise estimation, the overall growth trend is clearly reflected in these data. [14]

Table 2   Share of the Four Subclasses of the Middle Class, Urban China

Percent

Year	Capitalist	New middle	Old middle	Marginal middle	[Working][b]
1982	0.0	13.9	0.1	19.7	66.3
1988	0.1	17.2	3.2	23.8	55.7
1990	0.5	19.6	2.2	19.9	57.8
1995	0.6	22.1	5.5	26.6	45.2
2001	1.5	16.6	10.3	33.2	38.4
2002	1.1	23.6	11.1	29.1	35.1
2005	1.6	21.0	9.7	31.4	36.3
2006	0.6	18.8	19.6	25.4	35.7

Source:
a. Percentages for 1982, 1990, and 2005 are calculated from census data and the 1 percent population survey. Percentages for 1988, 1995, and 2002 are derived from the household income survey of Chinese cities. Percentages for 2001 and 2006 are from the national survey of social structure change and the China General Social Survey (2006); these data include cities and towns (with a lower percentage of new middle class and a higher percentage of old middle class). Others are data of cities.
b. The working class is not, according to the criteria, part of the middle class.

From 1982 to 2006 the new middle class increased by roughly 10 percentage points. The old middle class was almost nonexistent in the early 1980s but by 2006 was nearly 20 percent. This fast growth of the old middle class is one of the most significant characteristics of the development of Chinese middle class. In most Western countries expansion of the new middle class has been followed by a diminution of the old middle class. In Mainland China, however, the old middle class and new middle class have expanded simultaneously. Actually, the number of the old middle class in many midsized and small cities, especially towns, is larger than that of the new middle class.

The marginal middle class has also developed quite rapidly. Its percentage increased by about 10 percentage points during this period. The capitalist class first emerged during this period, but its percentage remains small compared to other classes. The rise of the middle class has resulted in a significant shrinking of the working class, which decreased by about 30 percentage points over the period.

The middle class accounted for about 64 percent of the urban popula-tion in 2006. If we exclude about 5 percent of the elite class and add in the farmer population in rural areas, the urban middle class is about 60 percent; the country's middle class is about 30 percent. However, if we use the more strict definition of middle class-that composed of only the new middle class and the capitalist class-the percentages of middle class among the urban population and the national population are, respec-tively, about 18 percent and 9 percent.[15]

Distribution of the Middle Class

As a newly rising class, China's middle class has some distinct charac-teristics in terms of its demography and socioeconomic situation.

Sector and Occupation. China's middle class has been emerging amid tremendous changes in the country's economic conditions, namely, the transformation from a planned economy to a market economy. Previ-ously almost all employees worked in the public sector. In 1982, for instance, all members of the new middle class and the marginal middle class worked in the public sector, and the capitalist class and old middle class did not exist (Table 3). As a result of the economic marketization since the 1980s, the capitalist class and the old middle class began to appear in the private sector. They became the new elements of the middle class.

At the same time, members of the new middle class and the marginal middle class gradually transferred into the private sector. However, most of the new middle class (62.2 percent) and the marginal middle class (54.2 percent) still work in the public sector. This has resulted in an important feature of China's middle class: public sector members have a closer relationship with the state than private sector members because they depend on the state for their socioeconomic well-being. Some of them, especially the upper new middle class, exert strong influences on policymaking and public opinion.

Table 3   Share of the Middle Class, Two Subclasses and Occupation, Urban China, 1982~2006

Percent

Year	New middle class		Marginal middle class		New middle class		
	Public	Private	Public	Private	Professional	Administrator	Manager
1982	100.0	0.0	100.0	0.0	…	…	…
1988	99.6	0.4	99.6	0.6	70.2	21.7	8.1
1995	99.1	0.9	98.2	1.8	63.7	12.3	23.9
2002	87.0	13.0	76.9	23.1	66.7	12.2	21.1
2006	62.2	37.8	54.2	45.8	71.2	10.3	18.5

Professionals, managers, and administrators of governmental orga-nizations are the three major occupations of the new middle class, but their respective percentages have changed over time. Professionals have accounted for the highest percentage consistently, although the exact figures have fluctuated. The percentage of administrators, however, has declined over time. The percentage of managers was the lowest of the new middle class in 1988, increased sharply in 1995, but has since decreased slightly. Its sharp increase in 1995 might be the result of the rapid development of township and villages enterprises in late 1980s and early 1990s. The slight decrease after 1995 was probably due to the shrinkage of these enterprises as well as to the bankruptcy of many state-owned enterprises.

Table 4   Years of Education and Age, Middle-Class Subclasses, China, 1988~2006

Years

Subclasses of the middle class	Education				Age			
	1988	1995	2002	2006	1988	1995	2002	2006
Capitalist	5.8	9.7	10.9	13.8	41.5	41.2	43.1	35.1
New middle	10.4	12.3	13.2	14.9	42.5	45.6	41.6	36.0
Old middle	6.4	8.1	9.2	9.8	35.1	35.6	39.7	38.3
Marginal middle	8.8	10.6	12.2	13.9	38.7	40.7	39.0	34.9
[Working][a]	7.3	8.5	9.4	9.3	34.8	41.9	40.7	37.25

Source: a. The working class is not, according to the criteria, part of the middle class.

Education, Age, and Sex.

China witnessed a fast expansion of secondary and tertiary education over the years

1988 to 2006. As a result, the educational level of the middle class also advanced rapidly (table 4). The years of school for the capitalist middle class increased by 8.0 years, that of the new middle class by 4.5 years, that of the old middle class by 3.4 years, and that of the marginal middle class by 5.1 years In 1988 the capitalists and old middle class had the lowest educational levels, even below that of the working class. By 2006, however, years of schooling increased greatly, especially those of the capitalist class, which was also the class with most economic capital and least cultural capital in the 1980s and 1990s. Now this class possesses not only economic capital but also cultural capital. Its average educational level is now close to that of new middle class.

As for age, the middle class seems to become younger over time, and this is especially true of the capitalist class, the new middle class, and the marginal middle class. The average ages of these three groups decreased by about six years from 1988 to 2006. One plausible reason is that China's overall workforce has become younger as the age of retirement has lowered and a tide of new labor has arrived. However, the average age of the old middle class increased by about three years over the same period.

The sex ratio of the middle class seems to have remained fairly stable over time. Men have consistently been more represented than women across all subsets of the middle class. For example, the female percentage of the new middle class was 38.2 percent in 1988, 39.9 percent in 1995, 38.4 percent in 2002, and 38.8 percent in 2006. That suggests that it is difficult to overcome the advantaged place of men in the middle class.

Table 5   Share of Middle-Class Subclasses by Gender, China, 2006

Percent

	New middle				Marginal		
	Capitalist	Professional	Administrator	Manager	Old middle	Marginal middle	|Working|[a]
Male	86.7	48.0	87.5	82.1	55.0	57.9	55.9
Female	13.3	52.0	12.5	17.9	45.0	42.1	44.1

Source: a. The working class is not, according to the criteria, part of the middle class.

The figures in Table 5 show that classes with more power or authority tend to have higher percentages of men. Indeed, the capitalist class has the highest percentage of men (86.7 percent). The gender gap in the new middle class is much smaller than that of the capitalist class because a higher percentage of females than males are professionals. More than 60 percent of the new middle class is male. However, the new middle class groups with most authority (administrators and managers) have higher percentages of men than groups with less authority (professional).

Multiple Identities of the Middle Class

Simultaneously possessing multiple status identities is a very important feature of China's middle class. Very few people self-identify as members of the middle class. According to the Beijing Middle Class Survey of 2007, among all subsets of Chinese middle classes-the capitalist class, the new middle class, the old middle class, and the marginal middle class-only about 10 percent admit that they are members of the middle class. Furthermore, less than one-third of the new middle class identify themselves as members of the middle class. Indeed most of the people whom sociologists define as middle class deny this status. However, they are more willing to admit being members of a middle stratum.[16] In their view, middle class and middle stratum are different concepts. As mentioned earlier, members of the middle class are supposed to be per-sons with high levels of income and consumption. And members of the middle stratum are thought of as regular people and not at the extremes of wealth or poverty.

Table 6   Share of Middle-Class Subclasses by Father's Class and First Occupation, China, 2001

Percent

	Capitalist	New middle	Old middle	Marginal middle	[Working][a]	[Farmer][a]
Father's class						
Capitalist	0.0	7.9	3.8	8.5	21.1	58.7
New middle	0.0	37.1	2.5	7.7	21.0	31.7
Old middle	0.0	6.6	10.0	2.7	24.3	56.4
Marginal middle	0.0	16.5	1.5	22.6	26.5	32.9
[Working][a]	0.0	7.1	2.2	4.8	39.5	46.4
First occupation						
Capitalist	2.1	9.1	8.5	13.2	31.2	35.9
New middle	0.9	37.1	2.0	23.7	22.2	14.1
Old middle	0.0	5.1	5.9	5.2	47.6	36.1
Marginal middle	0.0	15.8	1.5	28.2	34.7	19.8
[Working][a]	0.0	1.8	1.8	7.2	49.8	39.4

Source: a. The working class and the farmer class are not, according to the criteria, part of the middle class.

Family Class Background and First Occupation

As the first generation of the middle class, today's group includes heterogeneous family backgrounds and diversified occupational experiences, which prevent an identical status identity or class-consciousness from forming. Table 6-6 lists middle-class members by their fathers' class background and by their first jobs. [17] Most members of the capitalist class and the old middle class are from modest family backgrounds. Nearly 60 percent of these two classes came from farmer families and more than 20 percent from working-class families. Although many of the new middle class come from better-off family backgrounds, more than half of them are from farmer and working-class families. Of the middle class as a whole, 65.3 percent are from farmer or working-class backgrounds.

Most members of middle class (56.5 percent) held blue-collar jobs before they entered the middle class. The first jobs of two-thirds of the capitalist class (67.1 percent) were as farmers or blue-collar workers. For the old middle class, the share is 83.7 percent. For the marginal middle class, 54.5 percent were farmers or blue-collar workers before they became middle class. Even among the new middle class, 36.3 percent were first farmers or blue-collar workers.

These two factors-heterogeneous family background and diversified occupational experience, often having a close relationship to farmers and the working class-have had significant impacts on the formation of class identity of China's middle class. They have also erected barriers to the development of a middle-class identity and a common consumption culture.

Inconsistency between Social Status and Economic Status

One cause of a lack of middle-class status identity is an inconsistency between members' social status and their economic status, since income and consumption are the two most important criteria by which the public defines middle-class membership. The public-and the middle class itself-tend to think that the middle class should be composed of high-income earners.

A 2007 study by Li Peilin and Zhang Yi developed a method for determining high income. [18] According to their method, persons with an income more than 2.5 times the average income of an urban area are members of the high-income group. This high-income group is in closer accord with the public image of the middle class. Using the China General Social Survey data to calculate income, the baseline of the high- income group is a yearly income of 28,272 yuan. In other words, according to this income definition, persons with a yearly income of 28,272 yuan or greater are middle class. Based on sociologists' definition, a very low percentage of the middle class has an income higher than this baseline. Table 7 lists the average yearly incomes of the middle class's four subclasses and the percentage of each that is above this threshold.

Except for the capitalist class, only a low percentage of the middle classes meet this income criterion. Less than one-third of the new middle class, less than one-fifth of the old middle class, and slightly more than one-tenth of the marginal middle class have yearly incomes of more than 28,272 yuan. Among the middle class as a whole, only 18 percent reaches the income threshold. In addition, only the average income of the capitalist subclass is higher than this income baseline; the other three subclasses all have lower average incomes than this baseline. Based on this proportion, we may estimate that only 11 percent of the urban population and 6 percent of the entire population meet both criteria of middle class, that is, the sociological criterion and the public criterion.

Table 7   Average Yearly Middle-Class Income by Middle-Class Subclass, China, 2006

Unit as indicated

Class	Average yearly income (yuan)	Persons with yearly income of more than 28,272 yuan (percent)
Capitalist	49,495[a]	75.0
New middle	26,422	28.3
Old middle	18,630	16.7
Marginal middle	16,971	11.7
[Working][b]	11,371	3.7

Source:

a. Amount is much less than actual income because capitalist class data are based mostly on small-size entrepreneurs.

b. The working class is not, according to the criteria, part of the middle class.

This dichotomy between social and economic status has resulted in a bizarre phenomenon. Most members of the middle class, as defined by sociologists, deny that they belong to the middle class and complain about their inability to achieve middle-class living standards. At the same time, this is a strong motivating force for the middle class to pursue their economic interests and strive for such a standard of living. Indeed, more and more members of the middle class have moved into the high-income group in recent years. Table 8 shows an increasing percentage of persons and families reaching this income criterion over time. In 1988 only 0.5 percent of the adult population had incomes higher than 28,272 yuan, and 0.7 percent of urban families had per capita incomes higher than 20,715 yuan. These figures increased in 2006 to 8.6 percent and 5.8 percent, respectively, in cities and towns. Nationwide percentages also increased over time.

Table 8 Share of Urban Middle-Class Individuals and Families Making the Average Income, China, Selected Years, 1988~2006

Percent

Year	Income, middle-class individual[a]		Per capita income, middle-class family[b]	
	Urban area	Nationwide	Urban area	Nationwide
1988	0.5	···	0.7	···
1995	0.8	···	0.8	···
2001	3.4	2.1	3.4	1.7
2006	8.6	4.6	5.8	3.0

Source:

a. Percent having yearly income of more than 28,272 yuan. The calculation includes the price index for each year.

b. Percent having per capita yearly income of more than 20,715 yuan (2.5 times of average per capita family income). The calculation includes the price index for each year.

Conclusion

The middle class is expanding very rapidly in China. Its expansion has been especially obvious in income and consumption, but has also recently expanded in the sociopolitical domain. Since no consensus exists on the definition of middle class, it is hard to estimate the size of China's middle class in a definitive way and to clearly describe its characteristics.

There are many different definitions of middle class. In the public and government's view, the middle class is mainly considered an income group and defined by income and consumption criteria. Sociologists prefer to define the middle class based on occupation and employment. There is a major divergence between the income-defined middle class and the occupation-defined middle class. From a sociological perspective, the income-defined middle class is the upper part of middle class. But as the middle class emerges, the income-defined middle class has become the image most representative of a middle-class lifestyle and culture-and will likely remain so.

This diversity of definitions and the vague boundaries may be inevi-table when a middle class emerges in a society undergoing such rapid changes to its social structure. How can one estimate the size of this class under such complicated circumstances? Perhaps the pragmatic choice is to do so using a mixture of quantitative and qualitative methods, while incorporating multiple dimensions and different perspectives.

The sociological definition undoubtedly overestimates the real size of China's middle class. Based on occupational classification, it consid-ers all white-collar employees, employers, and self-employed people to be members of the middle class. However, many white-collar workers and self-employed people lack the socioeconomic status that one would expect of members of the middle class. Some have lower incomes, less education, and unstable employment.

The public definition of the middle class, defined by high income and consumption, usually underestimates the size of the middle class. The two definitions have narrowed the gap between their estimations of the size of middle class, so perhaps combining them will yield a definition that is broadly accepted. Thus the middle class includes these people: private entrepreneurs (the capitalist class); professionals, managers, and officials with stable middle or high incomes (the new middle class); and some small business owners or self-employed persons with stable middle, or high incomes (the old middle class). This definition is closest to the real meaning of the concept of middle class. According to such a defini-tion, the size of the Chinese middle class is 10~12 percent of the national adult population and 20~25 percent of the urban adult population.

The size of the middle class estimated by sociologists, and based on the four-subset classification (capitalist class, new middle class, old mid-dle class, and marginal middle class), is about 30 percent of the national adult population and 60 percent of the urban adult population, much higher than the percentages of the combined definition. However, such high percentages may not be completely unfounded. They may overes-timate the current situation but may become true in the coming years as long as the economy continues to grow steadily. The income of these four groups, after all, has been increasing significantly in recent years. It will not take long for most members of these four groups to reach the alleged economic status of the middle class.

Additionally, the sociological classification of the middle class intro-duced by this chapter is a useful framework within which to understand the present situation of China's middle class, although it does admit-tedly overestimate its size. China's middle class is made up of four major social groups with different socioeconomic characteristics. As a new and emerging class, it is a heterogeneous group that lacks a shared identity. Most members of the middle class have close relations with the working class. It seems impossible for such varied group to become a real class with a coherent identity, culture, and sociopolitical attitudes and values.

In other countries, the new middle class has led middle-class culture, which sometimes dominates the entire society's values. In China like-wise, the new middle class has played a key role in helping to develop a leading culture and certain values and political views. But the capitalist class and the old middle class (which run micro enterprises and small enterprises and are private entrepreneurs and small property owners, most of whom have modest backgrounds and low educational levels), have a very different culture and value system than the new middle class.

In addition, the new middle class itself is separated into two groups: public sector and private sector. These two parts of the new middle class have differing sociopolitical attitudes, especially concerning the state and its policies. More than half of the new middle class is located in the public sector. This part of the middle class has the most influence on the government's policies because of their close relationship to the govern-ment, but they are sometimes criticized by members of the middle class because of this perceived dependence on the authorities.

In summary, multiple orientations coexist among China's middle class today, and it has a long way to go before it forms a homogeneous middle-class identity and culture.

References

1. Li Chunling, "Zhongguo zhongchan jieji yanjiu de lilun quxiang ji guanzhudian de bianhua" [Theoretical orientation and change of focus in the study of the middle class in China], in Bijiao shiyexia de zhongchan jieji xingcheng: guocheng, yingxiang yiji shehui jingji houguo [Formation of the middle class in comparative perspective: process, influ-ence, and socioeconomic consequences], edited by Li Chunling (Beijing: Social Sciences Academic Press, 2009), pp. 53~54.
2. These data form the major database for the study of social stratification and also are the best data for research into China's middle class. The census is conducted each decade; the 1 percent population survey is conducted middecade. Household income surveys of Chinese cities are usually conducted every five or seven years; they comprise Q7,000~9,000 household cases and 21,000~32,000 individual cases selected from a nation-ally stratified sample. The national survey of social structure change and the China General Social Survey data have about 6,000~10,000 individual cases selected from the nationally stratified sample. The Beijing Middle Class Survey is a small survey of 800 cases selected by random sample from fifteen middle-class communities in Beijing. This author participated in three of these surveys: the national survey of social structure change, the China General Social Survey, and the Beijing Middle Class Survey.
3. Li, "Zhongguo zhongchan jieji yanjiu de lilun quxiang ji guanzhudian de hianhua," pp. 47~48.
4. Chen Xiaoya, "Zhongguo zhongcen jieji fuchu shuimian" [Emergence of China's middle classi, Business Culture 2 (2002): 42~45; Xu jiang, "Xin zhongcen jieji jueqi: Zhongguo fuyu shidai de kaishi" [The emerging new middle class: a beginning of the wealth age of China], Economy and Trade World 8 (2001): 4.
5. He Pin, "Dangxia wenxue zhong de 'xiaozi qindiao' he 'zhongcen jieji quwei'" [Sentiments of the petty bourgeois and the middle class in contemporary literature], Lit-erature Review 6 (2005): 50~55; Xiang Rung, "Xiangxiang de zhongcen Jieji yu wenxue de zhongcenhua xiezuo" [The imaging of the middle class and the writing of the middle class], Literature Review 3 (2006): 24~27; Zhang Qinhua, "Women shidai de zhongcen jieji quwei" [Emotion and taste of the middle class in the modern age], Southern Literature Forum 2 (2006): 13.
6. He Jianzhang, "Woguo suoyouzhi jiegou de tiaozheng he shehui jiegou de bianhua" [Adjustment of ownership system and change of class structure in the country], Sociologi-cal Research 3 (1987): 2; "Woguo xianjieduan de jieji jiegou" [Class structure of China in the present period], Sociological Research 5 (1988): 4; "Lun 'zhongcen jieji'" [A comment on middle class], Sociological Research 2 (1990): 1.
7. Qiang Li, "Guanyu zhongchan jieji he zhongjian jiecen" [Middle class and middle stratum], Transaction of Renming University 2 (2001): 19; Xueyi Lu, Dangdai Zhongguo sbehui jiecen yanjiu baogao [Report on social

classes of contemporary China] (Beijing: Social Science Academic Press, 2002), p. 62.

8. Li Chunling, Duanlie yu suipian: Dangdai Zhongguo shebui jiecen fenhua shizheng fenxi [Cleavage and fragment: an empirical analysis on the social stratification of contem-porary China] (Beijing: Social Sciences Academic Press, 2009), pp. 54–58.

9. Zhou Xiaohong, Zhongguo zhongchan jieji diaocha [Survey of the Chinese middle class] (Beijing: Social Sciences Academic Press, 2005).

10. Li, "Zhongguo zhongchan jieji yanjiu de lilun quxiang ji guanzhudian de bianhua," p. 53.

11. This classification of middle class is a revised version of class scheme developed by East Asian Middle Class Project. Hsin-Huang Michael Hisao, ed., East Asian Middle Classes in Comparative Perspective (Taipei Institute of Ethnology Academia Sinica, 1999), p. 9.

12. The capitalist class is not classified as a part of middle class in classifications of other societies. However, capitalists, named as private entrepreneurs, are supposed to be an impor-tant part of middle class in China. That is because the Chinese capitalist class is a new class, and its appearance is changing the original class structure and symbolizes the rise of middle class.

13. John H. Goldthorpe, Social Mobility and Class Structure in Modern Britain (Oxford: Clarendon Press, 1987); Li, Duanlie yu suipian: Dangdai Zbongguo shehui jiecen fenhua shizheng fenxi , pp. 71–73.

14. Calculation of the sizes of classes mainly depends on occupation and a few of other, related variables (such as the employment situation). However, different data have different categories of occupation and different definitions of the employment situation. In addition, census data (1882, 1990, 2000), the 1 percent population survey (2005), and the household income survey (1988, 1995, 2002) provide less detail. But the national survey of social structure change (2001) and the China General Social Survey (2006) have more detail for classifying classes. That makes it impossible to precisely estimate the exact size of subclasses. Though the percentages in Table 6-2 fluctuate, the trend-expansion of the middle class-is quite clear.

15. Although the old middle class and the marginal middle class are classified by the criterion of occupation into middle class, most people think of these two groups as between middle class and working class because their socioeconomic status is lower than that of the regular middle class and higher than that of the working class.

16. The surveys of 2001, 2006, and 2007 all ask about social stratum. Social strata have five categories: upper, upper-middle, middle, lower-middle, and lower. More than 90 percent of members of the middle class classify themselves as upper-middle stratum, middle stratum, and lower-middle stratum; about 60 percent classify themselves as middle stratum. However, only a few identify themselves as middle class. This confuses researchers who use the criterion of subjective identity to estimate the size of the Chinese middle class. If they use social stratum to calculate the size of middle class, about 60–70 percent of the total population is middle class. But the percentage becomes lower than 10 percent if they use class ("middle class") as the category.

17. The earliest class of a person is determined by his first occupation in the labor mar-ket. Present class position is probably different from the early position if his occupation changed. Sociologists study social mobility by observing changes of occupation and class position of individuals.

18. Li Peilin and Zhang Yi, "Zhongguo zhongchan jieji de guimo, rentong, he shehui taidu" [The scale, recognition, and attitudes of China's middle class], in Daguoce tongx-iang Zhongguo zhilu de Zhongguo minzhu: Zengliang shi minzhu [Strategy of a great power: incremental democracy and Chinese-style democracy], edited by Tang Jin (Beijing: People's Daily Press, 2009), pp. 183–201.

Chapter 6

Urban Chinese Class Structure and the Direction of the Middle Class

Liu Xin

In recent years, the emergence of China's middle class has received much attention from sociologists. While research has achieved important results relating to how and by what criteria to define the middle class, there results also diverge significantly. As a result, the size of the middle class calculated by different researchers are very different. How to realistically define China's middle class is a question that needs further academic investigation.

This paper attempts to define the place of the middle class within the China's social structure as a whole, looking at the middle class as situated between the other basic classes. Theory is used to illustrate a clear meaning of China's urban middle class, and a theoretical framework for analyzing China's urban class structure is put forward. The author relies primarily on data from CGSS2003, the "2003 China General Social Survey", and uses the class analysis framework to show the class structure of urban Chinese society, and the proportion of which is middle class. The effectiveness of this class analysis framework is verified by looking at aspects such as income, housing, and class self-identification of survey respondents.

1. How should the middle class be defined?

"Middle class" is a broad and unclear concept, with many different definitions. This author does not plan to discuss these different meanings, but rather thinks that meanings of the middle class defined just by income, career standing, wealth, and other valuable social resources are relatively meaningless. Defining the middle class in this way means that there must be a middle class in every society. The middle class, namely the "new middle class", is a product of modern society, from developed industrial nations in particular, and it refers to a class between the basic classes of society (upper and lower). Possessing income and status is the result of social class (Wright, 1979); therefore, definition of the middle class can only be carried out within the class structure of modern society as a whole.

Nevertheless, the main existing theories regarding the middle class – Neo-Marxist and Neo-Weberist theories – are generally analytically contextualized within a developed Western market economy social structure. Neo-Marxist middle class theory (Dahrendorf, 1959; Poulantzas, 1973, 1975; Wright, 1976, 1985; Carchedi, 1975), primarily defines the middle class in terms of relations of production or relations of domination. The middle class is considered in between the basic classes in terms of status. Wright created an analytical framework for class structure in developed capitalist societies based on people's relations of production regarding differing control of economic capital, organizational capital, or technological capital (Wright, 1985). He primarily uses control of capital as a standard, dividing people into owners (employers) [*suoyou zhe* 所有者] and nonowners (employees) [*fei suoyou zhe* 非所有者]; the framework further divides owners based on amount of capital into three categories: bourgeoisie, petty proprietors, and the petty bourgeoisie. It further divides employees, or nonowners, into nine categories based on the condition of their organizational and skills assets. In Wright's categorical framework, the middle class refers to employee-category managers and specialized professional workers. Neo-Weberist middle class theory tends to take market forces and work relations as fundamentally defining of the middle class (Lockwood, 1958; Giddens, 1973; Erikson & Goldthorpe, 1992). Goldthorpe's class categories are widely used in empirical research, and his most recently published class analysis framework (Erikson & Goldthorpe, 1992), relies primarily on employment relations to categorize employment into three broad categories, namely employer, self-employed, and employee. It again further uses employment relations, namely labor contracts, service contracts, and contracts between these two kinds to define employee work status into three categories. Finally, it further defines each employment category into 2-3 types based on specialized skill level. Thus Goldthorpe's analytical framework has 13 employment categories and 7 classes (Erikson & Goldthorpe, 1993:36). These 7 classifications can further be grouped into four classes, the upper class, the petty bourgeoisie, the white collar middle class, and blue collar workers. Within this analytical framework, the middle class is composed mainly of specialized technical personnel, government workers, low-level management in large companies, and skilled workers.

These theories certainly help provide meaning in understanding China's current middle class. However, China's unique socialist market economy means that there are many issues with taking definitions of China's middle class directly from these theories. Wright's theory focuses on analysis of social relations within a system of private ownership, and the process of production. This framework struggles to carry out class definition of public ownership elites in the expansive non-productive sector. As a result, Wright's theory cannot be used to analyze China's situation, with its state-led public economy, and pervasive proponents of state authority. Wright's theory attaches great importance to market contract relations, and overlooks state authority and its role in public capital. The principal status and management model of the composition of the public economy of the socialist market economy mean that China's realistic employment relations cannot be simply considered employment relations in Wright's sense. Furthermore, using a simple employment relations approach to define the status of the state authority elite class is impractical.

Chinese academics have attempted to use many approaches to define China's middle class (Zhang Wanli, 2002; Qi Weiping and Xiao Zhaoqing, 2003). For instance, according to 1) economic criteria, 2) statistical ranking, 3) lifestyle criteria, 4) according to subjective class status self-identification, 5) integrated criteria, and so on. These approaches each have their own characteristics, but generally speaking, understanding of the theorization of China's middle class is clearly insufficient.

The basis of class stratification is without a doubt certain capital differences. Regarding the definition of China's urban middle class, first, by examining the social relations between the people related to this capital, the basic class positions within the social class structure should be defined. Next, within these basic class definitions, the middle class can be defined. By contrast, factors such as whether people's income is high or low, whether their house is large or small, whether their car is big or small, or what their consumption level is, are all but differences according to class status, showing lifestyle opportunity differences. The relationship between class status and life opportunities is an intimately connected one, like how a tree's branches are connected to its roots. Defining the middle class based on these superficial criteria is not only an approach with questionable effectiveness, but the resulting categories are also likely to lack a consistent logical conceptual approach.

Although different theoretical genres have large disparities in their recognizing the connection between class stratification and social assets, (Grusky, 2001), they are still largely aware of the three main causes of social class stratification: wealth, power, and skills. In the author's opinion, today's social class structure is founded upon an array of socio-economic system factors. Within these factors, the connection between the system of property rights and state authority plays a decisive role. In contemporary Chinese society, public power and market power construct the primary foundation for class stratification.

Here public power refers to state authority, which appears in two ways: first is in the authority of public service managers, and second is through the capital rights of those representing the people. Market power refers to the capital rights controlled by people in market competition, including economic capital rights and labor capital rights, transposed with real transaction power. As this includes the fundamental economic ownership and control rights of people and their transaction potential, it also includes the transaction potential of people, based on their education, skills, and labor power. For example, the market power of a business owner lies in his ownership rights of economic capital; the market power of managers lies in their control rights of economic capital; the market power of specialized technical professionals lies in their education and skills; laborer market power lies in their labor power. Regarding the two different systems of public power and market power relating to the creation of class stratification, this author has already conducted close analysis of related theories (Liu Xin, 2005a, 2005b), so they will not be discussed at length here.

It is necessary to further explain the question of why public power is a primary factor behind class division, and why market power based on capital rights is set as a secondary factor. This is because in modern society, due to the universalization of bureaucracy, power relations exist in every form of social collaboration (Dahrendorf, 1957), and in China's current "socialist market economy with Chinese characteristics", the following situation emerges in particular: the public economy component is still the primary economic system, and is run by an administrative, contractual, and multileveled commissioned-representative system. The market is embedded within a market of political authority structure. Because of this system, public power is of primary importance in class division.

2. China's Urban Class Structure and the Proportion of Middle Class

So, how can this basic class structure of people relative to public power and capital rights connections be drawn, and how can the middle class be defined within these connections between people and capital?

Defining social classes according to capital relations systematically locates people within society. According to this social location, people with a corresponding socio-economic status are members of a class, and might even subjectively self-identify with this social class as a result of this status also. The unequal distribution of the two kinds of capital control rights described above make members of society divide into two basic categories, namely those with rights versus those without, or property owners versus laborers. Diagram 1 is an analytical structure of current China's urban social class structure.

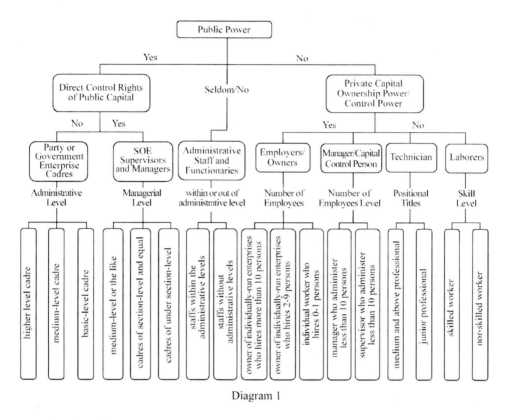

Diagram 1

First, based on the context of public power, social position is divided into two basic categories, namely those who enjoy public power, and those who do not. Furthermore, between these two groups are non-administrative-level low-level cadres, managers, and administrative workers and professionals.

Second, those social positions with public power are further divided into two groups based on whether they have direct control rights of public capital or not. Namely, into those cadres without direct control of public assets, and then those state-owned company managers and supervisors with direct capital control rights. Within these two groups, three more specific groups are further defined based on administrative or managerial level, namely board-level and higher Party or Government enterprise work unit leader cadres, department-level cadres, section-level cadres, department-level state-owned enterprise (SOE) directors, section-level SOE directors, and below section-level SOE directors. Third, regarding social positions that do not enjoy public power, this is broadly further divided according to market power. First according to whether they have economic capital control rights, which divides class status into two groups, those who enjoy economic capital control rights (including ownership rights), such as employers and managers, and those who do not, such as specialized skilled workers and laborers. These two social positions can be separated according to the size of control rights, and amount of skills assets, further defining specific class positions. Regarding employers, Wright's 1985 standards are used, according to the number of employees controlled, further separating employers into private entrepreneurs (more than 10 employees), small business owners (2-9 employees), and private laborers (0-1 employees). Regarding managers, the number of personnel under their supervision (with mid-level or higher employee classification) and low-level specialized skilled workers (low-level classification or no classification) is considered. Laborers are further defined by specialized skill level as skilled workers or unskilled workers.

In this way, we can define 17 types of social class position. Table 1 uses these classification standards to analyze China's urban class structure.

Table 1 Urban China Class Structure: CGSS2003

Multivariable Standards for Class Member Definition	Number	Ratio(%)	Class Type
1. Bureau and above Party-Government Enterprise Work Unit Leaders	1	0.0	I
2. Department-Level Work Unit Directors	14	0.5	II
3. Section-level Work Unit Directors	60	2.2	III
4. Dept.-level (or equivalent) SOE Directors	5	0.2	I
5. Section-level (or equivalent) SOE Directors	0	0.0	II
6. Below Section-level (or equivalent) SOE Directors	32	1.2	III
7. Administrative-level Personnel or Functionaries	163	6.0	III
8. Non-Administrative-level Personnel or Functionaries	303	11.2	IV
9. Private Entrepreneurs with 10 or more Employees	7	0.3	I
10. Small Business Owners with 2-9 Employees	12	0.4	II
11. Self-Employed with 0-1 Employees	252	9.3	V
12. Private Business Managers (10 or more Employees)	20	0.7	II
13. Private Business Managers and Small Business Supervisors	4	0.1	III
14. Mid-Level and Higher Classified Specialized Skilled Workers	162	6.0	II
15. Low-level and Unclassified Specialized Skilled Workers	361	13.3	III
16. Skilled Workers	396	14.6	IV
17. Unskilled Workers	924	34.0	V
Total	2715	100.0	

By looking at the categories in Table 1, the author's 5-level social structure framework for urban Chinese society can be seen. Upper levels of society have a leading status in the political authority structure or public economy capital control rights and private economy capital ownership/control rights structure. This group controls society as a whole. In contrast is the controlled class, including skilled workers, unskilled workers, and those professionals not quite endowed with rights to control, small business workers, etc. In between these two fundamental, archetypal classes is the middle class. Members of this class are again defined as upper- and lower-middle class depending on whether they enjoy public power, have capital control rights, or relatively high technical capital. Upper-middle class includes Party and government work unit mid-level leadership cadres, mid-level SOE managers, small business owners, entrepreneurs, highly specialized technical professionals, and so on. The lower-middle class includes low-level Party and government work unit cadres, low-level specialized technical professionals, administrative-level personnel and functionaries, low-level SOE managers, mid-level private business managers and supervisors, and so on. Table 2 illustrates the fundamental status of China's current urban class structure.

Table 2   Urban China's Class Structure: CGSS2003

Class	Number	Ratio(%)
I. Upper Class	13	0.6
II. Upper-Middle Class	207	7.6
III. Lower-Middle Class	619	22.8
IV. Skilled Workers and Professionals	699	25.7
V. Unskilled Workers and Small Business Workers	1177	43.3
Total	2715	100.0

The data from Table 2 shows the class structure of China's urban society, which is a kind of archetypal "pyramid" shaped structure. The proportion of the upper class is very small, while the lower class is huge. The upper-middle class is 7.6% while the lower-middle class is 22.8%, with a combined total of about 30%. This ratio of middle class would be much smaller if it also took into consideration the huge migrant population. Overall, current Chinese society's class structure, indeed urban society's class structure, is still relatively far from being an "olive-shaped" middle class society.

3. China's Urban Middle Class Income, Housing and Status Self-identification

By using the class analysis framework's interpretation of people's life opportunities and worldview, we can see the validity of this framework. In this paper, the data from CGSS2003 is used, and an attempt is made to use the class analysis framework to explain class status self-identification, feelings of happiness, personal annual income, household home size, and the difference between other such variables. The results show that the decreases in variation of these variables of this class framework all have high statistical significance.

Table 3 shows the results of subjective self-identification with class status by classes. The statistical conclusion shows that class variables and subjective class status self-identification variables have high a high relative statistical relationship. Objective class status can have an approximate diminishing variation of subjective class status self-identification of about 28%, and has a high relative statistical relationship (p<0.001). Specifically, objectively higher-class people subjectively self-identify as upper class 37.5% of the time, much more often than other classes. Likewise, objectively lower-class people (such as skilled workers and functionaries, and unskilled workers and private laborers) subjectively self-identify as lower-class 57.6% and 59.7% of the time, much more often than upper- or middle-class people self-identify as their class. Overall, from the objectively upper- to lower-classes of society, subjective self-identification as upper-class status shows a gradually decreasing trend, while self-identification as lower-class shows a clearly increasing trend.

In terms of the middle class, self-identifying as middle class is markedly more frequent than for workers and other lower-class people self-identifying as lower class, while compared to the rate self-identification in the upper-class, their ratio is relatively low.

Table 3   Interpretation of Class Status and Self-Identification of Status

Objective Class / Subjective Identification	Upper Class	Upper-Middle Class	Lower-Middle Class	Skilled Workers	Unskilled Workers, Laborers
Upper Class	37.5%	9.5%	10.0%	2.9%	3.9%
Middle Class	62.5%	58.0%	51.0%	39.5%	36.4%
Lower Class	0.0%	32.5%	39.2%	57.6%	59.7%
Total Number	8	169	518	582	993

Pearson Chi-sq = 126.9; Gamma = 0.28; n = 2270; df = 8; p < 0.001.

The results from Table 4 show that the class structure analysis framework is also effective at interpreting people's happiness. The relationship between the two variables has a high statistical relationship (p<0.001). Middle class and upper class people clearly have a much stronger feeling of happiness than lower class people, and the middle class has a much stronger feeling of happiness than other classes.

Table 4   Interpretations of Class Status and Feelings of Happiness: CGSS2003

Happiness	Upper Class	Upper-Middle Class	Lower-Middle Class	Skilled Workers	Unskilled Workers
Happy	53.8%	54.1%	50.8%	36.0%	32.2%
Average	38.5%	44.9%	46.9%	56.0%	55.8%
Unhappy	7.7%	1.0%	2.3%	8.0%	12.0%
Total	13	207	618	697	1172

Pearson Chi-sq = 123.3; Gamma = 0.28; n = 2707; df = 8; $p < 0.001$.

The table below again looks at the author's class analysis framework's two guidelines for reflecting the importance of people's life opportunities – using the interpretative ability of income and house size. Table 5 provides the results of analyzing the role of class status in variance in income and house size.

Table 5   Interpretation of Class Status and Annual Income and House Size: CGSS2003

Class Status	Personal Annual Income (RMB)			House Size (sqm)		
	n	Average	Standard deviation	n	Average	Standard deviation
Upper Class	13	28549.2	13797.1	13	100.6	57.8
Upper-Middle Class	193	20535.8	23318.9	203	92.6	60.0
Lower-Middle class	547	14472.8	12046.5	592	93.9	58.8
Skilled Workers etc	627	10586.2	8746.8	661	82.4	57.3
Unskilled Workers Etc	1021	9829.5	9838.8	1065	87.4	78.5
Total	2400	12041.6	12234.1	2535	88.1	67.6
Variance Source	Sum	DF	Variance	Sum	DF	Variance
Inter-group	26877816047.2	4	6719454011.8	48168.9	4	12042.2
Intra-group	332248330022.4	2395	138725816.3	11531929.3	2529	4559.9
Total	359126146069.6	2399		11580098.2	2533	
F	4.84			2.64		
P	<0.000			<0.05		

The results of analyzing variance in income show that there is a strong statistical relationship between variance in income and the class status variable. From upper- to lower-class society, the difference in income between classes is extremely clear. Class influence on home size also shows a similarly high correlation. But, due to the significantly disparate levels of economic development in different cities and areas in China, a more precise investigative approach of the influence of class on income and house size would be to introduce a suitable control variable, and conduct analysis using a multivariable statistical approach. Table 6 includes sex, age, and location control variables, and shows the results of analysis of income and house size after these additions.

The results in Table 6 show that after controlling sex, age, and location, the influence of class status on income and house size is typically still a strong statistical relationship. The difference in income between classes is clearly apparent, as from high to low class status there is a corresponding decrease in income level. House size also shows a similar trend, exceptions being skilled workers and petty functionaries, whose house sizes are not notably different from unskilled workers and private laborers.

Table 6   Individual Annual Income and House Size Multivariable Statistical Regressive Analysis Logarithm (OLS): CGSS2003

Dependent Variables	Regressive Coefficient B, Standard Deviation, Exp (B) and Level of Significance	
	Income	House Size
Class Status		
Upper Class	1.066***	0.330*
	(0.200)	(0.161)
Upper-Middle Class	0.722***	0.156***
	(0.056)	(0.045)
Lower-Middle Class	0.457***	0.145***
	(0.037)	(0.030)
Skilled Workers	0.088*	−0.003
	(0.036)	(0.029)
Unskilled Workers as Control Variable		
Sex (Male)	0.257***	0.002**
	(0.030)	(0.024)
Age	0.048***	−0.025**
	(0.011)	(0.008)
Age squared	−0.001***	0.000***
	(0.000)	(0.000)
Special Urban Zone	0.528***	−0.325***
	(0.047)	(0.038)
Prefecture-level City	0.316***	−0.114**
	(0.045)	(0.036)
County-level City	0.087	0.017
	(0.046)	(0.038)
Town as Control Variable		
Constant Variables	7.666***	4.815***
	(0.193)	(0.153)
n	2400	2535
R-square	0.19	0.07
F	55.3	17.8
P	0.000	0.000

Explanation: Numbers in parentheses are standard deviation from B; $*p < 0.05$, $**p < 0.01$, $***p < 0.001$

These results show, based on a sketch of the basic class structure formed by people's social connections related to public power and economic capital rights, and China's urban middle class defined in terms of people's appropriation related to these resources, whether in terms of life opportunities such as income or house size, or in terms of class status self-identification, these factors all take on a middle-level for the middle class. Their income level and house sizes are lower than those of the upper class, but clearly higher than those of the lower classes. They also tend to subjectively self-identify as middle class more than others classes do. The middle class, in particular the upper-middle class, has a good income, relatively large houses, a strong feeling of happiness, and tends to self-identify as middle class.

4. Conclusion

The author thinks that class status is a systematized, resource-related and defined social position, and definitions of the middle class should place it in the middle of the social class structure as a whole. The position of the middle class is in between that of other classes.

In order to illustrate the comprehensive class structure of urban China, the author put forward a theoretical model to define class status, based on public power, market power (based on capital control rights and skills assets), and further constructed a five-tiered class structure analytical framework consisting of the upper class, upper-middle class, lower-middle class, skilled workers and petty functionaries, and unskilled workers and laborers.

From this framework, the author used data from the "2003 China General Social Survey" (CGSS2003) to conduct analysis on China's current urban social class structure. Research results show that China's urban upper class makes up approximately 0.6% of the population, while the upper-middle class makes up 7.6%, the lower-middle class 22.8%, skilled workers and petty functionaries 25.7%, and unskilled workers and laborers 43.4%. These results show that China's urban social class structure is still an archetypal "pyramid-shaped" structure. Within this structure, the middle class makes up approximately 30% of the population. If these statistics also included the massive number of rural migrant workers, the proportion of the urban middle class would be much lower. Overall, China's current urban society's class structure is far from being an "olive-shaped" middle class society.

Regarding the author's class analysis framework and connections between individual annual income, house size, class awareness, and happiness, statistical analysis shows that the explanations this framework provides for variance between variables have strong statistical significance. This means that the author's analytical framework is suitable for use in current urban society in China. Looking at the urban middle class as defined by this framework, income, house size, life opportunities, and class self-identification all show classic characteristics of the middle class condition. China's urban middle class, especially the upper-middle class, is a social group with relatively high income, relatively large houses, a strong feeling of happiness, and a tendency to self-identify as a middle level social class.

References

Bell, Daniel. *The New Class: A Muddled Concept*. In Celia S. Heller, editor. *Structured Social Inequality*, 2d ed.. New York: Macmillan, 1987.

Bell, Daniel. *The Coming of Post-Industrial Society*. New York: Basic Books, 1973.

Carchedi, Gulielmo. "On the Economic Identification of the New Middle Class." *Economy and Society*, Vol.4, 1975.

Dahrendorf, Ralf. *Class and Class Conflict in Industrial Society*. Stanford: Stanford University Press, 1995.

Davis, Deborah S. "Social Class Transformation in Urban China: Training, Hiring, and Promoting Urban Professionals and Managers after 1949."*Modern China*, Vol. 26, 2000.

Erikson, Robert, and John H. Goldthorpe. *The Constant Flux: A Study of Class Mobility in Industrial Societies*. Oxford: Clarendon Press, 1992.

Giddens, Anthony. *The Class Structure of the Advanced Society*. London:Hutchinson & Co (Publishers) Ltd, 1973.

Goldthorpe, John. *Social Mobility and Class Structure in Modern Britain*. 2nd ed. Oxford: Clarendon Press, 1987.

Gouldner, Alvin. *The Future of Intellectuals and the Rise of the New Class*. New York: Seabury Press, 1979.

Grusky, David. *Social Stratification: Class, Race, and Gender in Sociological Perspective*. Colorado: Westview Press, 2001.

Dahrendorf, Ralph. *Class and Class Conflict in Industrial Society*. London: Routledge & Kegan Paul Ltd., 1959.

Kivinen, Markku. "The Middle Classes and Labour Process." *Acta Sociologica*, vol.32., 1989.

Li Chunling, *Duanlie yu suipian: dangdai zhongguo shehui jieceng fenhua shizheng fenxi* [Fragmentation and Rupture: Empirical Analysis of Contemporary China's Social Class Stratification] Beijing: Shehui Kexue Wenxian Chubanshe, 2005.

Li, He. "Emergence of the Chinese Middle Class and its Implications."*Asian Affairs*, 2006:67-83.

Li Lulu. *Zaishengchan de yanxu: zhidu zhuanxing yu chengshi shehui fenceng jiegou* [Continued Re-Production: Transformation of the System and the Urban Social Class Structure]. Beijing: Zhongguo Renmindaxue Chubanshe, 2005.

Li Peilin, editor. *Zhongguo xinshiqi jieji jieceng baogao* [Report on Class in China's New Era]. Ha'erbin: Heilongjian Renmin Chubanshe, 1995.

Li Peilin, et al. *Zhongguo shehui fenceng* [Social Stratification in China]. Beijing: Shehui Kexue Wenxian Chubanshe, 2004.

Li Peilin and Zhang Yi. *Xiaofei fenceng: Qidong jingji de yi ge zhongyao shidian* [The Consumer Class: An Important Viewpoint for Starting the Economy]. *Zhongguo shehui kexue*, 1999(1).

Li Qiang. *Zhuanxing shiqi de zhongguo shehui fenceng jiegou* [Chinas' Social Stratification Structure in the Transformation Era]. Ha'erbin: Heilongjian Renmin Chubanshe, 2002.

Li Qiang, *Guanyu zhongchan jieji he zhongjian jieceng* [On the Middle Class and the Mid-level Class], *Zhongguo Renmindaxue Xuebao*, 2001(2).

Li Youmei. *Shehui jiegou zhong de "bailing" jiqi shehui gongneng — yi 20shiji 90niandai yilai de shanghai weili* ["White Collar" Workers in the Social Structure and Their Social Function – Post-1990's Shanghai as an Example]. *Shehuixue yanjiu*, 2005(6).

Liu Xin. *Dangqian zhongguo shehui jieceng fenhua de zhidu jichu* [The System Foundations of China's Current Social Class Stratification]. *Shehuixue yanjiu*, 2005a(5).

Liu Xin. *Dangqian zhongguo shehui jieceng fenhua de duoyuan dongli jichu — yizhong quanliyanshenglun de jieji* [The Multi-factored Foundations of China's Current Social Stratification – A Power Discourse Explanation]. *Zhongguo shehui kexue*, 2005b(4).

Lu Xueyi, editor. *Dangdai zhongguo shehui jieceng yanjiu baogao* [Report on Research on China's Current Social Classes]. Beijing: Shehui Kexue Wenxian Chubanshe, 2002.

Lu Dayue and Wang Zhizheng. *Xianggang zhongchan jieji chujing guancha* [Observing the Emigration of Hong Kong's Middle Class]. Hong Kong: Sanlian shudian (HK), Co. Ltd., 2003.

Lockwood, David. *The Blackcoated Worker: A Study in Class consciousness*. London:Allen & Unwin, 1958.

Mills, C. Wright. *White Collar: The American Middle Classes*. New York: Oxford University Press, 1956.

Poulantzas, Nicos. "On Social Classes." *New Left Review*. No.78, 1973.

Poulantzas, Nicos. *Classes in Contemporary Capitalism*. London: Left Books, 1975.

Qi Weiping and Xiao Zhaoqing. *Lilunjie guanyu dangdai zhongguo shehui zhongjian jieceng de yanjiu zongshu* [Summary of Theoretical Research on Contemporary China's Middle Class]. *Shehui*, 2003(6).

Scott, John. *Stratification and Power: Structures of Class, Status and Command*. Cambridge: Polity Press, 1996.

Sun Liping, et al. *Zhongguo shehui jiegou zhuanxing de zhongjinqi qushi yu yinhuan* [Recent Trends and Hidden Perils in the Transformation of China's Social Structure]. *Zhanlue yu guanli*, 1998(5).

Xiao Wentao, *Zhongguo zhongjian jieceng de xianzhuang yu weilai fazhan* [The Current State and Future Development of China's Middle Class], *Shehuixue Yanjiu*, 2001(3).

Weber, Max. *Economy and Society*. New York: Bedminster Press, 1968.

Wright, Erik Olin. "Class Boundaries in Advanced Capitalist Societies." *New Left Review*, No. 98, 1976.

Wright, Erik Olin. *Class Structure and Income Determination*. New York: Academic Press, 1979.

Wright, Erik Olin. "Varieties of Marxist Conceptions of Class Structure." *Politics and Society*, Vol.9., 1980.

Wright, Erik Olin. *Classess*. London: New Left Books, 1985.

Wright, Erik Olin. *Class Counts*. Cambridge: Cambridge University Press, 1997.

Zhang Wanli. *Dui xianjieduan zhongguo zhongjian jieceng de chubu yanjiu* [Early Research on China's Middle Class in the Current Stage]. *Jiangsu shehui kexue*, 2002(4).

Zhou Xiahong, editor. *Zhongguo zhongchan jieceng diaocha* [Survey of China's Middle Class], Beijing: Shehui Kexue Wenxian Chubanshe, 2005.

How Should We View China's Current Middle Class?

Li Qiang

1. Exploring the Meaning of "Middle Class"

What is the middle class? It is a concept introduced from the West, which in Chinese has many translations (*zhong chan jie ceng* 中产阶层, *zhong chan jie ji* 中产阶级, *zhong jian jie ji* 中间阶级, *zhong deng jie ji* 中等阶级, *zhong ceng jie ji* 中层阶级, and so on). The middle class belongs to a kind of classist definition approach, which divides society into the upper, middle, and lower classes. This stratification is not based on attributes or qualities, and there are no strict boundaries between each class, furthermore, as a result of these vague class boundaries, there is no strong opposition between classes, but moderate conflict appears relatively easily. Thus middle class language belongs to a kind of moderate class perspective.

Internationally speaking, the middle class holds a majority in social structures as a whole, a phenomenon that emerged after the Second World War. After the 1950's and 60's, in the employment structure of developed industrial nations, the phenomenon of the white collar group overtaking blue collar workers emerged. There are four main white collar groups, namely managers, specialized skilled workers, salespeople, and typical office workers, and the number and proportion of these kinds of workers constantly grew. These four professional groups are also known as belonging to the middle class. As a result the theory of the middle class became popular internationally.

So-called middle class theory states that the middle class will continue to expand in modern society. When the middle class becomes the social majority, or the subject of society, lower classes, or low-income groups, necessarily become a minority. At this time, an important characteristic of society is that its structure is relatively stable. This is because the middle class gradually leads society's values and has a strong sense of self-identity, and so it plays a conflict-resolving and pressure-relieving role. However, when the middle class is still just a social minority, the lower classes, or low-income groups, occupy a relatively large proportion of society. At this time, society's structure will be in an unstable condition.

This is because lower-class incomes have a weak sense of self-identity in society, and have relatively strong anti-societal feelings. Furthermore, without the stabilizing role of the middle class, the upper and lower classes easily clash and fall into conflict.

The earliest academic to put forward the concept of the middle class was Eduard Bernstein, who first illustrated his comprehensive ideas on the middle class in a presentation in 1909. The first person to academically illustrate the concept of the middle class was German sociologist Emil Lederer, who published his first paper on the middle class in 1912, *The Private Foundation of Modern Economic Development.* After the Second World War, due to the large changes in the structure of society that had occurred, the white collar class continued to spread, and became a hot topic in middle class research. At this time, academic works on the middle class were relatively abundant, and the four most important works were Mills' *White Collar: America's Middle Class*, David Lockwood's *Black Collar Workers*, Theodor Geiger's *The Middle Class in the Furnace*, and Fritz Croner's *The Employee Class of Modern Society*.

2. The Structure of China's Middle Class

Compared with international middle classes, China's middle class has comparatively lagged behind modernization and development, thus the development of the middle class is also somewhat languid. But what cannot be ignored is that China's middle class is quite different from those of other nations. The author has already written on these differences, pointing out that the West's new middle class is constructed of employees, while the middle class created in China is mainly a non-employee class, like the mid- to small-scale business class, and independent businessman class. In fact divergences are not limited to this, and so this paper attempts to analyze the structure of China's middle class, through which we can further observe these differences. The author thinks that China's middle class primarily consists of the following four kinds of people:

First, mainland China's middle class is the most stabilizing force, it is a class of traditional cadres and intellectuals. If all the leaders (cadres) from all the state-owned enterprises (SOEs) and work units are counted in this class, it would comprise about 1.67% of the population. Of course, within this 1.67%, a small number would be higher than middle class, but since this number is so small, we can put it aside for now. Yet recent research shows that cadres and intellectuals are also diverging, for instance, traditional intellectuals are within the system, but in the recent years of market-based development, a number of these intellectuals have been drawn out of the system. Thus, while cadres can be considered a resource wholly within the system, it is hard to say whether intellectuals primarily count as a resource inside or outside the system. If intellectuals are considered equally a resource inside and outside the system, this is relatively more realistic.

Of course, inside or outside the system, if all specialized skilled professionals are counted as middle class, its current population would be 5.7%. This includes all those in government, departments, bureaus, schools, hospitals, research departments, professional work units, mines and factories, corporations, companies, and other private work unit workers employed as specialized skilled professionals. The statistic for number of professionals and the aforementioned statistic for leadership cadres in SOEs have no crossover at all, so if added together they make a total middle class proportion of 7.37% of China's population. Conceptions of specialized skilled professionals and traditional intellectuals are not entirely the same, but for simplicity's sake here the author temporarily groups them together.

Second is the so-called "new middle class": the author's past research already shows that a new "new middle class" is emerging in China's big cities (Li Qiang, 1999). The general characteristics of this class's members are that they are: relatively young of age, usually highly educated; have new specialized knowledge; speak foreign languages; are adept at computers; usually work for foreign-funded enterprises or new industries such as finance, bonds, information, or in the high-tech sphere. Because this group's high position in the production structure and its high skill level, a lot of its members work for foreign companies and capital, and as a result, their incomes are clearly higher. In terms of consumer behavior, they show a strong tendency towards high-end consumerism. In terms of lifestyle, they also have started to form a new "pattern". Recently popular terms such as "petty bourgeoisie", "Bo-bo", or "bourgeois and bohemian" refer to the kind of lifestyle indicative of this class. In actuality there is one indicator of this newly-developed class – they are not only the result of changing structures of production, but also the product of changing social structure. From the perspective of the population as a whole, the speed of the middle class's growth has not been fast at all, but in large urban areas their constant increase has been clear. Of course, recently the number of university graduates and graduate students has been increasing dramatically, which to a certain degree has created internal competition within the middle class. The number of middle class is not large, and there is no concrete statistic, but it should be about 1~2% of all employed peoples.

Third is the employees of relatively good State-Owned Enterprises (SOE), joint-stock enterprises, and other relatively good businesses, companies, and work units. The author's past research shows that, before Opening and Reform, SOE employees were comparatively the quintessential middle class in Chinese society at the time, and the author calls this the "middle class type". Compared to the majority (more than 80%) of farmers at the time, or to non-state enterprise workers of the time, back then employees in SOEs clearly held superior social and economic status. Since Opening and Reform, particularly after the mid-1990's, the status of SOE employees has showed clear decline. A large number of China's traditional middle class – SOE employees – has become the army of urban unemployed, laid-off workers, and early retirees, or the washed-up middle class in China today.

After the shocks of the mid-90's, until the beginning of the 2000's, the breaking up of SOEs had mostly finished, and as a result the economic status of employees of relatively efficient enterprises and companies was relatively stable This group made up approximately 3~4% of employed people.

Fourth is the large number of self-employed and private businessmen. In the countryside, this includes that relatively economically successful, rising wealthy class, while in urban areas it includes the large number of private entrepreneurs, small- to medium-scale business owners, independent businessmen, and small- to medium-scale company managers. This structure of this part of the middle class is the most complicated, and also embodies characteristics of change amidst the reorganization of China's social classes. Recently, this sub-group of the middle class has been growing the most rapidly, and currently represents about 5~6% of the employed population. If development continues along this trend, small- to medium-sized businessmen might become the primary middle class structural group.

The above four groups show some overlap, for instance specialized skilled professionals with the "new middle class" and employees of relatively efficient SOEs, and a few belong to classes higher than the middle class, for instance high-level managers in the managerial class would be upper class. Thus, the overall ratio of middle class in society is slightly smaller than of the four groups simply added together, so is most likely not more than 13% of China's employed population.

3. The Three Characteristics of China's Middle Class

Analyzing the four abovementioned groups of the middle class, it is apparent that China's middle class has three clear characteristics: First, there is no unified middle class in China, but there are massive differences between each sub-group. The economic interests, lifestyles, and cultural level, among other factors, are too divergent to be of a unified group. This means that, to China, forming a unified middle class is significantly difficult. In other words, it is difficult for China's middle class to meet the so-called need for united interests.

Second, the power of China's middle class is quite weak. In terms of numerical influence, the four groups described above as the middle class, regardless of which one, are an extremely small group compared to China's employed people, laborer, worker, or farmer populations. Together, they are only about 13% of China's employed population. Hence, in the following years, Chinese society cannot form a strong and powerful middle class. The chronic shortage of a middle class means it will be difficult to ameliorate the current "unstable structure" in a short timeframe. Therefore, in this new Century, we can only strive to cultivate the social conditions to form a middle class.

Third, from a "world-system theory" perspective (Wallerstein, 2000), the development of China's middle class is limited. If China is a marginal primary goods-exporting nation, and imports high-end products from abroad, China cannot avoid an expansive low-income population as a result of driving down primary-goods prices. But the result is that this bolsters the huge middle classes of developed nations, and does not help China produce its own large middle class. Therefore, this becomes a serious limitation to the development of China's middle class.

4. Conclusion

Currently, China has clearly stated its desire to expand the proportion of the middle-income group in society, as this clearly is beneficial to social stability and the building of a harmonious society. The expansion of the proportion of the middle class can be good for society in many ways. By investigating society's structure, it is apparent that an olive-shaped social structure is much more stable than the pyramid-shaped structure. Generally speaking, in any given society, the middle class is an important social force in maintaining social stability. First, the middle class is situated between the upper and lower classes, and is a cushion between them. When they become the primary body of society, social conflict between the upper and lower classes will be prevented, and social conflict will largely be reduced. This is the political reason for social stability. Second, the middle class represents moderate and conservative ideologies, and when these become leading ideologies, extremist thinking and conflict ideologies struggle to have a market. This is the ideological reason for social stability. Third, the middle class is also the key consumer group leading society. When the middle class becomes the social majority, middle class lifestyles ensure a broad and stable consumer market. This is the economic reason for social stability.

Naturally, it is important to realize that even today China is still a society primarily of farmers. Until the end of 2006, rural-registered residents made up 56% of the population, thus China still has not departed from the general structure of the "pyramid-shaped" society. According to the analysis in this paper, the number of the middle class does not exceed 13% of all employed people, which is to say that 87% of Chinese are not middle class. Therefore, on the one hand, our effort should be directed at pushing forward the development of the middle class, but on the other hand, we need to recognize how far from being a middle class society China is – there is still a huge disparity indeed. According to the author's research and calculations, for China to achieve a transformation from a pyramid-shaped society to the middle class-dominated olive-shaped social structure, it still needs about 40 years (Li Qiang, 2005).

References

Li Qiang. *Shichang zhuanxing yu woguo zhongdeng jieceng de daiji gengti* [Market Transformation and China's Middle Class's Abandonment of Generational Relations]. *Zhanlue yu guanli*, 1999(3).

Li Qiang. *"Dingzixing" de shehui jiegou yu "jiegou jinzhang"* ["T-shaped" Social Structures and "Structural Tension"]. *Shehuixue Yanjiu*, 2005(2).

Lockwood, David. *The Blackcoated Worker.* London: Allen & Unwin, 1958.

Wallerstein, Immanuel. *Xiandai shiejie tixi* [The Modern World-System]. Volumes 1-3. Translated by Lu Dan. Beijing: Gaodeng Jiaoyu Chubanshe, 2000.

Chapter 7

"Different Paths, Different People": A Typological Analysis of Contemporary China's Urban Middle Class

Li Lulu and Li Sheng

1. Background

It is common knowledge that the earliest middle class was a product of capitalist industrialization in the West. Later, the development of middle classes emerged in many post-industrial nations and areas, including socialist societies. Following the wave of system transformation and modernization in Chinese society since the 1980's, the issue of China's middle class within the context of China's changing social structure has received increasing attention. One of the main reasons for this attention is that many people think that the development of the middle class, and its social function, could influence the stability and future development of Chinese society.

This paper hopes to use a "mirror" investigative approach[36] to explore the nature and characteristics of contemporary China's middle class,[37] and discuss the social function of this class. Typical middle class theories from Western capitalist systems state that modern society is one where the middle class continues to develop and mature, and once the class reaches a certain scale, its values become mainstream social values, middle class culture

---

36 The "mirror" approach is the comparison of commonly-discussed Western versus Eastern models; in this paper this mainly involves the comparison of the socialist and capitalist systems, namely analyzing China's middle class by comparing it to the middle class produced by Western capitalist systems.

37 In *White Collar*, Mills says that the new middle class has four possible political directions: a) to develop into an independent political class, superseding other classes, and playing a role in pushing forward the transformation of modern society; b) while not an independent class, another is to become a stabilizing force in the balance between different classes; c) to become part of the bourgeoisie, becoming an anti-activist, conservative force; d) to develop according to a classic Marxist model: to unite with the proletariat and implement socialist policies (Mills, 1987: 326–327).

becomes mainstream culture, and the middle class will play a stabilizing function in society, cushioning conflict between the upper and lower classes. Simply put, in social development, the middle class is a "stabilizing agent", a "cushion class" for social conflict, and a "compass" for social behavior.

Even during early stages of the formation of the middle class in industrializing Western societies, researchers from different perspectives were already aware of the uniqueness and importance of the middle class in the social structure. For instance, thinkers such as Marx , Lederer (See Li Qiang, 2004: 284~286), and Bernstein (1981) fit this description.

Based on the massive transformations in the economic and social structure of the 20th Century United States, Mills, based on an "old-new" categorization of the middle class, systematically illustrated the nature and characteristics of the middle class and "white collar workers" and their function in the social structure. He described what is known as the "political rearguard" and "consumer vanguard" concept (Mills, 1987). Many other Western academics, such as John Goldthorpe, L. Corey, David Lockwood, and Daniel Bell, studied Western society within a context of economic and technological transformation over the turn of the 20th Century. While certain theoretical divergences regarding the middle class do exist, most of these academics support the idea that the middle class maintains a cushioning, stabilizing function in society (Zhou Xiaohong, 2005).

The above discourses on the nature, characteristics, and function of the middle class have dominated the majority of theoretical debates on the middle class.

However, the process of social structure transformation in later-developing, externally-supported modernizing nations show differences from earlier-developing, internally-supplied nations. Regarding debates on the nature, characteristics, and social function of these middle classes, many academics have put forward ideas different from the past, initiating a theoretical dispute on the middle class.

A quintessential example is research on Korea. Korea is a later-modernizing nation, and its middle class formed amidst sudden industrialization and social structural change, giving it emergent and complicated characteristics. As a result, the characteristics and social function of Korea's middle class show stark differences from those in Europe and America. Particularly after the 1980's, in terms of political participation, Korea's middle class shows great enthusiasm, becoming "a new kind of democratic force", with many exhibiting radical, reformist traits, becoming the vanguard of democracy. In terms of lifestyle, it also shows characteristics of continuing a kind of traditional culture (Leiter, 1998; Xiao Xinhuang, 1993; Wang Jianping, 2004; Zhou Xiaohong, 2005). Similar characteristics have also occurred in China and Taiwan's middle classes.

Yet, when Mills discussed the political characteristics of the middle class, his four possible political directions of the middle class also suggested this more radical possibility. After analyzing Shanghai's middle class, Li Youmei pointed out that the possibilities for social function and collective action of the middle class there suffered multi-factored limitations, and not just macro-scale factors (social structure, historical development stage, cultural traditions, system context, etc), but also micro-scale factors (social outlook, social attitude , etc) (Li Youmei, 2005).

The above analyses of the middle class in late-modernizing nations and areas indicate to different degrees the divergence in characteristics and social functions of different middle classes. This indicates the nature of the characteristics and social function of the middle class as defined by the process, path, and era of its context in different social structures.[38]

From this it is evident that in terms of middle class theory, these classes are all the products of specific socio-historical contexts, either facing the chaos before "revolution", or the period of the rise and prospering of capitalism and its continuing process of maturation, or the period of structural transformation of later-modernizing nations. Therefore, investigating the characteristics and social function of the middle class needs to occur within a certain social context, paying attention to the path taken in the formation of the middle class, and the resulting differences in characteristics and social function of this class.

As a result, a key assumption in this paper is that compared to the 2~300 years of middle class formation within a context of constant capitalist maturation in Western capitalist nations, contemporary China's middle class has emerged and gradually developed in the space of only 20~30 years.[39] It is a group "born" amidst much more sudden

---

38 Class personality belongs to a kind of societal personality, which has been described at length by American sociologist David Riesman. He points out that a group or class's personality structure is "a product of its experience", manifesting in its cultural and political life, defining people in terms of the majority culture,* and finally manifests as a kind of motivating identification and external behavior. Through analysis of the American middle class, Riesman and others pointed out the decisive influence of change in the social environment (social structure) on class personality (Riesman, D., N. Glazer, R. Denney. *Lonely Crowd: A Study of the Changing American Character*. Translated by Liu Xiangping.   Liaoning Renmin Chubanshe, 1989.

39 Of course, regarding the question of whether a middle class exists under the national socialist system, debate is ongoing. For instance Frank Parkin's analysis of middle classes in socialist societies (Parkin, 1968), Zhou Xiaohong and Li Qiang's analysis of "types of middle class" (Zhou Xiaohong, 2005; Li Qiang, 1999), Thomas Heberer and Nora Sausmikat's conclusion regarding the nonexistence of a middle class in national socialist societies in *Is the Western Idea of Civil Society Appropriate for China?*, in *Nankai xuebao* (zhexue shehui kexue ban), 2005(2). This paper does not intend to discuss this question especially, but to primarily analyze contemporary China's middle class from a social transformation perspective.

transformation of the social structure, and under these space-time conditions, the resulting middle class might have different characteristics and social function from those of the middle class in the West under a capitalist system. Therefore, the question this paper focuses on is: in contemporary China, what influence will the transformations as a result of the reallocation of the economy to a market system have on the characteristics and social function of the middle class?

2. Two Middle Classes: Theory and Research Assumptions

From a social stratification perspective, in analyzing a group in terms of a class, and placing it within the existing social structure, the key question is exploring what place this class holds in the social structure, and whether this social position fundamentally determines the social function this class performs. This kind of "structure → function" analytical paradigm is more specifically used in this paper as a "social structure → class characteristics → social function" analysis. That is to say, when analyzing the social function of the middle class, on the one hand the social position of this class needs to be determined in the social structure. Only a societal structure analytical perspective can clearly recognize the traits and social function of the middle class. This is much like when Mills said "you need to want to know how to grasp (recognize) their issues; in the constantly changing structure, white collar workers need to connect and start considering their interests and issues" (Mills, 1987:13). On the other hand, in terms of middle class traits, the process of formation should be focused on, as well as the resulting political and cultural traits formed, and through this approach explain the middle class's social function.

We will illustrate the research logic behind the "social structure → class traits" from two levels. The first level is utilizing the cultural theory of class formation. This theory states that moving from social structure to having class characteristics is carried out following two paths, namely class experience, and class self-identification. The other level is, when analyzing the class traits and social function of the middle class, it is necessary to carry out a kind of categorization. This categorization does not simply replace the "old-new" middle class from under the Western capitalist system, but is a special form of categorization from the perspective of China's transforming social structure. If the former were said to be the basic logic framework for this paper, the latter level would be the investigative strategy for analysis carried out with this framework.

I Cultural Theory of Class Formation: Roles Objectivity and Subjectivity Have in Common

What first needs to be clarified is that the concept of class used by this paper is a common group of people with the same interests, much like the meaning defined by Thompson: "As a result of common experience (regardless of whether this experience is from personal participation or that of earlier generations), when people feel and clearly show mutual interests specifically different from others (even occasionally in opposition), then a class has been formed" (Thompson, 2001:2). This meaning includes the two key factors of class experience and self-identification (class awareness). Class experience primarily indicates objective experience of the same economic circumstances, and here emphasizes the formation of a kind of continued or self-determining experience. Class self-identification primarily indicates the class level of awareness, meaning "proper" or "single" understanding of class interests, which mainly manifest in the possibility of the class forming unified social behavior (Leiter, 2006:244~246). Thompson performs a comparative analysis of class experience and class self-identification: class experience emphasizes that class self-identification is a reflection of a socio-economic situation, with reciprocity with the long-term objective world. Class awareness emphasizes that class self-identification is a kind of social construction, and is a product of the specific course of history, including the dynamic role of people (Thompson, 2001). Much like how John Smale pointed out that a class's experience constructs that class's self-identification as such, in this way it also self-constructs their place in society, and leads to class behavioral traits. This kind of class experience is produced of socio-economic conditions, through self-identification reflecting this socio-economic reality. Based on this understanding, Smale produced his "cultural theory on class formation" (Smale, 2006).

This theory is built on an attempt to counteract the divergence between Marxism and modern class theory regarding class formation issues. Marxism emphasizes the construction of classes by objective socio-economic realities (Leiter, 2006), while modern class theory emphasizes more the role of culture in constructing classes (Bourdieu, 1998); cultural theory of class formation largely brings these two theories together, posing objective socio-economic conditions and cultural formation as reciprocal, both playing a role in building a class. That is also to say that "class experience and class awareness are produced by a process, during this process a group simultaneously comprehends and constructs its socio-economic conditions," only by conducting analysis based on objective and subjective factors together can class analysis have specifically practical meaning (Smale, 2006:10). The cultural theory of class formation is also a practical theory, which is also to say that regarding class, cultural theory research asks: "experiences from what aspects compose an individual's world of self-interests, and in what ways does this composed world influences the individual's behavior – these individual behaviors successively further build up the reality they experience" (Smale, 2006). Smale thinks that class formation should be understood as a kind of cultural construction: "only by looking at class as a kind of culture can its meaning be understood. Within this culture, through conscious understanding of their position within production relations (production relations anchored within a certain cultural context), a group forms (but does not consciously decide) its own attitude, habits, and unique conception of the world related to itself" (Smale, 2006:262). Thusly, the focus of class analysis concentrates on the given world structure built by groups based on their self-experience (Smale, 2006). The middle class's feeling of self-identification with interests is similarly shown in the realms of economics, politics, and society.

An objective socio-economic reality constructs a class's experience and self-identification, and at the same time class experience and self-identification also construct the objective socio-economic reality. Through such a process of actualization, class culture and characteristics are constructed. Because changes to the social structure depend on objective socio-economic class realities, the "social structure → class traits" conceptual framework can be further defined as "social structure → class experience → class self-identification → class traits (cultural construction)". Once this process of actualization has occurred, a class's production of its social behavior and realization of its social function take on possibility. From this it can be deduced that the divergent traits of social structures reflect differing class experiences, thereby reflecting the creation of different class traits and social functions.

From the above debate on middle class-related theories and on the cultural theory of class formation, it is easy to observe that the traits and function of the middle class fundamentally depend on the characteristics of the social structure, and are further constructed through a certain process of actualization. Different social structures and processes of change, and different processes of actualization, will form different middle class traits and functions. The U.S.A., England, France, Germany, Korea, and other developed capitalist nations have, due to different social structure contexts, formed different middle class experience and awareness, as well as specific traits and social functions of remarkable divergence (Smale, 2006; Akihiro Ishii, etc, 1982).

Different results from "social structure → class traits" not only occur between different nations or areas, but particularly occur in those societies currently experiencing massive changes in their structure. For instance Chinese society is of particular analytical importance. Due to the uniqueness of China's social structure, and the massive changes occurring in its system, not only is an experience created for China's middle class different from that of those in capitalist systems, but China's middle class has also followed an extremely different formative path, resulting in different traits and social functions. This will be initially discussed below in terms of definitions of the middle class, then analyzed by categorizing China's middle class and using the aforementioned conceptual framework to conduct analysis of the middle class's traits and social function.

II Definition and Composition of China's Middle Class

Its very name suggests that the middle class finds itself with middle-level attributes, or social resources that put them in a place in the middle of the social structure. However, due to the variety of kinds of attributes or social sources,[40] a plethora of proposed definitions have also emerged in the academic world. According to different defining standards, within the same society different sized middle class groups can be defined. And precisely because of the multi-faceted nature of any definition for the middle class, whether the resulting group is homogenous or subdivided, or whether there is one unified middle class or a multi-faced middle class, continued and sizeable divergence in the academic world has resulted.

In actuality, in the past decade, the emergence of the middle class has caused sociology theorists to start focusing their attention, and typological analysis has always been a key topic in middle class research. In this kind of analysis, a common approach to defining the middle class is to differentiate between the old and new middle classes, and it is the new middle class that receives the most attention in terms of current theoretical debate on attributes and social resources (Mills, 1987).

The actualized development in East Asian nations and areas, including South Korea, Singapore, Hong Kong and Taiwan, shows that even though post-World War 2 capitalist East Asian development basically followed the two hundred year path of Euro-American capitalist development, even so regarding the occurrence of the middle class, the East Asian cases are quite different from the Western world. Of these differences, the two most important ones are: first, during East Asia's development, national governments used direct and applied force to intervene, which played an important role in reshaping the class structure. Second, in East Asian areas, although the new middle class continuously grew, the old middle class, or petty bourgeoisie, was also not getting smaller, and it steadily developed in the restructuring of daily life by countries following post-Fordist development. As a result, all four East Asian nations experienced the simultaneous growth of both old

---

40   David Grusky sums up seven categories of capital, resources and value assets for a basic class system, defined as those of economic type, political type, cultural type, social type, reputation type, civil society type, and individual type, from this outlining a multi-faceted class analysis approach (Grusky, 2006: 3).

and new middle classes (Wang Xiaoyan, 2005).

The middle class discussed in this paper was gradually produced and formed following the huge transformations of China's reallocation of its economy to a market-based system. The transformation of the system of reallocation, and the rise of the market system, created a continuous flood of new middle class in China's social class structure. This is what "middle class" or "middle group" refers to.

Therefore, contemporary China's "middle class" has a strong "emergent" quality: on the one hand it is a continuation of pre-Reform Chinese society, but on the other it is also emerging amidst the process of transformation in Chinese society today.

i) Typological Analysis: Reallocation and the Market

In fact, when looking at the process that produced contemporary China's middle class in terms of the formation of a path, the background already suggests a certain logic, namely a dualist "reallocation – market" mechanism. That is to say, contemporary China's middle class was formed under such a dualist mechanism. Regarding the differences in categories for China's middle class, some of China's academics have carried out characterizations of this composition from different perspectives.

Zhou Xiaohong has divided China's middle class into 6 categories, using multiple perspectives (Zhou Xiaohong, 2005:5). Li Qiang has raised his "four middle class groups" theoretical ideas (Li Qiang, 2004: 312). Other academics have also pointed out that due to the dual limitation and influence of the transformation of China's social structure, the middle class comes from three main paths: those that entered with the support of power relations (the administrative model), those that entered as a result of market transfer relations (the market model), and those for whom social connections capital played a role (the social network model). These academics point out that within these three models there exist fairly clear differences in cultural conceptions and values: "official circle culture" (the culture and values of officials), "business culture" (market actor culture and values), and "personal culture" (people-based culture and values) (Zhang Wanli, Li Wei, Gao Ge, 2004). Of course, there are academics that define the middle class from a multi-faceted approach, dividing the class into the employment-based middle class, income-based middle class, consumer-based middle class, and the subjectively self-identified middle class before characterizing and analyzing them (Li Chunling, 2003).

The discourse of these academics shows that the structure of contemporary China's middle class is complicated, and within the context of China's rapidly transforming social structure, the "emergent" class has not experienced a substitute for the "new" and "old", but has formed a symbiotic coming into being. Therefore, this kind of symbiotically emergent middle class group is certainly not a homogenous body, but different middle class sub-groups and their class experiences are different. As a result, they necessarily also form different characteristics.

Based on the academics discussed above, this paper conducts analysis on a "reallocation → market" transformation dualist framework, carrying out a concentrated typological categorization of China's middle class. From the perspective of society's changing structure, the formation of the middle class is on the one hand a result of Opening and Reform and the market economy. On the other hand, it also unavoidably bears the marks of the traditional system of reallocation. This is also to say that the formation of China's middle class has taken two paths: one path is the "internal" route, primarily referring to the middle class with continued characteristics of the system of reallocation. This paper calls this the "endogenous middle class". The other path is the "external" path, which is mainly market-based, having been produced by and developed in a more market-based system, and this paper calls this the "exogenous middle class". This paper considers these to be two significantly different paths of middle class formation. The typological differentiations by the academics discussed above are also certainly not disregarded, but because this paper follows a "social structure → class traits" analytical logic, the influence of changes in the system on the formation of the middle class are focused upon much more. In different system contexts, different class experiences will be created, and consequently different traits will be created within the middle class. In terms of a systems and process analysis of China's social transformation, there is already a large body of work, and this paper will not add to it. Regardless of the divergences within this body of research, the "system of reallocation" and "market system" compose a basic analytical framework.

ii) Characteristics Analysis of The Two Middle Class Groups: Research Assumptions

It needs to be pointed out that the middle class characteristics analyzed in this paper are primarily social function characteristics, and this paper mainly reflects these through three criteria: "generational continuation", "political awareness", and "consumer awareness".

First, since the two groups of China's middle class are a continuing one and an emergent one, the mechanism of class movement will naturally show differences: the continuation of the system of reallocation will make the endogenous middle class show a relatively high level of generational continuation–their career experience and social connections are deep, and continued from one generation to the next. Contrastingly, the rising market system has given certain members of society new opportunities to pursue, making the exogenous middle class display a certain generational discontinuity as a result. From this the following assumption can be made:

First assumption: The generational continuity of the "endogenous middle class" is much stronger than that of the "exogenous middle class".

Second, considering political ideology as part of the characteristics of class bears a strong meaning in terms of social function. The class experience of the "endogenous middle class" shows a much greater level of path dependence on the system of reallocation, possibly making the "endogenous middle class" retain a certain political conservativeness. While the class experience of the "exogenous middle class" was formed amidst a process of market competition, in contrast to the "endogenous middle class", this group is possibly more politically radical. From this the following assumption can be made:

Second assumption: In terms of political ideology, the "endogenous" and "exogenous" middle classes contrast: the former is relatively conservative, and the latter is relatively radical.

Finally, consumer tastes and living style have gradually come to be status symbols, consumer behavior and cultural tastes symbolic of differentiation between classes, and have become the symbols through which people recognize their own class position. Thus consumer taste and lifestyle have also become another symbol denoting class social function (Fussell, 1998; Bourdieu, 2001).

The consumer behavior of middle classes formed in different social structures should be different. Because the class experience of the "endogenous middle class" retains a strong continuation of tradition to it, this class also identifies with a more traditional lifestyle, that is to say a more traditional kind of consumer style. Furthermore, the class experience of the "exogenous middle class" has created a different kind of logic, namely what Mills identified, that they wish to display themselves through lifestyle, consumer behavior, and cultural tastes, in order to gain recognition of their status from others (Mills, 1987). Based on this, the following assumption can be made:

Third assumption: In terms of consumer awareness, the "endogenous" and "exogenous" middle classes contrast also: the former is relatively traditional, the latter more avant-garde.

3. Empirical Analysis of Categorization of Contemporary China's Middle Class

In the above sections, we analyzed the traits of China's middle class from a theoretical perspective, according to the "social structure → class traits → social function" conceptual framework, and within the fundamental context of "reallocation → market" transformation.

By typologically differentiating the middle class, the research assumptions of this paper were raised. In this section, we will analyze the data from the urban section of the 2003 China General Social Survey (CGSS2003) and verify the above assumptions.

I Variable Manipulation

i) Conducting categorization of the two types of middle class

This paper defines the middle class mainly in terms of the "managers, skilled professionals, public servants, and private entrepreneurs (including self-employed businessmen)" from the CGSS2003 survey.[41]

Regarding the typological categorization of the two kinds of middle class category, because the definitions rely on the dualist "reallocation – market" analytical framework, here a "state-owned department – non-state department" differentiation is utilized. This is mainly because: even though current "state-owned departments" are also undergoing market reform, most continuation of the system of reallocation is concentrated in state-owned bureaus, and the market system mechanism primarily manifests in the non-state sector. That is also to say that the "endogenous middle class" specifically refers to current state sector managers, skilled professionals, and office workers, while the "exogenous middle class" specifically refers to non-state sector managers, technical staff, and office workers.

The above differentiations are mainly conceptual in nature. The applicability of this differentiation can is validated by the interpretive power of this approach when using distribution results from other categorization criteria. The objective of this is, on the one hand, to better understand that under different definition criteria, the middle class will be structured differently. On the other hand, is to also possibly understand the distribution situations of the middle class under different criteria. Table 1 shows the two kinds of middle class and the interconnected results of income level, lifestyle level, and their class belonging (integrated household socio-economic status) level.

The results of analyzing Table 1 show that in the five income level groups, "endogenous middle class" has a higher ratio of higher level income, the upper 3 groups making up 32.6%, 21.8% and 21.8% respectively. While the "exogenous middle class" income level distribution is more average, the 4th and 5th groups, 20.1% and 21.9% respectively, somewhat higher than the 2nd and 3rd groups (14.7% and 17.9%). In terms of living standards and household socio-economic affiliation level distribution, the two middle

---

41   The criterion here for employment categorization is the employment category selected by survey respondents on the current employment section of the survey.

class groups are more closely correlated, both concentrated in the middle level (at the middle living standards level, "endogenous middle class" has 48.7% while "exogenous middle class" has 43.0%; at the household socio-economic class affiliation level, 47.8% of the "endogenous middle class" is mid-level, and 41.2% of the "exogenous middle class"). Thus it can be seen that this paper's definition of the middle class is still largely distributed in the middle-level even when using other definition criteria – under different standards, China's middle class groups still have the same shared characteristics.

Table 1   Integrated Analysis of Middle Class Income, Lifestyle, and Class Group Levels

Income Level						Total
Middle Class Group	1	2	3	4	5	
"Endogenous"	32.6%	21.8%	21.8%	14.3%	9.5%	1118
"Exogenous"	25.4%	14.7%	17.9%	20.1%	21.9%	224
Lifestyle Level						
Middle Class Group	1	2	3	4	5	
"Endogenous"	0.2%	7.7%	48.7%	31.4%	12.0%	1188
"Exogenous"	1.1%	6.5%	43.0%	28.0%	21.5%	279
Class Belonging Level						
Middle Class Group	1	2	3	4	5	
"Endogenous"	0.4%	7.7%	47.8%	30.3%	13.9%	1032
"Exogenous"	0.4%	7.1%	41.2%	31.1%	20.2%	238

Explanation: Ratio between three integrated kinds, from top to bottom. Income level, living standards, and household socio-economic class affiliation each have five groups from high to low. In each row, the upper value is the "endogenous middle class" results, while the lower value is the "exogenous middle class" result as a ratio.

ii) Operation of middle class characteristics

The divergence in generational continuity of the two middle class groups is mainly shown through the career changes of survey respondents, in comparison to the career their fathers. Through this career-based generational connection, from a Chinese social structure perspective the characteristics of this group can be clearly analyzed.

In terms of political and consumer attitude, the CGSS 2003's J9 and J2 questions provide a political attitude and consumer behavior scale.[42] These two scales differentiate "politically conservative → politically radical" and "traditional consumer → avant-garde

---

42   See appendix. The political attitude scale in J9 is calculated using three different levels representative of political sensitivity and conservatism, either 1, −1, or 0 points. After points are added there are 5 groups from low to high. J2's consumer behavior attitude scale is calculated using 5 different choices from traditional to avant-garde tastes, giving 2, 1, 0, −1, or −2 points each. Added together, respondents are classified as one of 5 groups. J6 looks at social participation, asking two participatory-related questions and two non-participatory-related questions. J3 provides festivals, of which 1, 3, 4, 5, 6, 7, 8, and 12 are traditional Chinese festivals, and of which the remainder are not.

consumer" from high to low, thus showing class differences. Aside from this, for the analytical needs of this research, J6, "social participation", and J3, "celebrations", are also included in the analytical range, because the former shows differences in political attitude, and the latter shows differences in consumer lifestyle.

II Analytical Results and Verification

i) Generational Continuation

First we will analyze the connections between the career status earned by the middle class compared to that of their parents and other factors, in terms of the comprehensive middle class as defined in this paper. Table 2 is a logistical analysis of the status achieved by the current generation. From the table below, we can see the as a whole the model for earning status of contemporary China's middle class.

Table 2   Logistical Regressive Coefficient, Career Status of Descendants

Independent Variable	Descendants(Logarithmic ratio)(Considering Self-employed and Entrepreneurs)									
	Managers		Skilled Workers		Office Workers		Farmers		Laborers	
Intercept	-4.106^{***a}		-3.149^{***}		-1.616^{***}		-6.077^{***}		0.179	
	$(0.375)^b$		(0.342)		(0.313)		(1.252)		(0.228)	
Parent Generation Employment Category — Mana-ger	1.360^{***a}	3.895^c	0.991^{**}	2.693	1.267^{***}	3.550	1.698	5.463	0.869^{***}	2.384
	(0.343)		(0.338)		(0.326)		(1.185)		(0.251)	
Skilled	0.604	1.829	1.176^{***}	3.243	1.224^{***}	3.399	2.328^*	10.259	0.809^{**}	2.245
	(0.365)		(0.343)		(0.336)		(1.129)		(0.264)	
Office	0.834^*	2.302	0.584	1.793	1.268^{***}	3.553	2.392^*	10.940	0.752^{**}	2.121
	(0.378)		(0.373)		(0.349)		(1.155)		(0.278)	
Farm	0.174	1.190	0.448	1.565	0.027	1.028	2.919^{**}	18.515	0.168	1.183
	(0.298)		(0.293)		(0.289)		(1.027)		(0.202)	
Labor	0.776^*	2.173	0.794^{**}	2.212	1.189^{***}	3.283	2.104^*	8.201	1.297^{***}	3.657
	(0.307)		(0.300)		(0.288)		(1.056)		(0.210)	
Descendent Education (Middle School)	1.291^{***}	3.637	2.143^{***}	8.522	1.304^{***}	3.682	-1.338^{**}	0.262	0.156	1.169
	(0.171)		(0.179)		(0.153)		(0.443)		(0.118)	
(University)	3.550^{***}	34.820	4.826^{***}	124.696	2.742^{***}	15.526	0.336	1.399	0.143	1.154
	(0.266)		(0.269)		(0.255)		(0.647)		(0.246)	
Descendent Gender	0.294^*	1.341	-0.800^{***}	0.450	-0.531^{***}	0.588	-0.644^{**}	0.525	-0.084	0.919
	(0.147)		(0.138)		(0.130)		(0.236)		(0.102)	
Descendent Political Status (CCCP Member)	2.816^{***}	16.704	1.412^{***}	4.104	1.780^{***}	5.932	-0.575	0.563	0.657^{**}	1.928
	(0.235)		(0.241)		(0.237)		(0.564)		(0.224)	
Descendent Location (Eastern China)	0.044	1.045	0.107	1.112	0.090	1.095	0.334	1.396	0.275^{**}	1.316
	(0.141)		(0.136)		(0.129)		(0.226)		(0.103)	

$N = 4793$; -2 Log Likelihood$=4301.58$; $df=70$; Chi-Square$=2898.03$; $*p<0.05$; $**p<0.01$; $***p<0.001$; a: Nonstandardized Coefficient; b: Standard Deviation; c: Occurrence Ratio

From Table 2 we can see that the status of current members of the middle class (referred to as descendants) has a close relationship with the work status of their parent generation, their own educational level, gender, and CCCP membership.

In terms of career, if the parent generation was managerial, skilled, or office-level, their descendants likewise have a correspondingly high ratio of managers, skilled workers, or office workers. This is also to say that their potential to become middle class is very high. Likewise, recipients of a high level of education who are male CCCP members are also much more likely to be members of the current middle class. However, our question is: does this kind of holistic analysis signify that the middle class actually displays certain unified characteristics? This requires further analysis according to the typological analytical strategy put forward in this paper.

First we must look at the two middle class groups' characteristic of generational continuity. Table 3 lists categorized middle class descendants related to the categories of their parent generation's work for analysis.

Table 3   Analyzing The Two Middle Class Groups Related to Parent Generation Work Categories

Parent Generation Work Category	Middle Class Group		Total
	Endogenous	Exogenous	
Manager	15.7%(19.2%)	1.0%(5.4%)	16.7%
Skilled Worker	12.1%(14.8%)	2.2%(12.0%)	14.4%
Office Worker	8.8%(10.8%)	1.7%(9.2%)	10.5%
Farmer	18.7%(22.9%)	7.3%(39.7)	26.0%
Laborer	24.4%(29.9%)	4.3%(23.4%)	28.7%
Self-Employed Entrepreneur	1.9%(2.3%)	1.9%(10.3%)	3.8%
Total	81.6%(100%)	18.4%(100%)	100.0%

Explanation: sample size: 1425, Correlation Coefficient $\lambda=0.89$, Sig. $p < 0.001$.

Cross-tabulated numbers show ratio of like people compared to total sample size, values in parentheses are percentage within column.

From the results in Table 3, we can see that the rate of the "endogenous" group's parent generation being middle class is higher than that of the "exogenous" group. Looking at the work categories of the "endogenous" group's parent generation, manager, skilled worker, and office worker percentages are 19.2%, 14.8%, and 10.8% respectively, while in the "exogenous" group, these work categories of its parent generation are only 5.4%,[43]

---

43   Here the ratio is the ratio of the column, that is, this type of account the ratio of the total number in this column, such as "inside source —— management" for 15.7%/81.6% = 5.4%, if not special instructions, the followings are all of this calculation method, that accounts for the ratio of the type of column.

12.0%, and 9.2%. Only in the "self-employed entrepreneur" category was the "exogenous" group's parent generation's percentage higher (10.3%) than that of the "endogenous" group's (2.3%). Thus to a certain degree this supports the first assumption described above, which is also to say that the "endogenous middle class" has a relatively more entrenched characteristic of generational continuation than the "exogenous" group.

ii) Political attitude

Table 4 below is about the political attitude characteristics of the two middle class groups, it lists the political attitude scale, CCCP membership status, and social participation responses. From these three interconnected factors the political distribution of the two middle class groups can be seen.

Table 4   Analyzing Interrelatedness of the Two Middle Class Groups and Political Attitude

Middle Class		Category		Total
		Endogenous	Exogenous	
Political Scale (Conservative to Radical)	1	4.5%(5.6%)	0.3%(1.6%)	4.8%
	2	25.9%(32.1%)	3.4%(17.7%)	29.3%
	3	35.8%(44.3%)	8.1%(42.2%)	43.9%
	4	13.1%(16.2%)	5.6%(29.2%)	18.7%
	5	1.5%(1.9%)	1.8%(9.4%)	3.3%
CCCP Member	Member	26.0%(32.0%)	1.0%(5.3%)	27.1%
	Non-Member	55.2%(68.0%)	17.8%(94.7%)	72.9%
Social Participation	Active	28.9%(35.5%)	10.8%(58.1%)	39.7%
	Inactive	52.5%(64.5%)	7.8%(41.9%)	60.3%
	Total			100.0%

Explanation: Sample size: 1425; categorization and political attitude scale Correlation Coefficient $\lambda=0.25$; Sig. $p<0.05$; CCCP Member Correlated Coefficient $\lambda=0.82$, Sig. $p<0.001$; Social Participation Correlation Coefficient $\lambda=0.33$, Sig. $p<0.05$.

Table values show percentage of like people within whole sample size, values in parentheses are percentage within column.

In Table 4, political scale levels from top to bottom (1-5) refer to conservative to radical leanings. Analyzing these results shows that the "endogenous middle class" and "exogenous middle class" do not have a single political attitude. Looking at the CCCP membership section, the "endogenous" group membership ratio (32.0%) is much higher than that of the "exogenous" group (5.3%). Thus it is not hard to understand why the "endogenous" group has a relatively low score on the political scale (more conservative), while the "exogenous" group's score is relatively high. Even though differences are not all that apparent, overall it is possible to discern the differences between the two middle class groups. For instance the "endogenous" group's 1st and 2nd groups on the political scale are practically twice as large as the last two groups (4.5%+25.9% versus 13.1%+1.5%). This is also to say that the "endogenous" group has a much stronger tendency towards more conservative views. Furthermore, the "exogenous" group shows much higher expectations for social participation (58.1% versus 35.5% of the "endogenous" group).

So, does the different distribution of political attitudes shown across these two middle class groups have statistical meaning, or in other words, are the above percentages of real significance? This requires further analysis. Table 5 is about the variance in political attitudes of the two middle class groups, more clearly displaying the differences between each group.

Table 5   Squared Analysis of Political Attitudes of The Two Middle Class Groups[44]

	Sum of Squares	df	Mean Square	F	Sig.
Between Groups	48.269	1	48.269	4.878	0.027
Within Groups	18930.972	1913	9.896		
Total	18979.241	1914			

Through a squared analysis, shown in Table 5, it is further visible that by placing the two middle class groups as two analytical categories, there is a clear difference between the political attitude scale scores of the two groups ($P=0.027<0.05$). The difference between these two groups provides statistical evidence of the difference between the two middle class groups. Thus Table 12.4* shows that the "endogenous group" is distributed more across the lower end of the political attitude scale, while the "exogenous group" is distributed towards the higher end of the scale. To a certain degree this supports the second research assumption, that regarding political attitude, the "endogenous middle class" is relatively more conservative than the "exogenous middle class".

iii) Consumer awareness Finally, the differences in consumer awareness between the two middle class groups will be looked at. Table 6 provides an interaction analysis between consumer behavior-related scores and "festivals" celebrated.

Table 6 displays the scores of survey respondents on the consumer awareness index, from low to high, which is to say from traditional to avant-garde. The statistical results

---

44   Variance

show that the "endogenous group" has different consumer awareness from the "exogenous group". The distribution of the "endogenous group" within the first two index groups is six times that of the last two groups (25.5%+31.0% versus 8.0%+1.4%). Furthermore, the first two index groups of the "exogenous group" are a measly 1/8.5 of the last two groups (0.3%+1.4% versus 5.6%+8.8%). In terms of the "festivals" question, the "endogenous" group also bears a much stronger tendency towards traditional Chinese festivals than the "exogenous group".

Table 6 Analysis Tabulations for Middle Class Group Consumer Awareness

		Middle Class Group		Total
		Endogenous	Exogenous	
Consumer Awareness Points	1	25.5%(31.6%)	0.3%(1.6%)	25.8%
	2	31.0%(38.4%)	1.4%(7.3%)	32.4%
	3	14.8%(18.3%)	3.1%(16.1%)	17.9%
	4	8.0%(9.9%)	5.6%(29.2%)	13.6%
	5	1.4%(1.7%)	8.8%(45.8%)	10.2%
Festivals Celebrated	Traditional Festivals	76.0%(93.6%)	7.0%(39.3%)	83%
	Non-Traditional	5.2%(6.4%)	10.8%(60.7%)	16%
	Total			100.0%

Explanation: Sample size: 1425; typological and consumer awareness Correlated Coefficient: λ=0.34; Sig. p<0.05; Festivals Correlated Coefficient: λ=0.80; Sig. p<0.01. Values show percentage of each type within whole sample size, values in parentheses are percentage within column.

Similarly, analysis of the variation between the consumer awareness values of the two middle class groups can further demonstrate their difference.

From the variation analysis in Table 7, when analyzing the two middle class groups separately there is a relatively clear difference between their consumer awareness index values ($P=0.045<0.05$), and the difference between these values provides statistical evidence for the difference between the percentages of the two middle class groups. Just like with political attitude, in terms of consumer awareness the two middle class groups also maintain difference, which corresponds to the typological differentiation of the groups themselves, showing the significance of this differentiation. Thus Table 6 shows that in terms of consumer awareness index scores, the "endogenous middle class" is distributed lower, while the "exogenous middle class" is distributed relatively high, meaning that the average index score of each group is different.

Table 7   Variation Analysis of Middle Class Group Consumer Awareness Values

	Sum of Squares	df	Mean Square	F	Sig.
Between Groups	19.016	1	19.016	0.693	0.045
Within Groups	48053.559	1752	27.428		
Total	48072.575	1753			

From the evidence above it can similarly be seen that the two middle class groups also show difference consumer characteristics. The "endogenous middle class" consumer outlook is clearly more traditional than that of the "exogenous middle class", thereby supporting research assumption three: that the consumer behaviors of the two middle class groups are significantly different, the "endogenous middle class" being more traditional than the "exogenous middle class".

Overall, even though the percentage of the "endogenous middle class" in contemporary China (81.6%) is clearly higher than that of the "exogenous middle class" (18.4%), it is still possible to see that in terms of "generational continuation", "political attitude" and "consumer awareness" how the two middle class groups show different characteristics. These different traits necessarily create different social functions for the middle class also, suggesting that the middle in China is not homogenous, or not even one group at all.

4. Conclusion

Thus this paper has used a "social structure → class traits" conceptual framework and middle class typological differentiation analytical approach to examine both theoretical and empirical arguments, and it has shown the different characteristics of contemporary China's two middle class groups. This is also to say that different social contexts will likely create different middle class characteristics, and analysis of the middle class's social function needs to occur from the perspective of different time-space conditions.

This paper carries out analysis of its subject – China's contemporary middle class – in terms of "endo-exo" categorization, categorizing the groups primarily according to this paper's "structure → function" goal, which takes a changing social structure analytical perspective. From this investigative perspective, we can see that China's middle class group is not at all homogenous, but has a divided structure. This division mainly appears in terms of the characteristics of the middle class. At this level, contemporary China's middle class is a diverse group, which cannot easily form unified social behavior.

The "endogenous middle class" created under the system of reallocation has a relatively strong generational continuation of status, and is relatively conservative in terms of politics and consumer habits. This makes this group, at least at this current stage, unlikely to become leaders of radical social movements. Moreover, the "exogenous middle class" created under market conditions bears much more market economy-oriented characteristics as a result of its formative environment, and so is politically rather radical, and in terms of consumer habits is more avant-garde. As a result, regarding the debate on the social function of contemporary China's middle class, it should be built on a diverse typological foundation. Given the different formative paths formed by the earlier system of reallocation and the process of social transformation, contemporary China's middle class is in actuality not a homogenous class, and its social function is very likely therefore diverse. Further analysis of the different social functions of different social groups needs a much more powerful analytical framework, which the authors intend to explore further in the future.

Since this paper has highlighted the two different middle class groups in China, and demonstrated their different characteristics and social functions, what is the development trend of these two groups given the continual social change of China's social structure, and the change of relatively power from a system of "reallocation" to the "market"? Whether the middle class's characteristics will change – for instance mutual transformation, or one group towards the other – is a big question. Will the social function of China's middle class tend towards that of Western middle classes under capitalist systems, or continue to be different? When we begin examining such questions of the middle class, it is also a reaction to the economic division and social structure transformation trends in China currently. Following market development of Opening and Reform, China's social and economic structures have experienced huge division. Moreover, this paper's analysis shows that, even though the middle class is rapidly increasing in size, it still shows relatively strong characteristics of path dependence in its development. We believe that following the continued growth of China's economy and the transformation of its social structure, the social function of the middle class will also correspondingly change, including the relationship and differences between the two middle class groups defined in this paper. Thus we need to better recognize the trends in China's changing economy, and within this better recognize the trends in China's transforming social structure. Due to the limitations of the data used in this paper, these issues cannot be further discussed, but further research with in-depth historical analysis is sorely needed.

5. Appendix: 2003 China General Social Survey (CGSS2003) Urban Survey Questions

Question J9 For the sentences below, do you agree, disagree, or have no opinion?

	Agree	Disagree	No Opinion
1. Democracy means the government making decisions for the people	(1)	(2)	(3)
2. It is only democracy when the common people have direct right of speech and control over national and local matters	(1)	(2)	(3)
3. If the people have the right to elect representatives to discuss national and local matters, that is democracy too	(1)	(2)	(3)
4. Regardless of education or other factors, every person has an equal right to discuss national and local matters	(1)	(2)	(3)
5. Only relatively intelligent and capable people should be allowed to discuss national and local matters, as these things require intellect and ability	(1)	(2)	(3)
6. In deciding national and local matters, the key factor is whether the results will benefit the people as a whole	(1)	(2)	(3)
7. In deciding national and local matters, the key factor is whether the correct process was taken	(1)	(2)	(3)
8. Rural migrant workers in urban areas should receive the same treatment as urban residents	(1)	(2)	(3)
9. Wealthier people should be taxed in order to help the poor	(1)	(2)	(3)
10. Currently some people make a lot of money, while others make very little, but this is fair	(1)	(2)	(3)
11. Through hard work and intelligence any child has the same opportunities to go to a good university	(1)	(2)	(3)
12. In our society, the children of laborers and farmers have the same opportunities to become rich, high-status people as everyone else.	(1)	(2)	(3)

Question J6 Assuming your work unit is adjusting pay or hours, resulting in unfair treatment of a large number of employees, including yourself, if someone were to call on everyone to mobilize and find a manager to settle things, what would you do?

1	Fervently support and participate mobilization
2	Participate, but stay in the background
3	Watch how things develop before deciding
4	Not participate, regardless of how things go
5	Other ( )

Question J2　Do the following statements correspond to your living habits or personal opinions?

	Highly correspond	Somewhat correspond	Barely correspond	Do not correspond at all	No response
1. Except when necessary, my family and I never impulse-buy products beyond necessities	(1)	(2)	(3)	(4)	b
2. When someone has a birthday or other important celebration, we always go to a restaurant to celebrate	(1)	(2)	(3)	(4)	b
3. I always buy from well-known shops	(1)	(2)	(3)	(4)	b
4. My work is always stressful	(1)	(2)	(3)	(4)	b
5. I always take taxis or drive to get around	(1)	(2)	(3)	(4)	b
6. Household durable goods are mostly brand label items	(1)	(2)	(3)	(4)	b
7. Our home is full of relatively good art, and has paintings on the walls	(1)	(2)	(3)	(4)	b
8. I never want to socialize with people from living conditions that are not-so-good	(1)	(2)	(3)	(4)	b
9. My life is currently very comfortable, secure, and is seldom very stressful	(1)	(2)	(3)	(4)	b
10. For leisure, I always want to listen to music, or enjoy works of art	(1)	(2)	(3)	(4)	b
11. Most of my leisure time at home is spent watching television	(1)	(2)	(3)	(4)	b
12. On weekends or during free time, I often play cards or Mahjongg with others	(1)	(2)	(3)	(4)	b
13. I often go to specialized gyms to work out	(1)	(2)	(3)	(4)	b

Question J3 Which of the following traditional Chinese festivals or Western festivals do you celebrate?

(e.g. eat traditional foods on a certain day)

1	Spring Festival	8	*Qingming* Festival
2	New Year's Day	9	Christmas
3	Mid-Autumn Festival	10	April Fool's Day
4	Lantern Festival	11	Valentine's Day
5	Dragon Heads-raising Day	12	the Double Ninth Festival
6	a lunar year	13	Father's Day
7	Dragonboat Festival	14	Mother's Day

Question D12 Based on your 2002 income, what class is your living standard in your area?

1. Upper Class	2. Upper-Middle Class	3. Middle Class	4. Lower-Middle Class	5. Lower class	a. Hard to say

Question D13 What class do you think your household belongs to versus the average socio-economic status in your area?

1. Upper Class	2. Upper-Middle Class	3. Middle Class	4. Lower-Middle Class	5. Lower Class

References

Bell, Daniel. *The Coming of Post-Industrial Society—A venture in social forecasting.* Translated by Gao Xian, Wang Hong Zhou, and Wei Zhangling. Beijing: Xinhua Chubanshe, 1997.

Bourdieu, Pierre. *Distinction: A Social Critique of the Judgment of Taste.* Harvard University Press, 1984.

Bourdieu, Pierre. *Fulfillment and Reflection.* Translated by Li Meng and Li Kang. Beijing: Zhongyang Bianyi Chubanshe, 1998.

Bourdieu, Pierre. *Principles of Art.* Translated by Liu Hui. Beijing: Zhongyang Bianyi Chubanshe, 2001.

China Central Compilation and Translation Bureau International Research Office. *Deguo shehui minzhudang guanyu boensidan wenti zhenglun* [The Debate on Issues Relating to Bernstein by the German Social Democrat Party]. Beijing: Sanlian Shudian, 1981.

Fussell, Paul. *Class: Style and Status in the USA.* Translated by Liang Lizhen et al. Beijing: Zhongguo Shehui Kexue Chubanshe (1998).

Goldthorpe, John. "On the Service Class, Its Information and Future." In Giddens & G. Mackenzie, editors. *Social Class and the Division of Labor.* Cambridge: Cambridge University Press, 1982.

Grusky, David. *Social Stratification.* 2nd Edition. Translated by Wang Jun et al. Beijing: Huaxia Chubanshe, 2006.

Lederer, W. *Zhongchan jieji* [The Middle Class]. In Li Qiang. *Zhuanxing shiqi zhongguo shehui fenceng* [China's Social Classes in the Era of Transformation]. Shenyang: Liaoning Jiaoyu Chubanshe, 2004/1937.

Leiter, E.O. *Class.* Translated by Liu Wei and Lu Liangshang. Beijing: Gaodeng Jiaoyu Chubanshe, 2006.

Lett, D. Potrzeba. *In Pursuit of Status: the Making of South Korea's "New" Urban Middle Class.* Harvard University Asia Center and Harvard University Press, 1998.

Li Chunling. *Zhongguo dangdai zhongchan jieji de goucheng yu bili* [The Formation and Proportion of China's Contemporary Middle Class]. *Zhongguo Renkou Kexue*, 2003(6).

Li Chunling, *Duanlie yu suipian: dangdai zhongguo shehui jieceng fenhua shizheng fenxi* [Fragmentation and Rupture: Empirical Analysis of Contemporary China's Social Class Stratification] Beijing: Shehui Kexue Wenxian Chubanshe, 2005.

Li Qiang. *Shichang zhuanxing yu woguo zhongdeng jieceng de daiji gengti* [Market Transformation and China's Middle Class's Abandonment of Generational Relations]. *Zhanlue yu guanli*, 1999(3).

Li Qiang. *Zhuanxing shiqi zhongguo shehui fenceng* [China's Social Classes in the Era of Transformation]. Shenyang: Liaoning Jiaoyu Chubanshe, 2004.

Li Qiang. *Guanyu zhongchan jieji de lilun yu xianzhuang* [On the Theories and Conditions of the Middle Class]. *Shehui*, 2005(1).

Li Youmei. *Shehui jiegou zhong de "bailing" jiqi shehui gongneng — yi 20shiji 90niandai yilai de shanghai weili*

["White Collar" Workers in the Social Structure and Their Social Function – Post-1990's Shanghai as an Example]. *Shehuixue yanjiu*. 2005(6).

Marx, K. *Kapital*. From Li Qiang. Li Qiang. *Zhuanxing shiqi zhongguo shehui fenceng* [China's Social Classes in the Era of Transformation]. Shenyang: Liaoning Jiaoyu Chubanshe, 2004/1975

Mills, C. Wright. *White Collar–America's Middle Class*. Translated by Yang Xiaodong. Hangzhou: Zhejiang Renmin Chubanshe, 1987.

Parkin, Frank. "Class Stratification in Socialist Societies". *The British Journal of Sociology*, No. 20, 1969.

Riesman, D. *Lonely People – Analysis of Changes in the American Personality*. Translated by Liu Xiangping. Shenyang: Liaoning Renmin Chubanshe, 1989.

Smale, John. *The Origins of Middle Class Culture*. Translated by Chen Yong. Shanghai: Shanghai Renmin Chubanshe, 2006.

Thompson, E.P . *Yingguo gongren jieji de xingcheng* [The Formation of England's Working Class]. Translated by Qian Chengdan. Beijing: Yilin Chubanshe, 2001.

Wang Jianping. *Zhongchan jieji yanjiu: lilun shijiao jiqi juxian* [Middle Class Research: Theoretical Perspectives and Limitations]. *Tianfu Xinlun*, 2004(3).

Wright, Erik Olin. "The Biography of a Concept: Contradictory Class Locations." In John Holmwood, editor. *Social Stratification*. London: Edward Elgar Publishing Limited, 1985.

Xiao Xinhuang. *Bianqian zhong Taiwan shehui de zhongchan jieji* [Taiwan's Middle Class in the Midst of Change]. Taibei: Juliu Tushu Gongsi, 1989.

Zhang Wanli. *Dui xianjieduan zhongguo zhongjian jieceng de chubu yanjiu* [Early Research on China's Middle Class in the Current Stage]. *Jiangsu shehui kexue*, 2002(4).

Zhang Wanli, Li Wei, and Gao Ge. *Xianjieduan zhongguo shehui xin zhongchan jieceng de goucheng tezheng* [The Characteristics Formed by the New Middle Class in China's Current Stage]. *Jiangsu Shehui Kexue*, 2004(6).

Zhou Xiahong, editor. *Zhongguo zhongchan jieceng diaocha* [Survey of China's Middle Class], Beijing: Shehui Kexue Wenxian Chubanshe, 2005a.

Zhou Xiaohong. *Quanqiu zhongchan jieji baogao* [Global Middle Class Report]. Beijing: Shehui Kexue Wenxian Chubanshe, 2005b.

Zhou Xiaohong. *Zai lun zhongchan jiji: lilun, lishi yu leixingxue* [Re-discussing the Middle Class: Theory, History, and Typology]. *Shehui*, 2005c(5).

石井晃弘等，1982，《みせかけの中流階級——都市サラリーマンの幸福幻想》，日本：有斐閣。

Part III   Identity and Attitudes of China's Middle Class

Chapter 8

The Scale, Self-identification and Social Attitude of China's Middle Class

Li Pei Lin and Zhang Yi

1. Introduction

In sociological research, the "middle class" has always been a concept with a certain charm, but one around which there also exists a lot of debate. While people have already carried out extensive research on middle class income, work, education, aspirations, gender, ethnicity, tastes, self-identification, and socio-political attitudes, such research has seemingly only provided new challenges, and it has been very difficult to form a single understanding of this class (Butler and Savage, 1995). Even though academics with different, even opposing, theoretical directions have started to come together on the definition and ways of surveying the middle class, namely primarily taking the standard of employment type to define the middle class (Goldthorpe, 1990; Erikson and Goldthorpe, 1993; Wright, 1997), regarding the role and function of the middle class, empirical research has shown very different results. Some illustrate the importance of the middle class as a force behind change in contemporary societies (Lash and Urry, 1987), some show the role of the middle class as maintaining the traditional social order (Goldthorpe, 1982), and some illustrate the middle class's role behind stable, gradual industrialization (Kerr, Dunlop, Harbins and Myers, 1973), while others depict the middle class as a radical force behind democratization (Huntington, 1973).

In East Asia's newly-industrialized nations and areas experiencing social transformation, the middle class has played an important role, resulting in widespread attention from sociologists. But empirical research in Korea, Singapore, Hong Kong and Taiwan all show that the middle class possesses radical traits, but also has a conservative character (Lu Dongyue, Wang Zhijing, 2003; Xiao Xinhuang, Jun Baoshan, 1999).

China is currently experiencing globally historic modernization and wide scale social transformation. Within a context of globalization, this social transformation shows extremely complex characteristics: industrialization, urbanization, marketization, and internationalization all occurring at once. The simultaneous transformation of the economic and social systems, the demand for capital accumulation of early industrialization, the demand for increasing production of mid-stage industrialization, and the demand for environmental regulation of late-industrialization, are all occurring together. These complex characteristics bring several unique challenges to research on the middle class:

First, the proportion of the middle class is small, and its social boundaries are unclear. On the one hand, the level of urbanization in China seriously lags behind industrialization. The level of industrialization has reached approximately 88% (the percentage of GDP of industry and the service economy), but urbanization has only reached 44%. This means that the middle class, by certain definitions an "urban group", is far from mature. On the other hand, the importance of reliance on industry in the Chinese economy is extremely clear. Industry and the service economy made up 47.5% and 39.7% of the 2005 GDP respectively, and in the employed sector, industry and service jobs make up 22.8% and 31.4%, meaning that the scale of the middle class, by certain definitions a "service group", is out of step with the level of economic development in China.

Second, because the respective levels of transformation in China's economy, politics, and society are all quite different, an employment-defined middle class shows a certain low-end bias in terms of economic status, which is largely at odds with the more subjective public opinion of the middle class, and is quite different from a middle class commercially defined in terms of income, consumption level, and consumer tastes.

Third, China's urban-rural and regional differences are quite large, making the middle class defined by employment type at odds with the subjectively self-identified "middle class" group in society, and there is even a phenomenon of significant deviation, as, for instance, within the farmer population, close to 42% of people self-identify as what they consider to be "society's middle class".

Within this context, this paper attempts to respond to the following questions: in contemporary China, what definition and measurement of the middle class more accurately reflects reality? What exactly is the scope of China's current middle class? Does an objectively-defined or subjectively-identified "middle class" group have a more consistent perception of social attitude?

This paper uses data from the 2006 *China General Social Survey* (CGSS2006) undertaken from March to May of 2006, which covered 28 province-level urban areas, 130 district-level urban areas (cities and their surrounding areas), 260 rural areas (towns and street-level), 520 villager/resident committees, and interviewed 7100 residents, receiving back 7063 valid questionnaires with less than 2% margin of error. Unless explained otherwise, all data in this paper is from the CGSS2006 results.

2. Research Strategy

The main challenge in researching the middle class is defining this class itself. Different academics, with different research objectives, have defined different "middle class" concepts. The criteria used to define the middle class used in academia are many, from subjective criteria to objective criteria. Objective criteria include employment status, income level, accessible capital, size and scale of control authority, specialized skill level, educational capital, social aspirations, consumption level, ethnicity and heritage, etc. Subjective criteria are relatively simple, and can be divided into self-identification and assessment by others: the former is whether people consider themselves to be "middle class", while the latter comes from whether other members of society consider someone to belong to a certain group. Economists have also used income to define the middle class, merely considering all those within a certain income bracket to be middle class. Sociologists most often use an employment perspective, using work-related criteria to differentiate people. Namely those who have left manual labor and have a certain special skill level are an example of middle class workers.

It is clear that different academics with different disciplinary needs will define the middle class they are researching differently. For instance, in the mid-20th Century, Mills mainly used work-related criteria to define the middle class in his research. He thought that America's middle class was composed primarily of administrative managers and skilled service workers from government organizations, large-scale businesses, and all kinds of enterprises (Mills, 1951/2006). But the U.S. Census Bureau only defined the middle class as those with average household income between 75%-125% of national average household income, defining an "income middle class" (Kacapyr, Francese and Crispell, 1996). Most recently, the China Statistics Bureau also defined those with household income of between 60~500,000 *yuan* annual income as middle class.

While work-defined and income-defined middle classes can both satisfy different interpretive needs, in academic research more and more people have started to integrate different representative, practically implementable concepts to define the middle class. In the U.S., seldom is the group that composes the middle class defined by one specific criterion, more often there is a tendency towards a holistic examination including income, education, employment, and other factors (Thompson and Hickey, 2005). Professor Lu Dayue pointed out during his research on Hong Kong's middle class that even though the perimeters of the middle class can be set based on a monthly salary of between 20~50,000 *yuan*, employment and career still should be an important typical defining process (Lu Dayue, Zhu Zhijing, 2003) In China, there are also those who define the middle class in terms of consumption level (Li Peilin, Zhang Yi, 2000), but more and more people are starting to approach the middle class from three different perspectives—income, employment, and consumption level—to examine the question of the middle class's composition (Liu Yi, 2006).

Certainly, defining the middle class from any one specific perspective lacks robustness. A classic example is on escort women (*san pei xiaojie* 三陪小姐), whose income is actually higher than most typical managers, but who socially very few people would classify as middle class. Thus, education and employment also need to be considered as factors, so that the biases of any one definition can be weeded out.

Therefore, our research strategy is as follows:

First, when defining the middle class, it is not necessary to use a single specific criterion and simplistically define a social group, but to choose three important criteria that are relatively easy to implement, and that have had a relatively large influence on the socio-economic status of people in current China: namely, income level, employment type, and educational level. We take these three criteria, and we call the group that all three apply to the "core middle class"; those that only two criteria apply to we call the "semi-core middle class", and those to whom only one criterion applies are the "peripheral middle class".

Second, a logistic model is used to analyze people's self-identification as middle class. Though social appraisals by others are of great academic value, when limited to survey results, we can only use self-identification as a criterion for analysis.

Third, when analyzing social opinions towards the middle class, in order to avoid random disturbances of certain specific criteria, we conduct a factor analysis by taking 15 test criteria of people's social attitude, of which three are chosen as dependent variables, after which linear regressive equations are used to verify the influence of class self-identification variables and objective class variables.

3. Definitions and Measures for China's Middle Class

i) Definitions and Measures for Middle Class Income Criteria

The middle class is a product of urbanization and industrialization, in terms of a certain meaning, it has "urbanite class" and "service class" characteristics. Thus, in terms of income, if the national average income is taken as the basis for reference to define the national middle income level, the huge number of China's farmers will be included in the range of China's middle class, and so this 'middle-level' standard will be lower. Therefore, we have chosen to use the average income limits of urban-registered Chinese as a basis for reference, defining those with 2.5 times or more the average income as the "high income group", and those with 50% or less of the average income (this guideline in many developed nations is often called "relatively poor") are called the "low-income level"; those between the low-income limit and the average income are "lower-middle income level", and those between the average income and the 2.5 times higher limit are called the "middle-level income level", namely the "income-based middle class". As the proportion of high-income people included in the survey is very small, we included them in the "income-based middle class".

According to this definition and the calculations of the 2006 survey data, the average household income of urban-registered Chinese in 2005 was 9340 *yuan*. Therefore those with 9341 *yuan* or more are considered middle-level income households, while those with 4671~93340 *yuan* are the lower-middle level income households, and those with 4670 *yuan* or less per annum are low-income households.

Additionally, based on the experience of China's national survey, due to the mentality of "not showing one's riches" and the   high frequency of existing hidden income in China, the income level questionnaire survey data is generally much lower than people's actual income levels. For instance, according to statistical data, the 2005 average officially-administered household income of Chinese urban residents was 10493 *yuan*, while average consumer costs came to 7942 *yuan*, meaning after consumption costs only 2551 *yuan* is left. Similarly, the average rural resident net annual income was 3255 *yuan*, while consumption costs were 2555 *yuan*, leaving 700 *yuan* for rural residents; however, in 2005 urban and rural resident average bank savings were 10787 *yuan*. According to this survey experience, people's real incomes are on average usually 1.5 times higher than their income response. Therefore, when determining a realistic standard, the income level standards should take the reported survey incomes, multiply them by 1.5, then round the numbers to the nearest thousand. Doing this, using the post-survey average income levels, an average Chinese household annual income above 35001 *yuan* is high-income level, 14001~35000 *yuan* is middle-level, 7001~14000 *yuan* is lower-middle level, and less than 7000 *yuan* is lower-income level (see Table 1).

Table 1 Income Level Standards Based on Urban Household Average Income Standards (*yuan*/year)

Survey Average Standard A		Upper Lower-Income Limit B=A/2	Lower-Middle Income Limits C: (B+1)→A	Middle-Level Income Level D: (A+1)and above
Pre-Survey	9340	4670	4671~9340	9341and above
Post-Survey(×1.5)	14000	7000	7001~14000	14001 and above

Making calculations based on these income level standards, in 2005, 57.4% of Chinese fell within the low-income level bracket, 24.8% fell within the lower-middle level income bracket, and 17.8% fell within the middle-level income bracket (see Table 2).

ii) Definitions and Measures for Middle Class Employment Criteria

Defining the middle class in terms of employment criteria is currently a common method in sociology. Some academics call the small-scale employer class the "old middle class", and call the white collar manager class and other non-laborer white collar classes the "new middle class". In this research, we call all kinds of wage-earning managerial-authorized or highly-skilled non-labor workers the "employment-based middle class" (does not include laborer supervisors), which also includes "self-employed" and employers. Laborers, partially-skilled laborers, and laborer supervisors are considered the employment-based lower-middle class, and farmers are the employment-based lower class. Based on these definitions, the employment-based middle class is 22.4% of the population, the lower-middle class 30.6%, and the lower class 47.0% (see Table 2).

Table 2 Comparison of Income-, Education-, and Employment-Based Middle Class Groups

Income Classes	Percentage	Education Classes	Percentage	Employment Classes	Percentage
Lower	57.4	Lower	77.9	Lower	47.0
Lower-Middle	24.8	Lower-Middle	9.5	Lower-Middle	30.6
Middle	17.8	Middle	12.7	Middle	22.4
Total	100.0	Total	100.0	Total	100.0
N=	4998	N=	4998	N=	4998

Explanation: Does not include unemployed survey-takers.

iii) Definitions and Measures for Middle Class Education Criteria

A lot of researchers have shown that the educational yield of the middle class is clear, and since Opening and Reform it has also clearly improved; the educational yield is higher than their length of service, namely their work experience yield (Zhao Weiren,

Li Shi, Li Siqin eds., 1999: 455~457). Education level, income level, and employment status are all closely related. Within China's specific context, we define those with a polytechnic school or a bachelor's degree or higher as the "education-based middle class"; those with high school or technical training education are the "education-based lower-middle class", and those with middle school education and below are the "education-based lower class". Based on these definitions, we calculate that China's education-based middle class is 12.7% of the population, the lower-middle class 9.5%, and the lower class 77.9% (see Table 2).

After adding together the results of calculating the middle class based on income, employment and education, we can see that the "core middle class" is that group that accords with the "middle level" of each aspect, and only accounts for 3.2% of the total survey group. The "semi-core middle class" that belongs to the "middle level" of two of the aspects makes up 8.9%, and those that only belong to one "middle level" aspect, the "peripheral middle class", makes up 13.7% (see Table 3). In other words, if the "core middle class", "semi-core middle class", and "peripheral middle class" are together considered the middle class, the total percentage of the middle class in the survey group would be 25.8%. If only the "core" and "semi-core" groups count as the middle class, it would make up 12.1% (see Table 3).

Table 3 Distribution of National Core, Semi-Core and Peripheral Middle Class

Category \ Item	Frequency	Percentage	Percentage	Percentage
Other Class	3711	74.2	74.2	74.2
Peripheral Middle Class	683	13.7	13.7	13.7
Semi-Core Middle Class	442	8.9	8.9	
Core Middle Class	162	3.2	3.2	
Total	4998	100.0	100.0	100.0

Explanation: Subject group logarithm uses weighted values

Table 4   Distribution of Urban Core, Semi-Core, and Peripheral Middle Class

Category \ Item	Frequency	Percentage	Percentage	Percentage
Other Class	1078	50.3	50.3	50.3
Peripheral Middle Class	520	24.3	24.3	24.3
Semi-Core Middle Class	395	18.4	18.4	
Core Middle Class	150	7.0	7.0	
Total	2143	100.0	100.0	100.0

Explanation: Subject group logarithm uses weighted values

From Table 4 it can be seen that if only the urban workforce is considered, the "core middle class" makes up 7.0%, the "semi-core middle class" makes up 18.4%, and the "peripheral middle class" makes up 24.3% of the workforce. Similarly, if just the "core" and "semi-core" middle class groups together compose the urban middle class, the middle class as proportion of urban residents would be 25.4%. From this it is also clear that the middle class primarily resides in urban areas.

It is necessary to explain that the main reason the "peripheral middle class" is bigger than the "education-based middle class" and "employment-based middle class" is because of the so-called old middle class, namely those who employ relatively few laborers or who are "self-employed" entrepreneurs. On the one hand their education level is usually relatively low, and on the other their income level is also not that high. Of course, in certain conditions, during our survey, as these people often are self-employed or have household workshops, their household consumption costs and business costs are often indiscernible, and therefore the wages they give themselves will be estimated rather low. Thus an acceptable calculation of the middle class proportion of employed persons in current China should be about 12%.

4. Social Identification as "Middle Class" and Influential Factors

Empirical research shows that people's objective socio-economic status and the socio-economic status they subjectively identify with are not at all the same. And in nations and societies with significant differences in levels of economic development and income distribution, social identification with the "middle class" can actually be very similar. For instance, in highly developed and economically equal Japan, social identification as "middle class" is actually very similar to that of people in Brazil, which is a country with contrasting conditions. China and India are two nations with huge populations, and dramatic differences in level of development and income distribution, and China's current per capita GDP is more than twice that of India's, but the proportion of people that identify as "middle class" in India is much higher than that in China (see Table 5).

From this it can be seen that people's subjective class identification is affected by many objective factors such as income, employment, education, family situation, and so on. It is also affected by systems of comparison and other subjective factors. Therefore, the objectively-defined middle class is both the same as and different from that of people's subjective identification as "middle class".

From Table 6 we can see, through analysis of the survey data, that 61.7% of the "core middle class" group thinks they are socio-economically of "middle class" status; 53.5% of

-158-

the "semi-core middle class" thinks they are part of the social "middle class", and 46.8% of the "peripheral middle class" thinks that they are part of society's "middle class". of the "other classes" outside our three criteria, 38.6% also identify as "middle class".

Table 5　Percentage of Public Subjective Class Identification in Different Nations (%)

Class Country	Subjective Class Identification					(Number)
	Upper	Upper-Middle	Middle	Lower-Middle	Lower	
West Germany	1.8	11.2	62.5	20.0	3.6	(1127)
U.S.A.	1.9	15.7	60.7	17.4	3.6	(987)
France	0.4	10.9	57.7	25.2	5.3	(993)
Italy	0.7	7.0	56.9	22.2	8.0	(1000)
Australia	1.1	8.6	72.8	10.4	2.7	(1104)
Canada	1.2	14.2	68.8	11.8	2.2	(1012)
Brazil	4.4	13.1	57.4	17.2	5.5	(1000)
Japan	1.1	12.5	56.0	24.4	5.0	(1042)
Singapore	1.0	3.9	74.2	16.2	3.0	(996)
South Korea	1.1	14.7	51.0	23.7	9.0	....
India	1.2	12.0	57.5	21.7	7.5	(1020)
Philippines	1.3	7.0	67.1	18.5	5.9	(1574)
China (2002)	1.6	10.4	46.9	26.5	14.6	(10738)
China (2006)	0.5	6.2	41.0	29.3	23.1	(6789)

Explanation: Data from Watanabe (1998: 333–334), from 11/9/1979 Gallup International international poll. Only urban areas were surveyed in Brazil, India, and South Korea, while other countries were nationally surveyed. China's 2202 data is from the China 2002 Urban Public Social Conflict Survey (see Li Peilin, etc, 2005:57), and the 2006 data is from CGSS2006.

Table 6　Cross-Analysis of Self-Identified Middle Class and Objective Middle Class

Identified Class	Other Class	Peripheral	Semi-Core	Core	Total
Upper Class	0.3%	1.3%	0.9%	1.9%	0.6%
Upper-Middle	3.5%	7.0%	13.1%	15.4%	5.4%
Middle Class	38.6%	46.8%	53.5%	61.7%	42.4%
Lower-Middle	31.0%	28.6%	27.2%	18.5%	29.8%
Lower Class	26.5%	16.4%	5.4%	2.5%	21.8%
$N=$	3514	1092	467	162	5235

$X^2 = 317.501$, $P < 0.000$.

It is evident that between the income-based, education-based, and employment-based middle class groups, the more these aspects overlap, the higher the proportion of people self-identifying as "middle class" gets. Additionally, the more dispersed the distribution the people of these three middle class groups, the lower the number of people self-identifying as middle class is. Therefore, the unity between objectively-defined middle classes and subjectively-defined middle class groups needs to be strengthened. The proportion of the "core middle class" needs to be increased, which requires improved equality of opportunity in the process of social mobility in China. This will in turn increase the possibility of overlap between the three middle class categories: income, employment, and education level.

In China currently, what exactly are the factors influencing class self-identification by members of society? In other words, aside from population characteristics, employment, income and education are our three factors used to define the middle class, but which one has decisive meaning in influencing people's subjective identification as "middle class"? Table 7 shows the results of statistical analysis, where it can be seen that "gender" has no influence on self-identification as "middle class", even though the calculated average female income is much lower than the average male income, and also despite lower average female education level. Empirical research shows that individual identification as "middle class" depends most on the socio-economic status of an individual's whole household, and individual class identification is heavily influenced by family background. For instance a wife's class identification goes beyond personal factors to perhaps include the various social status and income factors of her husband, creating an overall self-evaluation, and giving herself a class identity. After all, families have the ability to reallocate income and other resources to family members within the household.

In terms of political status, the ratio of "Party members" that self-identify as "middle class" is clearly higher than non-Party members. This is generally because within state-owned enterprises (SOEs), managers are much more often Party members than not. Earlier it was thought that people in Eastern China were much more likely to identify as "middle class" than those in Central or Western China, but empirical research shows that this is clearly not so. This says that in situations of relatively high inequality between areas, the reference standards people use when identifying as "middle class" are different. What is strange is that, compared with Western China, many more people in Central China identified as "middle class". This is a question in need of further research. Here it is explained that people do not differentiate their class based on actual inequalities, but the differences they experience compared to their reference group are what make them find their own class status. Therefore, the majority of actual inequalities are one thing, but the inequalities people really experience is something else.

In terms of age factors, compared to the "aged 66 and above" group, the "aged 26~35" group has a much higher rate of identifying as "middle class"— 1.403 times higher than the older group. The "aged 25 and below" group also identified as "middle class" much more than either the "aged 36~45" or "aged 46~55" groups. On the one hand this reflects the current "fathers less than sons" income phenomenon in China. On the other hand, it reflects the differences in consumption between different age groups. Of course, there is also another reason – that the average educational level of young Chinese is much higher than their parent generation. In modern society, the advance of science and technology and the vigorous development of new industry has meant that those with the most recent education always have higher-income work positions. There is an especially strong connection between income level and particularly specialized, rare skills. Thus, generational differences in educational level have created significant differences in class identification.

Table 7   Factors Influencing Class Identification by Members of Society (Logistic Analysis)

	B value	Standard Deviation	Wald value	DF	Sig.	Principal Value of Power
Gender(Male=1)	0.029	0.063	0.218	1	0.640	1.030
Party Membership(Member=1)	0.331	0.115	8.273	1	0.004	1.392
Eastern/Central/Western China(Control Group: Eastern China)						
Eastern China	−0.083	0.084	0.969	1	0.325	0.921
Central China	0.170	0.079	4.672	1	0.031	1.186
Age(Control Group: 66 and above)						
25 and below	0.331	0.291	1.291	1	0.025	1.392
26~35	0.339	0.284	1.422	1	0.023	1.403
36~45	−0.029	0.283	0.011	1	0.917	0.971
46~55	0.018	0.286	0.004	1	0.951	1.018
56~65	−0.069	0.297	0.054	1	0.816	0.933
Education Level(Control Group: Low Level)						
Lower-Middle level	−0.046	0.108	0.181	1	0.670	0.955
Middle level	0.243	0.107	5.137	1	0.023	1.275
Employment level(Control Group: Low Employment Level)						
Lower-Middle Level	−0.431	0.083	27.181	1	0.000	0.650
Middle Level	−0.206	0.089	5.350	1	0.021	0.814
Income Level(Control Group: Low Income Level)						
Lower-Middle Income	0.399	0.077	26.722	1	0.000	1.491
Middle Income	0.762	0.097	61.892	1	0.000	2.143
Constant	−0.552	0.284	3.778	1	0.052	0.576

N=4655; −2 Log likelihood =6542.027.

This shows that in terms of educational level as a criterion, compared to the low-educated class, the middle-level education class has much higher instance of identification as middle class, approximately 1.3 times greater than that of the low-education level class.

What is quite strange is that the main criterion in defining the middle class, "employment", actually had a negative influence on identification as "middle class" when other variables were controlled. This is a very interesting social phenomenon, because the defined lower employment class is a farming class, represented by field-planting farmers. The urban laborer and other classes actually show lower identification as "middle class" than the farmer class. This shows that the living standards of China's farmers have been improved, bringing with it a large amount of class identification. While it would be difficult to include the farmer class in the definition and analysis of the middle class, the self-identification of the farmer class, currently improving in terms of economic income and living conditions, is easily raised. This also shows that those we have defined as the middle class, and its comparison group, compared to the farmer class, does not have an outstanding sense of class identity. Therefore, in current China, when controlling other variables, the sense of identification as "middle class" of China's worker class and white collar class is not as clear as often imagined.

Statistical analysis shows that, relative to employment and education factors, income class is much more able to explain people's subjective class identification. Compared to the low-income class, the identification of the lower-middle income class as "middle class" is 1.49 times higher, and the middle-income class identifies as "middle class" 2.14 times as much as the lower-income class. This shows that currently in China, income level is the primary factor in people's sense of class belonging.

Therefore, it is the income variable that most decides people's identification as middle class. Those members of society whose income has reached a certain level compared to their surrounding reference group, regardless of educational level or employment status, are much more likely to attribute themselves as "middle class".

5. Primary Factors Influencing Middle Class Social Attitudes

Is the middle class a force for social stability? The hypothesis that the middle class can maintain social stability was actually established on the premise that the middle class is a group with unified interests and status, and common social attitudes and behavioral preferences. So, is the middle class a group that possesses class meaning and societal interests?

In order to validate this point, we carried out a factor analysis of a test for social attitude with 15 variables. These 15 variables are shown in Table 8 (according to the order of factors discussed later):

Table 8   Topics Used for Factor Analysis of Test for People's Social Attitude

1	The government wants to demolish houses and develop, the people should just leave	6	Make money by any means, even illegally	11	Financial Bureau Tax Policy
2	The people should obey the government, the lower classes should obey the upper classes	7	Good family background	12	Work and Career Opportunities
3	Democracy is the government controlling the people	8	Have important connections	13	Rural vs. Urban Wages
4	The government is responsible for national affairs, the people should not overly concern themselves	9	Some people are corrupt/embezzle state funds or public capital	14	Wages in Different Areas and Professions
5	The people pay taxes, the government can spend them how it likes	10	The rich pay fewer taxes	15	Social Security, e.g. retirement treatment
Agreement Index 1 Strong Disagree 2 Disagree 3 Agree Somewhat 4 Strongly Agree		Degree of Influence 1 Large 2 Significant 3 Slight 4 None		Degree of Unfairness 1 Very 2 Not too unfair 3 Somewhat fair 4 Fair	

Regarding these 15 four-point Likert scales, we used a principal component analysis method with three "factors". When extracting initial eigenvalues, Factor 1 can explain a percent variance value of 21.34%, Factor 2 of 12.077%, Factor 3 of 10.847%, and cumulatively an original attitude variable value of 44.299%. But, in order to synthesize and "name" what these values represent, we used a Varimax method to carry out rotational analysis. Table 9 shows that after rotational analysis, Factor 1 is able to explain a percent variance value of 15.951% of the whole social attitude scale, Factor 2 of 14.384%, and Factor 3 of 14%. After rotation, the three factors cumulatively can explain 44.299% of the contents of the original 15 variables. Compared to pre-rotation, this information was not missing, but changed the ability of various factors to explain the original variables, which made these factors easy to "name".

Moreover, from Table 10's factor matrix it can be seen that after rotation, the content represented by these factors primarily focuses on these three aspects: Factor 1 represents "Opinions on Fairness of National Policy", because Factor 1 is most related to opinions on policy. Factor 2 represents "Opinions on Fairness of Process of Accumulating Wealth", because it is most related to the variables represented by this index set. Factor 3 represents "Acceptance Level of Obeying the Government", because it is most related to the variables represented by this index set.

Table 9   Factor Extraction

Factor (Number)	Initial Eigenvalue			Post-Rotation Factor Explanation		
	Factor Eigenvalues	Percentage Variation	Cumulative Percentage Variation	Factor Eigenvalues	Percentage Variation	Cumulative Percentage Variation
1	3.206	21.374	21.374	2.393	15.951	15.951
2	1.812	12.077	33.452	2.152	14.348	30.299
3	1.627	10.847	44.299	2.100	14.000	44.299
4	1.095	7.302	51.602			
5	0.926	6.173	57.775			
6	0.863	5.756	63.531			
7	0.841	5.606	69.137			
8	0.734	4.895	74.032			
9	0.674	4.496	78.528			
10	0.628	4.184	82.712			
11	0.606	4.038	86.750			
12	0.581	3.872	90.622			
13	0.529	3.529	94.151			
14	0.468	3.121	97.272			
15	0.409	2.728	100.000			

Explanation: Extracted Using Principal Component Analysis

Table 10   Factor Coefficients Using Varimax Rotation

Factor Description	Extracted Factors		
	Opinions on Fairness of National Policy (Factor 1)	Opinions on Fairness of Process of Accumulation of Wealth (Factor 2)	Recognition Level of Obeying Government (Factor 3)
The government wants to demolish houses and develop, the people should just leave	0.107	−0.023	0.585
The people should obey the government, the lower classes should obey the upper classes	0.088	−0.051	0.705
Democracy is the government controlling the people	0.024	−0.073	0.563
The government is responsible for national affairs, the people should not overly concern themselves	0.068	−0.045	0.728
The people pay taxes, the government can spend them how it likes	0.140	−0.070	0.557
Make money by any means, even illegally	−0.167	0.700	−0.082
Good family background	0.029	0.548	0.030
Have important connections	−0.009	0.511	−0.108
Some people are corrupt/embezzle state funds or public capital	−0.128	0.740	−0.091
The rich pay fewer taxes	−0.070	0.694	−0.035
Financial Bureau Tax Policy	0.494	−0.153	0.174
Work and Career Opportunities	0.586	−0.177	0.153
Rural vs. Urban Wages	0.752	−0.012	0.144
Wages in Different Areas and Professions	0.782	0.031	−0.003
Social Security, e.g. retirement treatment	0.731	−0.022	0.024

Explanation: Rotated using Varimax method

On this basis, we made these factors dependent variables, and after controlling gender, age, and household registration, we established employment, income, and education factors, decisive to objective class and subjective class self-identification, as independent variables in an analysis model (this is primarily to avoid individual variables creating random biased influences). Analysis results are shown in Table 11.

Table 11   Factors Influencing People's Social Attitude

Independent Variables	(Model 1) Opinion on Level of Unfairness of National Policy		(Model 2) Opinion on Level of Unfairness of Reasons People Get Wealthy		(Model 3) Level of Recognition of Obeying Government	
	B	Beta	B	Beta	B	Beta
Gender (Male=1)	0.009	0.004	0.034	0.016	−0.013	−0.006
Household registration (urban=1)	−0.047	−0.023	0.281	0.133***	−0.216***	−0.104
Political Status (Party Member=1)	−0.134	−0.055	−0.063	−0.025	−0.078	−0.031
Age Group (Control Group: 66 and above)						
25 and below	0.980	0.400	−0.781	−0.303	−0.893	−0.355
26~35	0.865	0.419	−0.787	−0.362	−1.015	−0.479
36~45	0.887	0.410	−0.860	−0.378	−0.723	−0.325
46~55	0.905	0.315	−0.860	−0.284	−0.478	−0.162
56~65	0.826	0.155	−1.007	−0.179	−0.224	−0.041
Class Identification (Control Group: Lower Class)						
Upper Class	0.510	0.039	−0.725	−0.053	−0.040	−0.003
Middle-Upper Class	0.463	0.148***	−0.307	−0.093**	−0.423***	−0.131
Middle Class	0.271	0.138***	−0.451	−0.218***	−0.324***	−0.161
Lower Class	0.266	0.119**	−0.228	−0.097*	−0.229*	−0.100
Objective Class (Control Group: Other Class)						
Peripheral Middle Class	−0.120	−0.041	0.022	0.007	−0.168	−0.056
Semi-Core Middle Class	−0.070	−0.034	−0.019	−0.009	−0.079	−0.037
Core Middle Class	−0.038	−0.027	−0.007	−0.001	−0.023	−0.003
Constant	−1.057		1.075		1.005	
R^2	0.08		0.075		0.083	
$N=$	4699		4588		4576	

Note: "***"$=p < 0.001$; "**"$= p < 0.01$; "*"$= p < 0.05$.

It can be seen that while in Model 1 "household registration" (*hukou* 户口) is not a notable variable. But in Model 2 and Model 3, its statistical significance is extremely notable. Here, those of non-rural household registration – so of town or city registration–

have a much stronger motivation to become wealthy by any means necessary, including illegal.

To a certain degree it can be said that "farmers" have a somewhat stronger sense of fairness than "city people", and a different research project of ours has similar results: that "rural migrant workers" have higher feeling of fairness than "urban workers" (Li Peilin, Li Wei, 2007). This generally shows that people's subjective feeling guidelines, such as fairness, satisfaction, and happiness, are not influenced most by real employment status or income level, but by factors such as their anticipated life, ability to receive information, level of openness in society, and comparison to a reference group.

But the "age group" dummy variable has lost its statistical meaning. That is to say, when controlling other variables, compared to social attitude, clear differences are shown between age groups.

The objective class variable in models 1, 2, and 3, lacks clear statistical meaning. The following conclusion can be drawn from this: either the middle class is not at all a group that possesses unified interests or in social attitude, or by using employment, income, and education to construct the so-called "middle class", realistically speaking this is just a theoretical "invention".

But class identification is very clear in every model. This is basically consistent with our earlier discoveries (Zhang Yi, 2005). We know from Model 1 that the more a social group identifies itself as "middle class", or close to the "middle class" ("upper-middle class" or "lower-middle class"), the more these people think that the various current systems in China are fair. The more they identify as one of these three "middle class" social groups, the less likely they attribute factors in gaining wealth to "illegally gaining wealth" or through unfair competition. But in terms of attitude towards the government, those that identify as middle class also show an attitude opposed to inappropriate government administration.

Because these three variables were all picked up after our factor analysis, therefore through this validation we can basically say that members of society have relatively high class identification. As a whole, the stronger people's formed sense of social fairness, the stronger the enthusiasm of their identification with society. Thus self-identifying as "middle class" is a variable significant to social stability, as such people more easily form a common social attitude and behavioral tendencies.

6. Conclusion and Discussion

Concluding the above analysis, the following basic conclusions can be surmised:

One, regarding the scale of the middle class. Taking income as a sole criteria of measurement, of Chinese households, currently 16.3% have an annual income above 14001 *yuan* (which includes 3% with above 35000 *yuan* annual income), 22.8% has an upper-middle level income of 7001~14000 *yuan*, and 60.9% have a lower level income of below 7000 *yuan* per annum. If employment, income, and education are all used to define the middle class, a more broadly defined middle class would be approximately 25.8% of society (the old middle class, that is private entrepreneurs and small business owners, have raised this figure). Within this figure, the "core middle class" to which all three criteria apply makes up approximately 3.2%, the two-criteria "semi-core middle class" makes up 8.9%, and the single-criteria "peripheral middle class" makes up 13.7%. Therefore, if those to whom two or more criteria apply are thought of as the "middle class", then currently China's middle class would be about 12.1%.

Two, regarding the relationship between the "objective middle class" and the "subjective middle class". Using employment, income, and education as objective defining criteria, the closer people are to the core class group, the more they tend to self-identify as middle class. Within the "core middle class" group, 61.7% of people thought they belonged to the "middle class'. In the "semi-core middle class" group, 53.5% of people thought they belonged to the "middle class", while in the "peripheral middle class" group, only 46.8% of people thought they were "middle class", and in the "other class" group, 38.6% of people thought they were "middle class". Of the factors influencing people's subjective decision to belong to the "middle class", the most clearly influential factors are "income" and "age". Compared to the farmer class, the manual laborer class had a much lower instance of identification as middle class. The employment-defined middle class also did not at all show much higher instance of identification as middle class versus the farmer class. While education did have some influence, it was not as strong as that of income level. Therefore, in current China, high or low income level primarily decides people's identifying as "middle class".

Three, regarding the comparison of consistent social attitudes between the "objective middle class" and "subjective middle class". The consistency of social attitudes within the "subjective middle class" is extremely clear, while the "objective middle class" shows no consistent social attitude or behavioral tendencies.

Questions that deserve further discussion and debate are:

First, is the middle class actually mainly a concept constructed by displaying social career, used to explain the process of replacement of wage laborers with skilled workers, or a life situation concept, used to show the structure of income distribution, transforming from the pyramid-shaped model to the olive-shaped model? Or is it a concept of class analysis, used to show a new social force produced during the march towards modernization? In the future we cannot but continue to research the meaning of the middle class and its categories. After all, different definitions only satisfy different needs. If we analyze the middle class from a class relations and class formation perspective, we need to investigate typological questions of the middle class from a relations perspective.

Second, in China's current stage, in academic research on how to define the middle class to best comply with people's understanding of this class, according to what theoretical framework and objective criteria is the middle class constructed, and whether or not it will become a hollow theoretical "invention", are of no use at all in explaining people's values and behavioral tendencies.

Third, differences between rural, urban, and different areas in China are extremely significant, and the so-called "middle class" living in different contexts, for instance an employee at a foreign bank in Shanghai, or a middle school teacher in a poor district of Western China, could belong to totally different worlds, and therefore only by analyzing the middle class in areas that are largely of a similar stage of development can research have meaning.

Fourth, subjective identification as "middle class" is the primary deciding factor in social attitude. New cooperative action and social movements are most often founded on a sense of social identity, and so research on this aspect should be improved, and our research has shown that further investigation into the importance of income on class identification is also needed.

Finally, because China lacks a strict individual income and assets declaration system, the proportion of hidden income to real income is hard to estimate. We decided on a 1.5 times multiplier, but much deeper research is needed to verify this, and whether this coefficient can be applied to all income levels is also something that is worth of wrestling with, because theoretically hidden income accumulates much more in the upper classes, but a distribution coefficient is difficult to define.

References

Bulter, Tim and Mike Savage editors. *Social Change and the Middle Class*. London: UCL Press, 1995.

Chen Guanren and Yi Yang. *Zhongguo zhongchanzhe diaocha* [Survey of China's Middle Class Members]. Beijing: Tuanjie Chubanshe, 2004.

Erikson, Robert, and John H. Goldthorpe. *The Constant Flux: A Study of Class Mobility in Industrial Societies*. Oxford: Clarendon Press, 1993.

Goldthorpe, John H.. "On the Service Class, Its formation and Future", in *Classes and the Division of Labour:*

Essays in Honor of Ilya Neustadt, A.Giddens and G. MacKenzie, editors. Cambridge: Cambridge University Press, 1982: 162–185.

Goldthorpe, John H.. "A Response", in *Consensus and Controversy*, J. Clark, C. Modgil, and S. Modgil, editors. London: Falmer Press, 1990: 399–440.

Huntington, Samuel P.. "Transnational Organizations in World Politics", *World Politics*, (1973(25): 333-368.

Huntington, Samuel P.*The Third Wave: Democratization in Late Twentieth Century*. Norman: University of Oklahoma Press, 1991.

Koo Hagen. *Hanguo gongren: jieji xingcheng de wenhua yu zhengzhi* [Korea's Workers: Culture and Politics Formed by Class]. Translated by Liang Guangyan and Zhang Jing. Beijing: Shehui Kexue Wenxian Chubanshe, 2004.

Lash, S. and J. Urry. *The End of Organized Capitalism*. Cambridge :Polity Press, 1987.

Li Peilin and Li Wei. *Nongmin zai zhongguo zhuanxing zhong de jingji diwei he shehui taidu* [The Economic Status and Social Attitude of Farmers in a Transforming China]. *Shehuixue Yanjiu*, 2007(3).

Liu Yi. *Zhongchan jieceng de jieding fangfa ji shizheng cedu — yi zhujiang sanjiaozhou wei li* [Methods and Tests for Defining the Middle Class – The Pearl River Delta as an Example]. *Kaifang Shidai*, 2006(4).

Lu Dayue and Wang Zhizheng. *Xianggang zhongchan jieji chujing guancha* [Observing the Emigration of Hong Kong's Middle Class]. Hong Kong: Sanlian shudian (HK), Co. Ltd., 2003.

Mills, C. Wright. *White Collar: America's Middle Classes*, translated by Zhou Xiaohong, Nanjing: *Nanjingdaxue Chubanshe*, 2006.

Kacapyr, Elia, Peter Francese, and Diane Crispell. "Are You Middle Class? Definitions and Trends of US Middle-Class Households", *American Demographics*, 1996(10).

Kerr, Clark, J.T.Dunlop, F.Harbison, and C.A.Myer. *Industrialism and Industrial Man*. Harmondsworth: Penguin Books, 1973.

Thompson, William and Joseph Hickey. *Society in Focus*. Boston, MA: Pearson, 2005.

Watanabe Masao. *Xiandai riben de jieceng chabie qi gudinghua* [Class Differences and Entrenchment in Modern Japan]. Translated by Lu Zedong. Beijng: Zhongyang Bianyi Chubanshe, 1998.

Wright, Erik Olin. Class *Counts: Comparative Studies in Class Analysis*. Cambridge: Cambridge University Press, 1997.

Xiao Xinhuang and Jun Baoshan. *Taiwan, xianggang he xinjiapo zhongchan jieji de jiti shehui zhengzhi yishi* [The Collective Socio-Political Awareness of Taiwan, Hong Kong and Singapore's Middle Classes]. Shehui jieceng yantan hui (Hong Kong). Hong Kong Zhongwen Daxue Yatai Yanjiusuo, 1999.

Zhang Peilin and Zhang Yi. *Xiaofei fenceng: qidong jingji de yi ge zhongyao shidian* [Consumer Class: An Important Perspective to Starting the Economy]. *Zhongguo Shehui Kexue*, 2000(1).

Zhang Peilin, Zhang Yi, Zhao Yandong and Liang Dong. *Shehui chongtu yu jieji yishi* [Social Conflicts and Class Awareness]. Beijing: Shehui Kexue Wenxian Chubanshe, 2005.

Zhang Yi. *Zhongguo chengshi shehui jieji jeiceng chongtu yishi yanjiu* [Research on Class Conflict in Urban Chinese Society]. *Zhongguo Shehui Kexue*, 2005(4).

Zhao Renwei, Li Shi, and Carl Riskin. *Zhongguo jumin shouru fenpei zai yanjiu: jingji gaige he fazhan zhong de shouru fenpei* [Re-researching the Income Distribution of Chinese Residents: Income Distribution amidst Economic Reform and Development]. Zhongguo Caizheng Jingji Chubanshe, 1999.

Zhou Xiaohong, editor. *Quanqiu zhongchan jeiji baogao* [Global Middle Class Report]. Beijing: Shehui Kexue Wenxian Chubanshe, 2005a.

Zhou Xiahong, editor. *Zhongguo zhongchan jieceng diaocha* [Survey of China's Middle Class], Beijing: Shehui Kexue Wenxian Chubanshe, 2005b.

Chapter 9

Stabilizing Force or Destabilizing Force? Sociopolitical attitudes of the China's middle class and its implication on political transition

Li Chunling

Institute of Sociology
Chinese Academy of Social Sciences

Since the beginning of this century, a social group with higher income, higher education and higher occupational prestige has been emerging in Chinese cities. The public media refers to this group as the "middle class". Even though people dispute the definition of the middle class, there is no doubt that it exists in China and it is expanding quickly. The middle class is gaining attention from the public, businessmen, and policy-makers alike, as well as from sociologists, economists and political scientists. Sociologists, in particular, have devoted attention to this group, focusing on its sociopolitical functions. Chinese sociologists are debating questions such as: What are the sociopolitical consequences of the emergence of the middle class? Is the middle class a stable or unstable influence with respect to existing authority? Will the middle class promote a democratic transition or preserve the existing political order? Social analysts give two opposite answers to these questions. Some argue that the middle class is a social force that promotes democracy and hence constitutes a destabilizing force for the government. They expect the government will take careful measures to control this group. But others consider the middle class to be a stabilizing force that supports the existing political and social order. Hence, they advise the government to act to enlarge it. This paper adjudicates between these contrasting perspectives by examining public opinion data on the sociopolitical attitudes of the Chinese middle class.

Controversy over the sociopolitical functions of the middle class

Since Chinese researchers began to discuss the possibility of an emerging middle class in the 1980s, there has been a lively controversy over the sociopolitical functions of the middle class. In the 1980s, radical intellectuals were expecting a democratic movement, propelled by the rising middle class, who were perceived as the "most active supporters of democratization"[45]. By the 1990s, most sociologists had changed their stance, describing the middle class as a stabilizing force for the political order, supporting the government's policies of economic reform and thus serving as a driving force of economic development[46]. However, in recent years, a few sociologists have questioned the view that the middle class is a "stabilizing force," claiming that the middle class could, in fact, destabilize the political authority[47].

The middle class as a destabilizing force

Sociopolitical theorists from the West, such as Lipset, Huntington, and Glassman, suggest that there is a correlation between the emergence of the middle class and the development of a political democracy[48]. Lipset developed a wealth theory of democracy, arguing, "the more well-to-do a nation, the greater the chances that it will sustain democracy"[49]. Democracy is related to economic development because, in wealthy countries, there is a diamond-shaped system of social stratification in which the majority of the population is situated on the middle stratum of the social hierarchy, the stratum most likely to support a democratic government. Huntington supports Lipset's argument, suggesting, "the most active supporters of [the third wave of] democratization came from the urban middle class."[50] Other theorists cite the East Asian and Southeast Asian countries and regions (South Korea, Taiwan, Philippines and Thailand, etc.), where the rising middle

---

45 Han Hulong, "Middle class and China's democratization", Theory and Exploration (1989) No.2, pp. 27~29; Liu Debin, "Middle class: a driving force of Western democratization", Free Views (1988) No.2, pp. 62~63.

46 Li Qiang, "Middle class and Middle stratum", Transaction of Renming University (2001), No.4. pp.17~20. Li Qiang, "Market transition and generational replacement of China's middle class", Strategy and Management (1999) No.3 pp. 35~44. Zhang Jianming, "Status quo and trend of middle class in urban China", Transaction of Renming University (1998) No.5 pp. 62~67.

47 Zhang Yi, "Is middle class a social stabilizer?" In Li Chunling (ed.) Formation of Middle Class in Comparative Perspective: Process, Influence and Socioeconomic Consequences. (Beijing: Social Science Academic Press, 2009).

48 Seymour Martin Lipset, *Political Man.* (Garden City, NY: Anchor, 1963). Samuel P. Huntington, *The Third Wave: Democratization in the Late Twentieth Century.* (Norman and London: University of Oklahoma Press, 1991). Ronald M. Glassman, *The Middle Class and Democracy in Socio-Historical Perspective* (The Netherlands: E. J. Brill, 1995). Ronald M Glassman, *The New Middle Class and Democracy in Global Perspective.*(London: Macmillan Press, 1997).

49 Lipset 1963, p. 31

50 Huntington 1991, p. 67

class has brought about democratic movements and a series of sociopolitical turbulences. Many scholars with Western academic background have followed this view to discuss the sociopolitical function of China's middle class.[51] Some Chinese sociologists, such as Li Lulu and Zhang Yi, take a similar position, arguing that the middle class will become a potent agent in the sociopolitical transition toward democracy and civil society[52].

The middle class as a stabilizing force

However, the most influential Chinese sociologists argue that the Chinese middle class is a sociopolitical stabilizer because middle class individuals tend to be politically conservative. Li Qian and Zhou Xiaohong suggest the following potential explanations for Chinese middle class conservatism: 1) They benefitted the most from the economic reforms and subsequent rapid economic growth, 2) They depend heavily on the state, which treats them favorably and protects their interests, and thus they have a propensity for state authoritarianism, and 3) They show apolitical attitudes and prefer materialism[53]. Scholars holding this view insist that middle class in most societies is a stabilizing force for existing regimes because: firstly, middle class as a buffer layer between upper class and underclass may ease the tension between these two classes; secondly, middle class with modest attitudes and conservative ideology will be helpful to prevent breeding of politic radicalism in society; thirdly, middle class as the most active consumer group will be helpful to stimulate economic growth which ensure political stability.[54] Some researchers who study the East Asian middle class propose an additional explanation. Because of traditional forms of political culture, the East Asian middle class prefers political conservatism and relies on the state for economic security[55]. Members of the Asian middle class thus hold contradictory attitudes about politics. On the one hand, they are inclined to support

---

51 Jie Chen, and Chunlong Lu. "Does China's Middle Class Think and Act Democratically Attitudinal and Behavioral Orientations toward Urban Self-Government." Journal of Chinese Political Science, (2006).Vol.11, No.2, Fall, p.1~20. Alastair Iain Johnston, "Chinese Middle Class Attitudes Towards International Affairs: Nascent Liberalization?" The China Quarterly, (2004) Vol. 179, pp.603~628. Goodman, David S. G. ed.. The New Rich in China. Future rulers, present lives. (London: Routledge, 2008)

52 Li Lulu, "Social function of middle class: a new perspective and multi-dimension framework", Transaction of Renming University, (2008) No.4. Zhang Yi, 2009.

53 Li Qiang, "Middle class and Middle stratum", Transaction of Renming University (2001), No.4. pp.17~20. Zhou Xiaohong. Survey on Chinese middle class, (Social Science Academic Press 2005)

54 Li Qiang, 2001, p.18.

55 David Martin Jones, "Democratization, Civil Society and Illiberal Middle Class Culture in Pacific Asia," Comparative Politics 30 (2). 1998 pp. 147~169. David Martin Jones and David Brown, 1994, Singapore and the myth of the liberalizing middle class. Pacific Review 7(1) 1994 pp.79~87.

liberalism and democracy. On the other hand, they desire sociopolitical stability and are subservient to the authoritarian state for economic security.[56] These studies find that East Asia middle class is usually rising in the period of rapid economic growth, in which authoritarian states implement policies to promote economic growth. Middle class benefits a lot from these policies so as to support authoritarian states for economic security and benefits.

Government's query on the sociopolitical function of a rising middle Class

Above controversy is not just involved in academic discussion but also politics. China's authorities have long disliked the term *middle class* for political reasons. The term was almost prohibited from formal publications during 1990s. This was because the term had acquired political connotations when it was referenced by liberal scholars during the 1980s. At the time, middle class mainly denoted private entrepreneurs, a newly emerging social group in the 1980s, which developed quickly in the 1990s. Liberal intellectuals thought the growth of this social group would bring about political changes, such as political democratization. Official theorists in the late 1980s and early 1990s asserted that liberal scholars tried to overthrow the socialist system through creating a middle class. Accordingly, authorities had continued to deem the middle class a threat to the existing political system.[57]

In the late 1990s a few influential sociologists argued that a large middle class was one of the general characteristics of modern societies and could be a stabilizing force, not a destabilizing force, for society[58]. These sociological arguments have become more prevalent since the late 1990s and seem to have gradually convinced Chinese policymakers that a rising middle class could be a positive element in maintaining political and social stability. These sociologists especially stressed that the growth of the middle class would help to reduce the income gap, which the state considered to be one of Chinese society's most serious problems, one that could even trigger political unrest.

Although political leaders seemed to partly accept this view, they have remained

---

56 Hsiao Hsin-Huang Michael, East Asian middle classes in comparative perspective. Taipei:Academia Sinica 1999. Hsiao Hsin-Huang Michael, Exploration of the middle classes in Southeast Asia, Taipei:Academia Sinica 2001. Hsiao Hsin-Huang Michael, The changing faces of the middle classes in Asia-Pacific, Taipei:Academia Sinica 2006.

57 He Jianzhang, "Adjustment of Ownership System and Change of Class Structure in the Country], Sociological Research 3 (1987): 2; He Jianzhang, "Class Structure of China in the Present Period, Sociological Research 5 (1988), p.4; He Jianzhang, A Comment on Middle Class, Sociological Research 2 (1990), p. 1.

58 Lu Xueyi, Report on Social Classes of the Contemporary China. (Beijing: Social Science Academic Press, 2002), p. 62. Qiang Li, 2001, p.19.

politically distrustful of the middle class. Undoubtedly, the rising middle class will be conducive to economic development. This is especially evidenced in consume market when middle class has been showing increasing spending power. Even during financial crisis in 2009, China's middle class remained its strong sending power. However, the political influence of the middle class remains uncertain for the authority. The political leaders of the government continue to prefer the term *middle-income stratum* to the term *middle class*. In November 2002 Jiang Zemin, then secretary general of the Chinese Communist Party (CCP), stated in his report to the Sixteenth National Party Congress that "expanding the middle-level-income group" was one of the policy targets of the government. Some analysts considered this statement to be a signal that the government would make an effort to develop the middle class, or middle stratum. Since then "cultivating" and "expanding" the middle stratum, as an income or consume group but not a social group, have been becoming a goals of social development the Chinese government pursue. However, the government has not yet determined whether it should develop a truly middle class and whether it would be good or bad thing for its political ruling. The current top priority of the Chinese government is to preserve social and political stability. Therefore, it is a critical issue for the government to make clear the political function of a rising middle class.

Research framework and measurement method

How to clarify the sociopolitical function of the middle class? Is the middle class stabilizing force or destabilizing force? Chinese sociologists try to answer this question by examining attitudes of the middle class. They build a link between the sociopolitical function and sociopolitical attitudes of middle class. Middle class is a stabilizing force if its members take conservative attitudes. On the contrary, middle class become a destabilizing force if middle class holds liberal or radical attitudes. Following this logic, a few of researchers tried to examine sociopolitical attitudes of China's middle class so as to judge the function of middle class[59]. However, such researches attained conclusions based on simple measurements of several scattered items of opinion questions but not a systematic measurement of sociopolitical attitudes. That results vague and weak evidences in support of the conclusions. In addition, it remains ambiguous statement on the concepts of conservative or liberal sociopolitical attitudes. It is impossible to reach a convincing conclusion by lack of a clear distinction between conservative and liberal attitudes. This paper tries to construct an ideal dichotomy of conservative and liberal sociopolitical

---

59   Zhang Yi 2009; Jie Chen, and Chunlong Lu 2006.

attitudes, measure related attitudes of middle class and other class based on this dichotomy framework, and finally answer the question about the sociopolitical function of middle class.

Features of political conservatism or liberalism

In order to constructing such dichotomy framework, we need to clarify distinct preferences of conservative and liberal sociopolitical attitudes toward certain issues, and then find specific measurement tool to test them.

Conservatism and liberalism as major two political ideologies have had long history and have been deemed as opposite ideologies in the political field of many countries. However, the specific meanings of conservatism and liberalism differ partly in different periods and countries[60]. Here we choose several major features of conservative and liberal sociopolitical attitudes generally identified by political scientists, especially concerned with the specific situation of China. The most notable distinction between conservatism and liberalism is the attitude toward sociopolitical change or evolution. Conservatism is inclined a skeptical attitude to change and enjoys the present while liberalism prefers social evolution and dissatisfied with the situation If the change is inevitable, conservatism like gradualism but liberalism favor radicalism. The second difference between conservatism and liberalism is related to the attitudes toward state or authority. Conservatism distrusts democracy and prefers authoritative leadership or strong state while liberalism proclaims the freedom of the individual and advocates political democracy. The third disparity of two ideologies involves social justice or egalitarianism. Conservatism pays more attention to the defense of property than justice and equality while liberalism stresses equality before the right of property[61].

Three criteria for distinguishing conservatism and liberalism

Based on these features of conservative and liberal attitudes mentioned above, we may propose three dimension criteria to classify different attitudes of conservatism and liberalism toward certain issues. These three criteria are all related to the hypotheses of "stabilizing force" and "destabilizing force" that theorists debate upon the sociopolitical function of middle class.

First criterion is *Satisfaction* which is to test individuals' feeling toward the current

---

60   In addition, political conservatism and liberalism is very different from conservatism and liberalism of economics.

61   Robert Eccleshall, Political Ideologies: an Introduction, (London: Routledge, 1994). Robert Leach Political Ideology in Britain. (London: Palgrave, 2002). Robert Nisbet, Conservatism.(Buckingham: Open University Press,1986).

situations. High satisfaction implies less expectation for change (conservatism) but less satisfaction hints more expectation for change (liberalism). Second criterion is *Authoritarianism* which is to examine individuals' attitudes toward the state and government. More favor of the existing government and authoritarian state indicates a desire to keep political stability (conservatism) but less favor of the existing government and authoritarian state denotes a wish to promote political change (liberalism). The third criterion is *Egalitarianism* which is to test individuals' value on social justice. Less egalitarianism signifies a wish to remain the existing institution and social order (conservatism) and more egalitarianism represents a willing to adjust the institution and social order (liberalism).

Table 1   Ideal dichotomy of sociopolitical attitude of conservatism and liberalism

Criteria	Conservatism	Liberalism	Index of measurement
Satisfaction: basic feeling toward the current situation	Feeling Satisfying and disliking change	Feeling dissatisfying and hoping some change	① satisfaction of individual living (life-satisfaction index) ② satisfaction degree of social situation (social-satisfaction index)
Authoritarianism: basic attitudes toward the state and government	High confidence in government; preference for authoritarian state	Low confidence in government; preference for political democracy	③ confidence in government (government-confidence index) ④ acceptance of state authoritarianism (authoritativeness index)
Egalitarianism: basic value on social justice	High acceptance of inequality; concealing interest conflict between groups	Low acceptance of inequality; sympathy for disadvantaged groups and low class	⑤ toleration of social inequality (inequality-perception index) ⑥ perception of social conflict (conflict-consciousness index)

Six indexes for measurement of criteria

In order to test these three criteria through attitude measurement of public opinion survey, six multi-item indexes are designed to represent the criteria, two indexes for each criterion. *Satisfaction* is represented re by life-satisfaction index and social-satisfaction index; *Authoritarianism* is represented by government-confidence index and authoritativeness index; and *Egalitarianism* is represented by inequality-perception index and conflict-consciousness index. The values of indexes are calculated by the scores of two or more questions the respondents answer in the survey. The scores of the questions are calculated based on Likert scale score. Table 2 lists theses questions and the scores of answers. The measuring items (questions) of each index are selected through Cronbach's Alpha and fact analysis.

Table 2 Measurement of indexes

Index	Question	Score
Life-satisfaction	*1 Comparison with five years ago, your current living condition is:* *2 You think your living condition after five years will be:*	*2)much better; 1)better;* *0) no change ; -1) worse ;* *-2) much worse*
Social-satisfaction	*3 How do you think about the current situation of social stability in our country?* *4 How do you feel about the current situation of our society in general?*	*2)very stable 1)stable 0)I don't know -1)unstable -2)very unstable* *2)very harmonious 1) harmonious 0) I don't know -1) disharmonious -2) very disharmonious*
Government-confidence	*5 Do you trust below governmental organizations or affaires?* *A. Central government* *B. Local government* *C. Government media* *D. Statistics released by the government* *E. Petition institutions* *F. Judge and policemen*	*2)strongly trust 1)trust 0)I am not sure -1)distrust -2) strongly distrust*
Authoritativeness	*6 Do you agree with statements below:* *A. Democracy means the government rule.* *B. Government is responsible for managing important affairs of our country, so people should not care about these affairs.* *C. People should comply with the government, just like subordinates should comply with their superiors..* *D. The government and party have capabilities to manage our country.* *E. People should move out of their houses if the government wants to build public constructions in the location of their houses.* *F. People pay tax and the government may decide how to spend it without taking into account of people's viewpoint.*	*2)Strongly agree 1) agree 0) I am not sure -1)don't agree -2) strongly don't agree*
Inequality-perception	*7 Do you think it is fair or unfair in the below aspects of our society?* *A. Wealth and income distribution* *B. Public finance and tax policies* *C. Opportunities of job and employment* *D. Opportunities of individual development* *E. College entrance examination system* *F. Promotion of the government's officials* *G. Public health care* *H. Compulsory education* *I. Political right* *J. Judicatory and administrative system* *K. Welfare in different regions and industries* *L. Welfare in urban and rural areas* *M. Social security* *N. General situation of social fairness*	*-2) very fair -1) fair 0) I am not sure 1) unfair 2) very unfair*
Conflict-consciousness	*8 Do you think there is interest conflict among social groups in our society?* *9 Do you think it is possible the interest conflicts among social groups will become intensifying?*	*1) no conflict 2) I don't know 3) a little conflicts 4) many conflicts 5) very much conflicts* *1)definitely impossible 2)impossible 3)I don't know 4)maybe possible 5)definitely possible*

Class classification and the definition of "middle class"

Before analyzing the responses to the questions above, it is necessary to define the middle class. While I recognize that there exist many classification schemes, the various ways of classifying the middle class is not the focus of this paper. Rather, in this paper I employ the classification developed by the East Asian Middle Class (EAMC) project[62]. The EAMC project is directed by researchers from Asian countries such as South Korea, Japan, Hong Kong, and Taiwan, who are conducting comparative research on the Asian middle class. The EAMC proposes the following classification system, based on John Goldthope's class scheme[63].

Table 3   Goldthorpe and EAMC's class scheme

Goldthope's class scheme	EAMC project's scheme
I Higher-grade professionals II Lower-grade professionals	1) Capitalists (employers who hire 20 or more employees) 2) New middle class
IVa Small employers with employees IVb Small employers without employees	3) Old middle class
IIIa Routine non-manual employees IIIb Personal service workers	4) Marginal middle class
V Technicians and supervisors VIa Skilled workers VIIa Semi-/non-skilled workers	5) Working class
IVc Farmers VIIb Agricultural workers	6) Farmers/farm laborers

Among the 6 classes in the EAMC scheme, three are middle class (new middle class, old middle class and marginal middle class). New middle class is constituted by professionals, managers and government's officials. New middle class is usually deemed as a key part of middle class. Old middle class is composed of small employers, small owners and self-employed people. Marginal middle class includes low white-collar workers or routine workers. Sometimes marginal middle class is considered as a marginal group between middle class and working class. That implies the definition of middle class is plural, namely middle classes, not middle class. The further presupposition proposed by the EAMC project is that there is internally intra-class diversity among middle classes in

---

62   Hsiao Hsin-Huang Michael. 1999; 2001; 2006.

63   John H. Goldthorpe, Social Mobility and Class Structure in Modern Britain. (Oxford: Clarendon Press, 1987).

attitudes. Different groups of middle class have different sociopolitical attitudes. Capitalist class is generally believed as upper class above middle class while Working class and farmers are lower class or underclass beneath middle class.

A small revision to the above scheme is required when using the EAMC classification system to define the Chinese middle class. The capitalist class, which is not part of the middle class according to the EAMC scheme, is actually a key part of the Chinese middle class. The Chinese capitalist class is new class whose rise changed the original class structure. The rise of the Chinese capitalist class is unlike the emergence of middle classes in other societies. Typically, an expanding middle class changes the original class structure, to include not only the capitalist and working class, but also a middle group of professional and managerial employees. In China, by contrast, the capitalist class is not the most dominant or advantaged social group. Most of the capitalists are owners of small or medium-sized enterprises. Even though they possess a large amount of economic capital, there is a limit to their social and political influence. In China, the most dominant and advantaged group is comprised of high-ranking government officials and CEOs of state-owned enterprises. They have great power and control over many social-economic resources that capitalists do not. Because of this idiosyncrasy, capitalists are defined as a part of the middle class in China.

An advantage of this class classification is to not only examine the difference of sociopolitical attitudes between middle class and working class but also may investigate the difference of subgroups of middle class. Such framework regarding heterogeneous composition of middle class is helpful to apprehend the true situation of China's middle class and clarify its sociopolitical attitudes. Many Chinese sociologists discover the different groups of middle class have different economic conditions, living standards and sociopolitical attitudes. Some sociologists prefer middle classes to middle class. They argue that distinguishing different groups among middle classes is as important as distinguishing middle class from working class or middle class from upper class. As for the four subgroups of middle class in above classification, disparities in socioeconomic and political status are easy to be acknowledged by empirical observation. That inevitably results differences in sociopolitical attitudes and related functions.

New middle class is generally considered as the key part of middle class which dominates the mainstream of whole middle class because the members of the new middle class occupy important positions in social, political and economic fields. They have some institutionalized paths to influence policy makers and elite groups. Capitalist class, named as private entrepreneurs in China, is an active actor in economic fields and might be a politically active actor in the future. This group has been increasing in its influence on the policies of local governments. But their influence has been restrained in the process of policy making of the central government since top leaders of the Chinese Communist Party have kept suspicious of their political loyalty. The other two groups, old middle class and marginal middle class, have the socioeconomic status apparently lower than that of new middle class and capitalist class. Sometimes sociologists deem them as marginal groups between the working class and typical middle class. However, some members of these two groups probably join in the queue of new middle class and capitalist class in the future. Old middle class is usually omitted out of middle class in the most western societies because of small proportion but absolutely can not be ignored in China in which old middle class holds a large proportion in China's middle class, especially in small cities and towns. Marginal middle class, the major part of this group is considered as a younger generation of middle class with higher education, more democratic consciousness and more capacities of political participation, has been becoming more and more active in the domain of the public media, mass culture and especially internet community. They are the most actively participants in the recent social movements. Younger members of marginal middle class are believed to have much more political liberalism than other members of middle class. Some analysts imply that the mainstream of relative politically conservative consciousness among China's middle class would be changed when these young people enter into new middle class. Based on these discussions, we may expect differences in sociopolitical attitudes not only between middle class and working class but also inside middle class. Because this research is based on a national sample survey data which did not include sample cases of elite group, below analysis can not examine the difference between middle class and elite group or upper class.

Data, variables and methods

Data

The data used for this research is national sample survey data on social stability collected in 2006 by the Institute of Sociology at the Chinese Academy of Social Sciences. The sample size is 7061. Because most members of the Chinese middle class reside in cities, only urban areas are included in this analysis, reducing the sample size to 2894.

Methods and variables

6 OLS linear regression models are used for examining the sociopolitical attitudes of members of the middle classes. One model is run for each attitude index. The indexes are

the dependent variables, and the five classes—the capitalist class, the new middle class, the old middle class, the marginal middle class and the working class—are the independent variables. Control variables include sex, age and education. Table 4 contains the descriptive statistics of each of the variables in the regression analysis.

Table 4 Descriptive statistics of variables (N = 2894)

Variable	Minimum	Maximum	Average	Standard error
Age	18	69	39.8	13.0
Schooling years	0	20	9.7	4.1
Scores of SSL index	−4	4	0.7786	1.6146
Scores of SSC index	−4	4	1.1399	1.6596
Scores of DCG index	−12	12	3.7487	4.0239
Scores of PDSA index	−12	12	0.1703	4.0923
Scores of ASI index	−28	28	−0.2880	8.8481
Scores of PCI index	2	10	6.2458	1.8043
		Ratio(%)		
Sex(male)		45.1		
Capitalist class		0.3		
New middle class		19.0		
Old middle class		19.8		
Marginal middle class		25.2		
Working class		35.7		

Results and interpretation

Table 5 shows average scores of five classes in 6 indexes which indicate roughly the differences of classes in attitudes and feelings of life-satisfaction, social-satisfaction government-confidence, authoritativeness, inequality-perception and conflict-consciousness. Table 6 lists the results of regression models which further examine the differences among classes by controlling gender, age and education.

Life-satisfaction

Average scores and regression coefficients display similar result. There are significant differences of life-satisfaction among classes. Higher status of class in social hierarchy, higher score in life-satisfaction. Capitalist class and new middle class have two highest score of life-satisfaction and following by old middle class and marginal middle class. Working class has the lowest score. Since the number of capitalists' cases in survey data is too little, the coefficient for capitalist class is not significant in the regression model. Other three coefficients of middle classes all are significant. That means there is difference in the satisfaction degree of individual living between working class and three middle classes (new middle class, old middle class and marginal middle class). In addition, these coefficients are positive figures and the coefficient of the new middle class is the largest one. That means three middle classes have higher satisfaction degree of individual living than working class. New middle class has highest satisfaction degree of individual living among middle classes. Sex coefficient and education coefficient indicate that there are no gender difference and no difference among different educated groups in satisfaction degree of individual living. However, age coefficient is significant and negative. That means there is difference among different age group. Older people have low satisfaction degree of individual living than younger persons.

Table 5   Average sores of five classes in 6 indexes

Class	Life-satisfaction index	Social-satisfaction index	Government-confidence index	Authoritativeness index	Inequality-perception index	Conflict-consciousness index
Capitalist class	1.2708	1.7208	4.4877	0.5825	−6.0967	5.8448
New middle class	1.4845	1.2581	3.5607	−1.5608	−0.2890	6.7455
Old middle class	1.0383	1.2957	3.7236	0.7055	−1.5397	6.0649
Marginal middle class	1.0218	1.0647	3.6022	−0.8535	−0.0533	6.6232
Working class	0.7479	1.0830	3.7317	0.5009	−0.3740	6.2349
Total	1.0160	1.1555	3.6668	0.2662	−0.5225	6.3953

Table 6   Unstandardized OLS Coefficients for the Linear Regression of Attitude indexes on Classes

Dependent variable / Independent variable	Life-Satisfaction index	Social-satisfaction index	Government-confidence index	Authoritative-ness index	Inequality-perception index	Conflict-consciousness index
Class (reference group: working class)						
Capitalist class	0.542(0.768)	0.706(0.812)	1.031(1.966)	1.543(1.903)	−6.339(4.329)	−0.844(0.857)
New middle class	0.787**(0.105)	0.231*(0.111)	0.072(0.268)	−0.806**(0.260)	−0.415(0.591)	0.104(0.117)
Old middle class	0.424**(0.095)	0.188(0.100)	−0.020(0.243)	0.222(0.235)	−1.378**(0.534)	−0.054(0.106)
Marginal middle class	0.326**(0.089)	0.002(0.094)	0.039(0.228)	−0.577**(0.221)	−0.033(0.502)	0.211*(0.099)
Sex(male)	−0.002(0.059)	0.007(0.063)	−0.106(0.152)	0.004(0.147)	−0.401(0.335)	0.109(0.066)
Age	−0.017**(0.002)	0.000(0.003)	0.017**0(.006)	0.031**(0.006)	0.006(0.014)	0.001(0.003)
Schooling years	0.008(0.009)	−0.015(0.009)	−0.039(0.022)	−0.222**(0.021)	0.062(0.030)	0.098**(0.010)
Constant	1.179**(0.153)	1.231**(0.161)	3.475**(0.390)	1.226**(0.378)	−0.730(0.860)	5.170**(0.170)
Adjusted R^2	0.056	0.001	0.004	0.098	0.002	0.058
N	2894	2894	2894	2894	2894	2894

Note: Standard error shown in parentheses. **: $P \leqslant 0.01$; *: $P \leqslant 0.05$.

Social-satisfaction

Average scores and regression coefficients of social satisfaction also show differences among classes and more advantageous classes have higher values in social satisfaction than less advantageous classes. However, it does mean that all middle classes have higher social satisfaction than working class. Capitalist class has the highest score, and new middle class and old middle class have significant higher scores than working class but marginal middle class has the score slight lower than that of working class. All coefficients of social satisfaction in Table 6 are not significant except the coefficient of new middle class which is a positive figure. That means new middle class has significant higher satisfaction of social situation than other middle classes and working class. The coefficients of capitalist class and old middle class are bigger positive figures but not significant. Marginal middle class have same level in social satisfaction as working class. There are no gender difference, no age difference and no educational difference.

Government-confidence

Average scores of government-confidence of classes seem to be very similar except capitalist class. The score of capitalist class is much higher than ones of other classes. All coefficients of government-confidence in Table 6 are not significant except age. That means no class difference in government-confidence by controlling gender, age and education. The coefficient of capitalist class is larger than others but not significant because of few cases. It is probably that capitalist class has higher confidence in government than other classes. At the same time, there are no gender difference and no educational difference in government-confidence. But old people have higher confidence than young people.

Authoritativeness

Average scores and regression coefficients of authoritativeness display a salient division inside middle classes. The scores of new middle class are much higher than other groups of middle classes and working class. The coefficients in Table 6 indicate that there are significant and large differences among classes, age groups and educational groups. New middle class and marginal middle class have negative coefficients which mean that new middle class and marginal middle class are less likely to support an authoritarian state than working class, old middle class and capitalist class. In other words, new middle class and marginal middle class have more democratic consciousness. In addition, higher educated group has more democratic consciousness and less state authoritarianism than lower educated group. Older people have more state authoritarianism than young persons.

Inequality-perception

Average scores and regression coefficients of inequality perception manifest again a salient division inside middle classes. The scores of capitalist class and old middle class are much bigger negative figures than ones of new middle class and marginal middle class. Two latter middle class have scores approaching to working class. All coefficients of inequality-perception in Table 6 are not significant except the coefficient of old middle class. The coefficient of old middle class is negative figure and quite large figure. That means old middle class has much lower inequality-perception than other classes. In addition, capitalist's coefficient, even though it is not significant because of few cases, is very large negative figure. That seems to imply that middle classes with economic capital (such as capitalist class and old middle class) have higher tolerance of social inequality or lower expectation of social justness. There are no differences of gender, age and education groups in inequality perception.

Conflict-consciousness

Average scores of conflict consciousness do not display large differences among classes although new middle class and marginal middle class have slight higher scores than working class and working class have slight higher scores than capitalist class and old middle class. Among coefficients of conflict-consciousness in Table 6, only two coefficients for marginal middle class and education are significant. That means marginal middle class has more conflict consciousness than other classes. And higher educated group has more conflict consciousness than lower educated group.

Summary and conclusion

Summary of results

The middle classes show significantly higher level of satisfaction with their standard of living than the working class. New middle class shows the highest level of satisfaction, with 71.8% indicating that their standard of living to improve in the past five years, and 68.6% indicating that they expect their standard of lives to improve in the next five years. These findings suggest that members of middle classes, especially new middle class, will likely hold conservative attitudes and be resistant to sociopolitical change, as they do not want their standard of living to be negatively affected.

The new middle class has a higher degree of satisfaction with the social circumstances in China than the working class and the old and marginal middle classes. 80.1% of the new middle class responded that the social circumstances in China are "stable". 76.6% of the new middle class indicated that the social situation is "harmonious". Stability, in this context, refers to social order, whereas harmony refers to the relationships between people or social groups. These findings imply that the new middle class is the most likely to want to maintain the existing social order and to object to changes that might bring about any social turbulence. The further implication is that the new middle class may have a more conservative attitude in this respect.

There is no significant difference between classes in the degree of confidence they have in the government. All classes view the government in a relatively positive light, but there are some differences evident in terms of particular issues. For example, all classes show a high degree of confidence in the Central government, but express a lower degree of confidence in official statistics. 94.1% of the new middle class, 94.8% of the old middle class, 95.4% of the marginal middle class, 94.2% of the working class and 89.9% of the capitalist class indicate that they somewhat believe or very much believe in the Central government. These findings suggest that the middle classes have a high degree of confidence in the government and thus are likely to want to preserve the existing political order.

The new middle class and the marginal middle class view state authoritarianism less favorably than the working class and the old middle class. The new middle class is the least likely to support an authoritarian state. However, while they prefer a less authoritarian (i.e. more democratic) government, results of analyses discussed above suggest that they do not want change that will bring about sociopolitical turbulence.

The capitalist and old middle classes are much more accepting of social inequality than the new and marginal middle classes and the working class. These findings suggest that there is diversity between the middle classes on their attitudes about social inequality. More specifically, the middle classes with economic capital are less concerned with social equality than the middle class with cultural capital, implying that the capitalist and old middle classes are more likely to have conservative attitudes, while the new middle class is more likely to have liberal attitudes.

The marginal middle class perceives there to be significantly more conflict of interest in Chinese society than other classes, namely the capitalist and old middle classes. Echoing the findings on social inequality, these results suggests that the middle classes with economic capital are more likely to hold conservative views, while the marginal middle class (the lower strata of the middle class) is more likely to hold liberal views and be more sympathetic towards disadvantaged groups and lower classes.

Final conclusion

There are striking differences in sociopolitical attitudes between classes, particularly between the new middle class and the working class. However, we cannot conclude that the middle class is simply more conservative or liberal than the working class. In some respects, such as in perceptions of social circumstances in Chinese society, the middle class is more conservative than the working class. In other respects, such as preferences regarding state authoritarianism, the middle class is more liberal than their working class counterparts.

More importantly, there are differences between the middle classes themselves in sociopolitical attitudes. The new middle class—the middle class with high cultural capital—holds a contradictory sociopolitical attitude. On one hand, they view state authoritarianism unfavorably, preferring a more democratic state; on the other hand, they display the highest levels of satisfaction with their current living standards and thus want to avoid sociopolitical change. The capitalist class and the old middle class—the middle class with high economic capital—hold relatively conservative political views. They are more likely to support state authoritarianism and are more accepting of social inequality. The marginal middle class—the lower strata of the middle class—holds the most liberal views. They are the least accepting of social inequality and state authoritarianism, and are the most sympathetic to the lower class.

Regression analyses suggest that age and education have partial effects on sociopolitical attitudes as well. Education is a significantly positively correlated with liberalism, especially with having a preference for a more democratic government. As the middle class becomes more educated, liberal democratic attitudes may become more common in the future. It is worth noting that younger people also prefer a less authoritarian state and have lower confidence in the government, further implying that liberalism and support for democracy may be on the rise among the middle class as more young people enter it in the future.

Within the Chinese middle class, there is a diverse set of sociopolitical attitudes, ranging from conservative to liberal. Members of the middle class are largely satisfied with the current sociopolitical situation and have a high degree of confidence in the government. However, a portion of the middle class also has high expectations for political democracy and social justice. Such contradictory attitudes imply that the Chinese middle class may be inclined to choose the Third Road, a gradual sociopolitical transition. In that case, the Chinese middle class is presently serving as a sociopolitical stabilizer. However, there is a possibility that it may become a destabilizing force on the sociopolitical order in years to come.

Chapter 10

New Middle Class Politics in China:
The Making of a Quiet Democratization?

Alvin Y. So and Su Xianjia[*]

Division of Social Science
Hong Kong University of Science and Technology

Please address all the correspondence to Alvin Y. So, Division of Social Science, Hong Kong University of Science and Technology, Clear Water Bay, Hong Kong. Phone: 852-2358-7780, e-mail: soalvin@ust.hk

In December 2008, 300 middle class members signed a document entitled Charter 08. The document calls for an entirely new constitution, an independent judiciary, direct elections, freedom of religion, speech and assembly, and the right to form independent political parties in China (Ramzy 2008). Charter 08 is very radical because it amounts to a manifesto calling for democracy and genuine rule of law to replace China's one-party system. Those who signed the document chose December 10, the anniversary of the Universal Declaration of Human Rights, as the day on which to express their political ideas and to outline their vision of a constitutional, democratic China. They want Charter 08 to serve as a blueprint for fundamental political change in China in the years to come.

Charter 08 has been snowballing on the internet. It received more than 500 signatures on December 10, 2008 and more than 2,000 signatures on January 15, 2009 (Ramzy 2008, Link 2009). Despite the party-state's efforts to censor the issue, the document has obtained more than 7,000 signatures in support from people of all levels and places in society by February 2009 (China Digital Times 2009).

Since many supporters of the Charter 08 event are members of the middle class, this incidence has rekindled the interest of studying the politics of the middle class in China. Researchers would want to know whether the middle class could act as an agency to propel the democratization project forward in China. The aim of this paper is to examine the role of new middle class in China's democratization. This paper first briefly reviews the theories of democratization by S.M. Lipset and S.P. Huntington. Then it will present the political activism of the Chinese new middle class. Finally it will discuss the role of new middle class in the democratization of China. In the concluding section, this paper will argue that the emergence of new middle class politics may lead to a new kind of democratization what we called "Quiet Democratization" in China.

Theories of Democratization and Middle Class

Observing the wave of democratization after World War II, S.M. Lipset (1963) developed a wealth theory of democracy, namely, "the more well-to-do a nation, the greater the chances that it will sustain democracy" (Lipset 1963, p.31). Democracy is related to economic development because there is a diamond-shape social stratification with an expanded middle class in wealthy countries. Since middle class members are the ones most likely to join voluntary political organizations, they provide a countervailing force to check the power of the state, form a source of new opinion for the mass media, and help to train citizens in political skills and to arouse political participation. Lipset asserts that a large middle class also tempers conflict by rewarding moderate and democratic parties and by penalizing extremist groups.

Studying a new wave of democratization in the late twentieth century, Samuel P. Huntington (1991, p.67) support Lipset's argument by reporting that "the most active supporters of [the third wave of] democratization came from the urban middle class." In the Philippines, the middle-class professionals and business-people filled the ranks of the demonstrations against Marcos in 1984. In Spain, economic development had created a nation of the modern middle class which made possible the peaceful transition to democracy. On Taiwan, the main actors for political change were the newly emerged middle class-intellectuals who came to age during the period of rapid economic growth.

Since China has also undergone very rapid economic development at the turn of twenty-first century, it is interesting to ask the question whether the rise of China as a world economic power will lead her to democratization. In other words, since economic development has led to an expanded middle class, will the middle class become a political agent to pursue democratization in China?

The Literature on the Chinese Middle Class's Democratic Potential

The China field presents a contradictory view on the democratic potential of the middle class. On one hand, the Chinese middle class is said to be "conservative" and "moderate". Jonathan Unger (2006, p.31) argues that "the Chinese educated middle class has become a bulwark of the current regime." Unger warns: "don't expect regime change or democratization any time soon. The rise of China's middle class blocks the way." He Li (2003, p.88) similarly concludes that "the new middle class as a whole does not pose any significant threat to the current regime. It quietly endorses the leadership in Beijing." Examining the case of homeowners' resistance in the cities, Yongshun Cai (2005, p.777) also reports that "the Chinese middle class are largely moderate because of their intention to maintain the political order and limited ability to stage disruptive action."

On the other hand, a democratic orientation is usually found from the surveys on the attitudes of the Chinese middle class. For example, Min Tang et al. (2009, p.91) find that "Chinese middle class has a greater degree of democratic orientation on all aspects." When people say that they belong to the middle class, they choose to identify with such "pro-democratic values like individualism, pluralism, and liberalism, and recognize their responsibility to facilitate progressive social political changes." In another survey conducted in Beijing, Jie Chen and Chunlong Lu (2006, p.2) also find that "Chinese middle-class individuals, especially in an urban setting, do think and act in accordance with democratic principles."

What explains the above contradictory views of the Chinese middle class? One possible explanation is that different studies use different definitions of the middle class. For example, Lipset, Huntington, He, Chen and Lu's middle class include both business people (who own property and engage in capitalist relations, i.e., the entrepreneurs) and educational professionals (like lawyers, teachers, technicians, and managers who hold a higher education degree, do not own any productive assets, and are dependent on a monthly salary for their livelihood). To avoid the confusion over definition, we use the term "*old middle class*" to denote the property owners and entrepreneurs, while we reserve the term "*new middle class*" for educational professionals whose superior market situation (income, security, prestige, etc.) is based on their knowledge and expertise rather than on property. Since So (2003) has already examined the old middle class in another study, we want to focus on the new middle class in this paper.

Another possible explanation of the contradictory findings is the studies use different levels of analysis. The survey findings are based on an individual-level analysis, while the other studies conduct their investigation at a highly level. It is possible that members of the middle class exhibit attitudes of democracy and talk democratically, but they have a different behavior when they act collectively. As such, this paper aims to go beyond an individual-level analysis by focusing on how the middle class acts collectively to protect its interests and lifestyle.

Political Activism of the Chinese New Middle Class

Since the Chinese new middle class has just emerged during the reform era a couple of decades ago, it belongs to the first generation and still has not attained a clear-cut identity and pattern of behavior to distinguish it from other classes.

Nevertheless, by the turn of the twenty-first century the Chinese mass media and the foreign press has began to talk about a new collective identity called "the middle class" ("*Zhong Chan Jie Ji*") (China Daily 2004; Phoenix TV 2006; The Economist 2002). Focusing on the income level and the consumer power, the mass media reported that a middle class member is one earning a monthly salary of 5,000 Yuan in 2004, and more than 80 million Chinese people can be categorized into the middle class. The mass media also optimistically predicted that within ten years, some 400~500 million Chinese would enjoy a "middle income", making China's consumer market much bigger than that of the United States.

From the mass media's perspective, the Chinese new middle class began to form at the cultural level, as distinguished by its unique consumption pattern and life style. Thus, members of new middle class are reported to live at a high-priced residential neighborhood, shop at the brand name department stores, join overseas tours, hire a helper at home to take care of the mundane household chore, take elaborate effort to decorate their home in their gated community, and safeguard their privatized, individualized lifestyle (Liu 2009).

Aside from the above cultural formation, the new middle class also began to form at the political front too, as they are getting more active in the following three political activities.

First, the middle class is getting more active in their "professional association" activities through voicing their professional interests and raising other political issues. For example, when the ACLA (All China Lawyers Association) was first set up in 1986, it was aimed to be a legal organization to enforce rules of conduct, professional ethics, and professional competence on its lawyer members. However, over the past few years, ACLA began to go beyond its professional boundary and raise issues that have far-ranging implications.

In 2005, 100 lawyers has put forward a petition at the Sixth Annual Meeting of the ACLA to demand the Public Security office to remove the barriers (like bars and wires) to separate the lawyers from their clients in the Public Security meeting rooms. The lawyers frame their petition not only as a means to defend "lawyers' rights," but also as a means to defend their "clients' rights". The lawyers said their clients should be taken as innocence until they are proven guilty by the court. The Security Office is wrong in treating the persons it arrested as criminals, denial them the rights of communication to their lawyers. By framing their petition as a right-defending issue, the lawyers not only have challenged the authority of the Public Security officials, but they also have helped to expand the legal rights of Chinese citizens.

Aside from this petition to remove barriers from the Public Security Office, the ACLA proposed other laws to expand the legal rights of Chinese citizens. For example, the ACLA proposed a new slavery law to protect coal miners and other people who are put into a slave-like condition, and proposed a new competitive law to protect the rights of consumers from the powerful phone company who has monopolized the communication market.

Second, members of the new middle class join social movements to articulate their concerns and to protect their lifestyle and interests. Homeowner's resistance movement, for instance, is a means to defend the consumer rights of the new middle class, to safeguard the new middle class's privatized lifestyle, and to protect the autonomy of the new middle class community (Liu 2009). Homeowner's resistance movement frequently draws upon the essential resources of the new middle class, like lawyers' familiarity with private property laws, architects' design knowledge about building construction, managers' sophisticated negotiation skills, former state officials' extensive interpersonal networks and contacts with the news media. With these new middle class resources behind the movements, homeowners in a middle class neighborhood often can win battles against powerful developers and corrupted local officials. These battle victories, in turn, have greatly empowered the new middle class.

Similarly, when intellectual (including writers, scholars, scientists, other professionals, and college students) become more vocal in their demands for a cleaner environment, these new middle class demands are very hard to contain and the Chinese environmental movement is gaining strength over the past two decades. As environmental activists often exposes the institutionalized corruption and the lack of accountability of the entire system of governance, many new middle class environmental activists later have expanded their demands and became closely linked with democracy activists who agitated for broader political reforms (Economy 2005; Lee et al. 1999).

Third, there is a "pre-existing democratic party" route in new middle class politics. Several small democratic parties were formed before 1949, and they are tolerated after the Communist Revolution because the Chinese Communist Party (CCP) put forward a united front policy of multi-party cooperation and political consultation under the leadership of the

Communist Party. For example, the "China Democratic National Construction Association" (CDNCA) is one of small democratic parties survived before the reform era. By 2008, CDNCA has 114,347 members in 361 local branches. It includes a large number of intellectuals and professionals working in the private and the public sector. In 2008, CDNCA has a total of 17,363 members represented in various levels of the National People's Congress (NPC) and Political Consultative Conference (PCC). With such a large representation in NPC and PCC, CDNCA is also getting more active, providing a variety of comments and voicing many new ideas at the NPC and PCC meetings. Comments and ideas of CDNCA include: poverty reduction, the development of the non-public sector, strengthen the links with the Hong Kong and Macao professionals, etc.

Through the above three routes (the professional associations' route like the ACLA, the new social movements' route like home owners' resistance movement, and the pre-existing political parties route like the CDNCA), the new middle class is beginning to emerge as a political actor, voicing its concerns and participating in Chinese politics in order to protect its interests and lifestyle.

The New Middle Class's Mode of Political Participation

Although the Chinese new middle class has just emerged and its political formation is highly rudimentary, it has presented a unique mode of political participation that is different from the other classes. In general, new middle class's political participation has the following characteristics: moderate, high-tech mobilization, and stay within the existing state limit.

First, new middle class's political participation tends to rational and moderate. It is willing to engage in negotiation and compromise, and it tries to avoid violent confrontation with other classes or the state. Because the new middle class is resource-rich (they have professional expertise, extensive social network, and negotiation skills), they need not resort to such radical actions as blocking the highway and engaging in violent demonstrations in order to attain their goals.

Second, members of the new middle class tend to use new communication technologies (internet bulletin board, web blogs, SMS wireless service, etc.) to mobilize their members for collective action. They need not resort to face-to-face mobilization at the community level because they are at the cutting edge of high tech development, and they highly value privacy and respect individual autonomy (Liu 2009).

Third, the middle class often acts within the state limits, because they're better educated and always rational to use the existing legal channels. As Cai (2005: 779) points out, the middle class is "fully aware of the boundaries of state tolerances; fear of punishment compels them to take action acceptable to the state." In homeowner's resistance movement, for example, lawyers are usually involved in waging collective lawsuits against the developer or the management company because the home owners want to make sure that their protests are within limit set by the party-state. The new middle class can afford to go through lengthy legal processes because their economic resources and their professional expertise enable them to do so.

Fourth, the new middle class's politics tend to the form of "voice" like speaking out of their own interests, giving advices and comments on policies, appealing the demands on behalf of other classes or groups through legal channels (litigation), the mass media (newspapers and TVs), and the internet.

Although a small radical segment of the new middle class could be quite critical to the party-state and call for such structural transformation as democratization (like the Charter 08 event discussed at the beginning of this paper), the new middle class as a whole is moderate, avoid taking a confrontation position, tends use existing institutional channel to articulate its concerns and works inside the party-state, and feels contented merely to have a voice.

As such, why the Chinese new middle class is contented with the existing institutional structure and seldom challenges the communist party-state?

The New Middle Class and the Party-State

During the 1950s-1970s, the new middle class had an uneasy relationship with the party-state in China. The Communist Revolution was founded on the support of workers and peasants, and the communist party-state did not trust the middle class. In the Hundred Flowers Campaign and the Cultural Revolution, many new middle class members were humiliated, downgraded, and sent to the labor campus in the countryside for re-education.

However, the communist party-state has drastically changed its relationship with the new middle class during the reform era. Instead of taking a hostile stand, the communist party-state is now friendly to the new middle class, as can be seen by the following processes.

To start with, the party-state's general reform policies during the past three decades are in harmony with the interests of the new middle class. Policies such as the expansion of higher education institutions, the setting up of high-tech developmental zones, attracting foreign investment, and adopting an export-led industrialization strategy naturally would enhance the interest of the new middle class because China will need more professors to teach in the universities, more engineers to work on the machines and construction industry, more scientists to work on the high tech industries, more lawyers to handle the legal complications in forming business partnership with foreign corporations, more social workers to handle the social problems created by the sudden shift from a post-socialist economic to neo-liberal capitalism, etc.

In addition, the party-state has adopted policies that are particularly aimed to boost the well-being of the new middle class. For example, during the past two decades, the state has raised the salary of the university professors several times so the Chinese professors' income is much higher than that of the average urban workers. University professors are also given very generous housing benefits, such as they could buy an apartment from their work unit at a discount price or they are given generous housing allowances so they could afford to buy or rent at a very nice middle-class neighborhood (Liu 2009).

Moreover, unlike the situation in Maoist China where the new middle class had to keep their mouth shut or risk political prosecution, the new middle class now feels that they have a voice and their voice are respected by the state officials and the party leaders. Members of the new middle class are often recruited into the think tank or invited to join the consultation committees to give comments or voice opinions. Irrespective whether their opinions are accepted by the party-state or not, members of the middle class highly value that they have a chance to participate in the decision-making process and believe they could influence the decision-making through the existing political channels (Dong Fang Zao Bao 2005).

Finally, there is a "fusion" between the new middle class and the communist party-state. On the one hand, there is a professionalization of the party leaders and state cadres. For example, in 2006, it is reported that out of the 35,637 communist party members in Beijing Xuanwu District, 12,989 (or 36.5 percent) have the educational qualification of post-secondary or university education (Beijing Xuanwu District 2006).

In order to encourage the professionalization of state officials and party leaders, the party-state put up such policy of bureaucratic promotion and recruitment: An applicant who has a B.A. degree will be appointed as a member; an applicant with a master degree will be appointed as Vice Head; while an applicant with a Ph.D degree will be appointed as Head of the department (Beijing Xuanwu District 2006)

Besides, the party-state also invests a lot of money in sending the cadres to advanced nations (like the U.S.) to undergo training. Guangdong Province, for instance, is reported to have spent 100 million yuan in five years to send 300 higher-level cadres overseas for training. The Guangdong government requires that the overseas trainer must be under 47 years old if he/she is a city-level cadre, must have a university B.A. degree, and must have a foreign language proficiency equaled to a 4-year university level. The news reported that after going overseas, the cadres feel themselves more professionalized and more confident in managing their departments (Nan Fang Du Shi Bao 2003).

On the other hand, members of the new middle class are being recruited into the communist party-state. As the Communist Party has maintain a high degree of support in the Chinese society, university students are not deterred to be a member of the communist party as it could provide an advantage in the job market in both the private and public sector. Similarly, university graduates and professionals are attracted to enter the state bureaucracy because it has instituted a policy which favors the hiring of the applicants with a B.A., a Master, and a Ph.D degree (Nanping Shi 2004).

Conclusion: Toward a Quiet Democratization?

In this paper, we have shown that rapid economic development over the past two decades has led to the expansion of the new middle class in China. At the turn of the twenty-first century, a new middle class began to form not only at the cultural front (as shown by the gated community and their pattern of consumption) but also at the political front. The new middle class is becoming more active in politics through the following three routes: First, the professional route, as the middle class professional associations began to raise wide-ranging concerns that often go beyond their professional boundary. Second, the social movement route, as the bulk of leaders and members of the social movements come from the middle class. Third, the existing political party route, as the bulk of leaders and members of the existing small democratic parties come from the middle class and these small democratic parties are becoming more active in voicing their concerns over different issues.

Examining the above routes of political participation show that the Chinese new middle class tend to adopt a rational and moderate position and it tries to avoid confrontation with the state and other classes. It also tends to works within limit set by the party-state and uses the existing channels to voice their concerns and grievances.

The new middle class adopts the above modes of political participation because it is having a good relationship with the party-state. Aside from the fact that the reform policies are in harmony with the interests of the new middle class, the party-state also set up many specific policies that are aimed to enhance the interests of the middle class. Thus, the new middle class is the beneficiary of the reform era, and that is why it is a supporter of the party-state.

Besides, there is a fusion between the party-state and the new middle class. On one hand, there is the professionalization of the party leaders and state officials. On the other hand, the new middle class are recruited into the party-state. If this trend continues, the communist party-state will soon become a new middle class party-state in several decades; its members are full of educated professionals who are prided of their technical knowledge and expertise.

What is the implication of the above analysis for the prospects of democratization in China? In developing countries, democratization emerged when the authoritarian state is overthrown by the noisy protests on the street, with the new middle class acted as leaders and organizers of the "noisy" democratization revolution. The third wave of democratization that Huntington talks about is full of examples of this "noisy democratization".

However, it is obvious the Chinese situation is different. Despite the Chinese new middle class is getting more politically active, despite there are incidences of mass disturbances in the countryside and in the cities, and despite many pundits predict that communist party-state would fall after the 1989 Tiananmen Incident, there is little sign to show that the democracy movement is becoming alive again and the communist party-state is losing its mandate to rule. The Charter 08 event that this paper talks about at the beginning may soon vanish without a trace.

It seems that China will not take the route of "noisy democratization", given the fact that the new middle class is moderate and rational, and there are fusion between the new middle class and the party-state. It seems unlikely that members of the new middle class would turn themselves into democratic martyrs, sacrificing their superior market condition and high status to fight and died for the cause of democracy.

But does the new middle class need to adopt a confrontation stand to promote a democratic revolution in China? Does the "communist" party-state need to be overthrown in order to have a multiple-party free election in China? Does democratization in China need to go through a revolutionary phase with open, violent confrontation, abrupt and radical structural changes?

If our analysis is correct, the Chinese new middle class is actually in a good position to push for another mode of democratization, what can be called a "quite democratization", in China. Over the past decade, the new middle class has been voicing political issues, raising concerns, and setting new practices (like expanding the rights of citizenship, implementing the rule of law, enlarging the scope of civil society, pressing more accountability and transparency from the party-state) that are important in laying the groundwork for democratization.

The mode that the new middle class is doing it is also conducive to democratization. New middle class's moderate, non-confrontation stand shows that it shares with the communist party-state's goal of political stability and avoiding class polarization, and the new middle class is not a threat to the party-state. Thus, the party-state would see the new middle class as its chief supporters and allies. Couple with the fusion of membership between the party-state and the new middle class, the new middle class will gradually have a stronger voice on policies. As times go by, the party-state policies will reflect more and more the agenda of the new middle class.

In sum, instead of taking a confrontation position to impose democratization on the party-state, the new middle class have been quietly laying the groundwork for democratization by working inside the party-state. If the middle class party-state feels empowered by the professionalization of its cadres, if the party-state thinks that it has strong societal supports from the Chinese citizens, and if the party-state does not feel any threats from outside forces, then it is foreseeable in the near future that the party-state could initiative democratization from above so as to consolidate its basis of legitimacy. Should such event take place, a quiet democratization will emerge in China without any open, noisy confrontation like the third wave democratic revolution happened in the Philippines, Korea, and Eastern Europe.

Of course, the new middle class has only recently emerged and it may be too early to say anything definitive on its impact on Chinese politics. But the structural trend analyzed above is quite promising. Should that trend continue in the near future, the new middle class could act as an agent to bring a quiet democratization in China. We only hope that the global economic financial crisis started in 2008 would not distract China from following this path of quiet democratization.

References

Beijing Xuanwu District. 2006. Year Book of Beijing Xuanwu District. Pp. 151~152. Available on the website: http://xwnj2006.bjxw.gov.cn/06XWNJxxxsh.ycs? GUID=388080

Chen Jie and Chunlong Lu. 2006. "Does China's Middle Class Think and Act Democratically? Attitudinal and Behavioral Orientations toward Urban Self-Government." Journal of Chinese Political Science 11 (#2): 1~20.

Cai, Yongshun. 2005. "China's Moderate Middle Class: The Case of Homeowners' Resistance." Asian Survey 45 (#5): 777~799.

CHINAdaily. 2004. "Middle Class Becomes Rising Power in China." CHINAdaily Nov. 6, 2004.

China Digital Times. 2009. "Beijing University Law School Requires Students to Boycott Charter 08". China Digital Times Feb 11, 2009.

Dong Fang Zao Bao. 2005. "Zhuan Jia Jian Yan 3G Pai Zhao Fa Fang, Jian Yi Yin Wai Zi Yu Min Ying Zi Ben (Expert suggest to set up a 3G licence, to attract both foreign capital and local capital). Dong Fang Zao Bao June 23, 2005. Available on the website http://www.chinabyte.com/telecom/201/2020701.shtml

Economy, Elizabeth. 2005. China's Environmental Challenge. Current History 104 (#683): 278~283.

Huntington, Samuel P. 1991. The Third Wave: Democratization in the Late Twentieth Century. Norman and London: University of Oklahoma Press.

Lee, Su-Hoon, et al. 1999. "The Impact of Democratization on Environmental Movements." Pp. 230~252 in Asia's Environmental Movements: Comparative Perspective, edited by Yok-Shiu Lee and Alvin Y. So. Armonk: M. E. Sharpe.

Li, He. 2003. "Middle Class: Friends or Foes to Beijing's New Leadership." Journal of Chinese Political Science 8 (#1&2): 87~100.

Link, Perry. 2009. "China's Charter 08: translated from the Chinese by Perry Link." New York Review of Books 56 (#1), January 15, 2009.

Lipset, S.M. 1963. "Economic Development and Democracy." Pp. 27~63 in Political Man. Garden City, NY: Anchor.

Liu Shuo. 2009. The Ordinary Middle Class in an Ordinary Community: The Formation of the New Middle Class in China. Unpublished dissertation. Department of Sociology, the Chinese University of Hong Kong.

Nan Fang Du Shi Bao (Southern City News). 2003. "Guang Dong Gao Pei Ban Tou Shi: Wu Nian Hua Yi Yi, Guan Yuan Yang Jin Xiu" 2003-08-30

Nanping Shi. 2004. Nanping Jiao Yu Ju Dui Fa Zhan Jiao Shi Dang Yuan De Diao Cha Yu Si Kao (Nanping City Education Bureau's Survey and Rethinking on the Prospect of Recruiting Teachers into the Party), June 28, 2004. Available on the website http://www.npjy.com/newsInfo.aspx?pkId=495017

Phoenix TV. 2006. "China's Middle Class: Reality or Illusion." Phoenix TV July 17, 2006.

Ramzy, Austin. 2008. "A New Call for Chinese Democracy." Times December 10, 2008.

So, Alvin Y. 2003. "The Making of the Cadre-Capitalist Class in China." Pp. 475~502 in China's Challenges in the Twenty-First Century, edited by Joseph Cheng. Hong Kong: City University of Hong Kong Press.

Tang Min, Dwayne Wood & Jujun Zhao. 2009. "The Attitudes of the Chinese Middle Class towards Democracy." Journal of Chinese Political Science 14:81~95.

The Economist. 2002. "To Get Rich is Glorious." The Economist Jan 19, 2002.

Unger, Jonathan. 2006. "China's Conservative Middle Class." Far Eastern Economic Review. April. 2006: 27~31.

Part IV   Socioeconomic Status of China's Middle Class

The Existence of Contemporary China's Middle Class: The State of its Social Life

Li Lulu and Wang Yu

This paper is a component of ongoing research on the middle class. The main objective of this research is, within the context of China's transforming society, is to confront the process of emergence and formation of China's middle class, and to describe and analyze the social conditions the middle class exists in. It is expected through this work to analytically clarify in social areas, to what degree, and having formed what characteristics the middle class exists in urban China, and to provide a "whole picture" of the middle class.

1. Analytical Strategy, Framework, and Data

i) Analytical Levels and Subject

The authors of this paper have already discussed the existence of contemporary China's middle class in another paper: First, it is different from developed "middle class society", middle class issues in contemporary China have unique meaning; Second, research on the middle class can be divided into two mutually related, but significantly different topics, namely "identifying" the middle class and then the issue of its social function. The former focuses on the conditions of its existence and middle class characteristics, while the latter focuses on the influential role of the middle class in the social structure and regarding social change. The former is to a certain degree the foundation of analysis for the latter,[64] and this paper continues the "identification" of this pursuit.

Identification of the middle class can in turn be divided into two basic sections, namely a "population statistics" meaning and a "socio-cultural" meaning of identification.

---

64 See Li Lulu and Wang Yu, *Dangdai zhongguo zhongjian jieceng de shehui cunzai* [The Social Existence of Contemporary China's Middle Class]. *Shehui KexueZhanxian*, 2008(10).

The former looks at the quantitative characteristics of the middle class (for instance population and employment, etc.), while the latter focuses on the middle class's class awareness, political ideology, and socio-cultural characteristics as well as their formation mechanisms. The authors show the different conditions and characteristics of class recognition, political ideology, and interest trends from the sphere of middle class system traits and class-political awareness.[65] This paper continues this kind of analytical strategy, from the social living sphere of the middle class, descriptively analyzing the existence of the middle class.

This paper's analysis of the middle class's social living sphere includes two interrelated topics: first, whether there are traits of class stratification in the upper social living sphere, or in other words, whether the middle class manifests unique characteristics. Second, what are the specific manifestations of these characteristics?

ii) Analysis

Different from the political sphere, the social living sphere this paper focuses on primarily refers to the living style of the middle class, its social communication, marriages, and consumption style – all these varied activities of the social sphere. Compared to the political sphere, the varied social sphere should be a much better indicator at "verifying" the level and process of formation of the middle class, because to many researchers, the formation of the middle class is not only specially located in the social structure, but also in the unique characteristics of their lifestyles, culture, and ideology.[66] At the same time, following the rise of the cultural model in class analysis, past researchers paid much more attention to the lifestyles and consumer lives of the middle class. The scope of analysis of this paper will be large, and social living conditions will be used to summarize this paper's area of focus. Hopefully this will enable more extensive analytical description of the formation and characteristics of contemporary China's middle class.

Residence Model

Many academics have already shown that in both the system of reallocation and the market system, where people reside (what houses they live in) is always an important

---

65 See Li Lulu and Li Sheng, *"Shutu yilei: dangdai zhongguo chengxiang zhongchan jieji de laixinghua fenxi"* ["Different Paths, Different Groups": Typological Analysis of the Urban and Rural Middle Class in Contemporary China]. *Shehuixue Yanjiu*, 2007(6).

66 Bourdieu, P. *Distinction – A Social Critique of the Judgement of Taste*. Translated. by Richard Nice. London: Routledge & Kegan Paul Ltd., 1984. *Principles of Art*. Zhongyang Bianyi Chubanshe, 2001. Mills, C. Wright. *White Collar: America's Middle Class*. Zhejiang Renmin Chubanshe, 1987.

socio-economic class indicator, despite system differences. Where people live (their home and neighborhood) is a product determined by their employment, effort, income, and other socio-economic variables. Therefore, the difference between residences is an important aspect of class difference.[67] Difference between houses can be analyzed from two points of view: one is in terms of property rights, quality and size of homes, and real estate price, to show differences between classes.[68] Bian Yanjie and others have used China's "Five Censuses" data to show that in China's cities, class has a notable influence on property rights, housing quality, and house prices, and think that in China's process of social transformation, mechanisms of class division will still continue, and alongside the growth of the market system, the distribution of real estate capital to social elites will be notably superior.[69]

The other aspect is the "residence differentiation" perspective. "Residence differentiation" is a human ecology perspective that shows how social class is reflected in residence spaces, focusing on the location, grouping, and differentiation situation of different social group's areas of residence.[70] Social classes or socio-economic status differences are an important mechanism in forming residence differences. This is a characteristic of urban residence space ecology, and is a kind of reflection of social class relations: different classes of different socio-economic status manifest differences in their residence spaces. The ancient saying "choosing one's residence by one's neighbors" is a common expression for this residence differentiation.[71] In a manner of speaking, residence differences are not just a product of class division, but also strengthen class differences, and are even a mechanism behind the re-production of class.

Social Relations

The authors of this paper have previously discussed the meaning of social relations subject analysis in class stratification analysis,[72] and this is one analytical foundation,

---

67 See Bian Yanjie and Liu Yongli. "Shehui fenceng, shufangquan yu juzhu zhiliang – dui zhongguo "wupu" shuju de fenxi" [Social Stratification, House Rights and Quality – Analysis of the "Five Census" Data in China". *Shehuixue Yanjiu*, 2005(3).

68 See Bian Yanjie and Liu Yongli, above.

69 See Bian Yanjie and Liu Yongli, above.

70 See Li Zhigang. "Zhongguo chengshi de juzhu fenyi". *Guoji chengshi guihua*, 2008(04). And Xu Jufen and Zhang Jingxiang, "Zhongguo chengshi juzhu fenyi de zhidu chengyin jiqi tiaokong yijiyu zhufang gonggei de shijiao". *Chengshi Wenti*, 2007(04).

71 Wu Qiyan. "Chengshi shehui kongjian fenyi de yanjiu lingyu jiqi jinzhan". *Chengshi Guihua Huikan*, 1999(03). And Bin Menghua. "Zhongguo chengshi juzhu fenyi yanjiu". *Chengshi Wenti*, 2007(3). And Li Zhigang, above.

72 See Liu Jingming and Li Lulu. "Jiecenghua: Juzhu kongjian, shenghuo fangshi, shehui jiawang yu shehui renting". *Shehuixue Yanjiu*, 2005(03).

namely the "proximity hypothesis" described by P. Blau's macrostructure theory,[73] and the conceptual origin of relation strength analysis in social network research is also founded on this hypothesis. In terms of research on social capital and resources, class status influences the forms and scope of social relations, and is directly an important explanatory variable: individual and household social resources are distributed in a pyramid-shaped way within the social class structure, and this class structure is composed of different structural limitations of social relations between members of different classes, because social capital can be explained from the perspective of class order status.[74] Social relations analysis provides a perspective to analyze class: for persons of a specific class position, social relations are largely confined to within their same class. To a certain degree this means that the class structure of society as a whole exhibits a relatively high degree of structure, and as a result becomes an important aspect in "confirming" the formation and existence of the middle class.

Marriage Matchmaking

Selecting a partner, or marriage matchmaking, is the most important area of social life, and one of the most basic social behaviors. While choosing a partner is influenced by many factors, for instance living space proximity factors, level of overlap at work, interests, hobbies, and so on,[75] research on selecting a partner and social class shows that in marriage choices, there is a "marry one's kind" model. Namely, in selecting a partner, both parties maintain similarity in many aspects, including ethnicity, religion, culture, and individual social attributes (education, socio-economic status, family background, etc.), which can be called "homogenous matchmaking". The process of marriage matchmaking is a process of self-construction, replication, and reproduction carried out by society.[76] Within this, similar class status is of great significance, and academics have pointed out

---

73   That is: people most often communicate with members of their class or like social group, as those in similar social positions have common social experience and perspective, as well as belonging and attitude, which are all conducive to communication between such people, for instance regarding relations such as marriage and friendship. See Blau, P. *Inequality and Difference*. Translated by Wang Chunguang and Xie Shengzan. Zhongguo Shehui Kexue Chubanshe, 1991: 57–59, 67.

74 See Bian Yanjie. "Chenshi jumin shehui ziben de laiyuan ji zuoyogng: Wangluo guandian yu diaocha faxian". *Zhongguo Shehui Kexue*, 2004(03). Linnan, Walter. M. En Saier, John. C. Vaughan, "Social capital and the power of connections: the structural factors in receiving employment status". From *Guowai Shehuixue*, 1999(04).

75   Xu Anqi. "Zeou biaozhun: Wushi nian bianqian jiqi yuanyin fenxi". *Shehuixue Yanjiu*, 2000(06).

76   See Li Yu and Xu Anqi. "Zeou moshi he xingbie pianhao yanjiu – xifang lilun he bentu jingyan ziliao de jieshi". *Qingnian Yanjiu*, 2004(10). And Xu Anqi, as above. See also Li Yu and Lu Xinchao. "Zeou peidui de tongzhixing yu bianqian – zizhixing yu xianfuxing de pipei". *Qingnian Yanjiu*, 2008(06).

that, the vast majority of marriage partners (in China), are from the same social class, or a class of equal social status. Therefore, marriage is the combining of social status of both man and woman, and can be called an "intra-class marriage system". This system of intra-class marriage not only exists in traditional China, but after Opening and Reform there has been an increasing trend of intra-class marriages, which will continue for a long time.[77] Especially in the highly-educated, young population, the socio-economic status of a potential future spouse has taken on an increasingly important role.[78] Therefore, in "confirming" the formation and existence of the middle class, the situation of "marriage matchmaking" can be considered an important criterion.

Lifestyle

The connection between lifestyle and class has always been a key question in class research. Weber defines lifestyle and social reputation as the basis for status distinction between social groups;[79] Bourdieu, Giddens, and others use Weber's understanding to connect lifestyle and class status, emphasizing that lifestyle is an important symbol of class distinction and status. Bourdieu's "habitus" mainly refers to the traits and tendencies of the daily life outlook and behaviors of people of a certain class, and therefore the process of creating habits is also the process of forming class.[80] Even more so, Mills considers lifestyle an important trait of the middle class, due to the "vague position" of the middle class in production and power relations.

Even though postmodern theorists think that the meaning of lifestyle is removed from "traditional" class concepts and in modern society has gradually become people's "constructed" symbol of self-identity, regardless of the connection between lifestyle and objective class status, academics have accepted that lifestyle is an important symbol of social differentiation, and is a sign of people's recognition of their class status.[81] Therefore, lifestyle is an important sphere in confirming the formation and existence of the middle class, just like Mill's famous conclusion: America's middle class is the "political rearguard, and consumer vanguard", and the latter is a notable symbol of the middle class.

---

77 See Zhang Yi. "Zhongguo jieceng neihunzhi de yanxu". *Zhongguo Renkou Kexue*, 2003(04).

78 See Xu Anqi, as above.

79 See Weber. *Economy and Society*. Vol. 2. Shangwu Yinshuguan, 1997: 253~260.

80 See Bourdieu, "What Makes a Social Class? On the Theoretical and Practical Existence of Groups", *Berkeley Journal of Sociology*, 1987(2).

81 See Fussell. *Class: Social Class and Lifestyle Tastes*. Zhongguo Shehui Kexue Chubanshe, 1998. Bourdieu. *Principles of Art*. Zhongyang Bianyi Chubanshe, 2001.

iii) Class Categorization Framework

Just as its name suggests, a basic premise of class issues, including the "middle class", is its relative independence. Especially in terms of the "(new) middle class", the unique characteristics it has manifested, different from other classes, have been the basis for inciting much interest. Only by confirming the connectedness of these traits with the middle class can the question of the middle class really have meaning, and only then can its social function be further explained. In order to achieve this analytical goal, establishing a class framework which includes at least the upper class, middle class, and lower class, is a necessary precondition. But since the data used in this paper comes from individual-focused sample surveys, only very few survey respondents can be considered upper class, and so there is no effective way to conduct this analysis. This situation, in research based on such methods, is quite normal.[82] Therefore, this paper's class analysis framework only includes the (new) middle class, the lower class, and the self-employed class (the old middle class). While this may not be ideal, it can still achieve one of this paper's basic objectives: to show the relative independence of the middle class. The three abovementioned classes compose the foundation for this paper. At the same time, considering the different levels of stratification in different, transforming societies, and the complexity and heterogeneity of the middle class itself, this paper by analytical necessity also divides the middle class itself into the upper-, middle-, and lower-middle class groups, in order to better demonstrate the middle class sphere in contemporary China, and the different degrees of its existing characteristics.[83]

The data used in this paper comes from the *2003 China General Social Survey* (CGSS2003),[84] and the total number of valid surveys is 3468, and they are categorized in Table 1 according to the analytical needs of this paper.

---

82   Robert Erikson and John H. Goldthorpe. "Concepts, Data, and Strategies of Enquiry", in *The Constant Flux: A Study of Class Mobility in Industrial Societies*, Oxford: Clarendon Press, 1992: 28–63.

83   Of course, society's lower classes similarly possess complicated internal differences. Yet since this paper focuses on the middle class's existing characteristics, these differences are not taken into account this time, but rather the lower class is considered unified. In this paper, occasionally due to analytical needs, we further define the above four classes: in the lower-middle class mid-level managers and skilled workers as well as general managers and skilled workers are separated in order to clarify the upper and lower middle classes. This paper calls this further differentiation the middle-upper-, middle-middle-, and middle-lower-middle class. In the lower class, labor supervisors, skilled laborers, unskilled laborers, and unemployed people are differentiated, forming the upper-, middle-, and lower- lower class—three classes within this one class.

84   Original data and materials from CGSS2003 and CGSS2005 have been made public for research use. To examine them, see www.gsschina.org or www.cssod.org.

Table 1 Class Categorization Definitions

Three Classes	Four Classes	Composing Members	No. of Surveys
Middle Class	Upper Middle	High-level Managers (administrative), Highly specialized personnel	120
	Lower Middle	Mid-, Low-level Managers, Mid-, Low- specialization personnel, office workers	1167
Lower Class	Lower Class	Supervisors, skilled workers, unskilled workers, and unemployed	1702
Self-Employed	Self-Employed		479
Total			3468

2. Middle Class in the Lifestyle Sphere

i) Residence Model

One goal of this section is to "confirm" whether the middle class has formed a different residence model from other classes. In China's urban society, two characteristics make this analysis somewhat difficult. First, under the system of reallocation, housing was a state-allocated "benefit", and inequalities mainly exist in the "elites—public" structure. Second, urban Chinese society has a special "work unit system" which led to the formation of all kinds of inequality, even within work unit housing allocation, but in the broader urban sphere it is mainly between work units that differences manifest, and within work unit neighborhoods people of different socio-economic classes live together. Since Opening and Reform, especially since the commodification of real estate in 1998, the mechanism of marketization in the housing distribution sphere has started to play an increasing role, meaning difference in people's socio-economic status or class status have begun to have an increasingly important influence on people's home and residential environment choices.

Research shows that residence differentiation occurs in many transforming societies, including China, especially in large cities and rapid urban development.[85] But in China the commodification of real estate has followed two development paths, namely: marketized house sales and welfare sales. Therefore, while the work unit system has gradually disassembled, the historically-formed work unit neighborhood has still not totally disappeared as a spatial mode. Many work unit neighborhoods, due to historical reasons, took up the best locations in cities, and through welfare-style purchases, their residents received the property rights to these places. This includes a large number of members of the middle class, and also many from the lower class. Therefore, urban China's residence

---

85   See Li Zhigang, as above.

differentiation will likely display extremely complex conditions, and this should be expected.

This paper divides urban neighborhoods into the categories described below, according to neighborhood quality and location, then describes the differences between residents in terms of two dimensions. First, different classes are distributed differently in certain types of neighborhood (see Table 2). It can be seen that the middle class and lower class do not exhibit clear class differences, but rather show a certain commonality, namely: these two classes both have approximately half their members living in wholly or partially work unit neighborhoods. The self-employed class show a special trait, that within this class only one quarter of its members live in work unit neighborhoods. Relatively speaking, the differences between classes only appear in terms of: first, compared to the middle class, the lower class has many more members living in unchanged, old neighborhoods; while compared to the lower class, the middle class has more members living in typical commercialized neighborhoods. Second, the self-employed class shows no special residence model.

Table 2   Analysis of Different Classes Living in Different Neighborhoods

	Middle Class	Lower Class	Self-Employed
Neighborhood Type	%	%	%
Unchanged Old Neighborhood	10.96	24.09	25.47
Wholly or Partially Work Unit	54.62	43.6	22.55
Typical Commercial Neighborhood*	17.72	13.87	16.08
"Combined Neighborhood"**	16.71	18.45	35.91
Total	100.0	100.0	100.0

* Original categories included a "High-end Neighborhood", but due to low number of survey responses, this was combined with typical commercial neighborhoods to form one category.

** This category includes migrant communities, market towns, and new urban areas recently transferred from urban village areas.

Second, the class composition of residents of different neighborhoods (see Table 3). In terms of social dimensionality, the results of similar class dimensions can be seen, namely that in work unit and commercial neighborhoods, most residents are middle or lower class, and the discrepancy between the two classes is small. The only difference between these two classes is: in unchanged, old neighborhoods, most residents are members of the lower class, in those neighborhoods of a slightly worse environment, the number of lower class members greatly outnumbers those of the middle class or self-employed class. That is also to say that, because the number of lower class people is vast, while there are some work unit or commercial neighborhoods with more than half lower-class residents, in unchanged, old neighborhoods and combined neighborhoods it is still mainly lower class people that reside there.

Table 3   Distribution of Class Members in Different Types of Neighborhood

	Middle Class	Lower Class	Self-Employed	Total
Neighborhood Type	%	%	%	
Unchanged, Old Neighborhood	20.95	60.92	18.13	100.0
Wholly or Partially Work Unit	45.27	47.78	6.95	100.0
Typical Commercial Neighborhood*	42.14	43.62	14.23	100.0
"Combined Neighborhood"**	30.67	44.79	24.54	100.0

* As above. ** As above.

To summarize the above two dimensions, the conclusion is: residential differentiation, especially the middle class neighborhood model, is not at all extremely notable; but, in those older neighborhoods and "combined neighborhoods", lower class and self-employed residents make up the vast majority, indicating a certain degree of residence differentiation.

If within the three-class framework there were no notable class differences, then only further, more detailed, analysis could answer: under what kinds of levels can class differences exist? Therefore, we separate the middle class into three more particular groups (the upper-middle class, middle-middle class, and lower-middle class), and also divide the lower class into three (upper-lower class, middle-lower class, and lower-lower class), keeping the self-employed as one class. A comparative analytical scatter diagram of the seven classes (Graph 1) shows much more residential differentiation information:

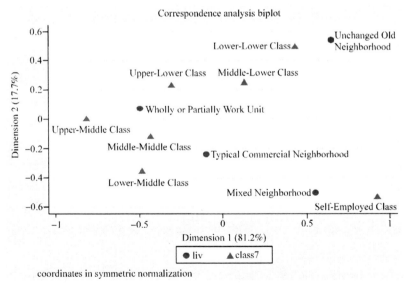

coordinates in symmetric normalization

Graph 1   Comparative Scatter Graph of Neighborhood Type and Class

First, lower classes (including the upper-, middle-, and lower-lower classes) mostly concentrate in "wholly or partially work unit neighborhoods". Of these, the lower-lower class and upper-lower class show relatively clear residence traits, namely that the lower-lower class is more connected to "unchanged, old neighborhoods", while the upper-lower class concentrates in work unit neighborhoods.

Second, the middle class (including the upper-, middle-, and lower-middle class) are distributed more in work unit and typical commercial neighborhoods. Aside from the connection evident between the upper-middle class and work unit neighborhoods, the middle-middle class and lower-middle class do not show any concentrated distribution traits.

Third, the self-employed class is concentrated in "combined neighborhoods".

ii) Social Relations

Analysis of social relations directly shows the degree of class structuring. Survey questionnaires inquired about respondents' 5 most important social relations in the last six months, including spouse, family, relatives, coworkers, old schoolmates, neighbors, friends, and other people. This paper only selects "friends" as an object of analysis, because, relative to other categories, "friends" receives the most influence from class status similarity. Within this data, there are 1324 respondents who placed "friends" as the most important social relation,[86] and based on this, the social relations model of members of different classes is analyzed.

It is necessary to explain that due to population distribution influences, the distribution of peripheral frequencies (structural factors) influence the percentages of cells. Therefore, the values in parentheses in Table 4 are the ratio of observed frequency to expected frequency. This value screens the influence of structural factors, and reflects the chance of each class choosing friends from different classes. From the table below, it can be seen that the friends of every class member have the highest likelihood of being from their own class (for the middle class this is 1.5 times the chance for the lower classes, and 3 times for self-employed), or in other words, the chance of close friends being from a different class is quite remote. Simple percentage distribution also shows the same results: 73.86% of middle class respondents' close friends are from their own class; for the lower classes this ratio is close to 60%, and for the self-employed it is also modally distributed. This is also to say that every class tends to choose friends from the same or a similar class. A comparative

---

86 There were some respondents who put "friends" for all 5 responses, so those who placed "friends" as the first response are those whose closest social relation is "friends".

analysis scatter graph displays this information visually (Graph 2).

Table 4   Social Relations of Different Classes (3 Classes) (Closest Friends)

Closest Friend Class Status	Respondent Class Status			
	Middle	Lower	Self-Employed	Total
Middle Class	73.86%	30.51%	26.00%	48.49%
	(1.5)*	(0.6)	(0.5)	
Lower Class	20.00	59.21	35.00	38.67
	(0.5)	(1.5)	(0.9)	
Self-Employed Class	6.14	10.29	39.00	12.84
	(0.5)	(0.8)	(3.0)	
Total	100%	100%	100%	100%

* Values in parentheses are ratio of observed frequency to expected frequency

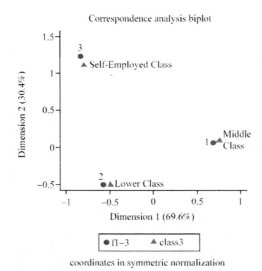

Correspondence analysis biplot

coordinates in symmetric normalization

Graph 2   Comparative Analysis Scatter Graph of Class Social Relations

If the middle class is divided into an upper- and lower-middle class, much more particular class traits can be seen (see Table 5). The upper-middle class is 2.2 times more likely to choose friends from its own class, and is also more likely to choose upper-middle class friends than lower-middle class (1.5 times). The lower middle class is almost as likely to choose friends from higher class or the same class as itself (1.6 and 1.5 respectively), so to the lower middle class the segregation of the upper middle class is not all that apparent. But to the social lower class and self-employed class, the situation is completely different: not only is the instance of choosing friends from the same class high, but the chance of choosing from a different class, especially the upper class, is extremely low. The lower class only has a 0.03 chance of choosing members of the upper class as a friend, and the self-employed class only has a 0.5 chance. Similar information is shown in a comparative analysis scatter graph.

Table 5   Social Relations of Different Classes (4 Classes)

Class of Closest Friend	Respondent Class Status (4 Categories)				
	Upper-Middle	Lower-Middle	Lower	Self-Employed	Total
Upper-Middle Class	28.85	20.46	7.4	6	13.14
	(2.2)	(1.6)	(0.03)	(0.5)	
Lower-Middle Class	51.92	52.7	23.1	20	35.35
	(1.5)	(1.5)	(0.7)	(0.6)	
Lower Class	17.31	20.27	59.21	35	38.67
	(0.4)	(0.5)	(1.5)	(0.9)	
Self-Employed Class	1.92	6.56	10.29	39	12.84
	(0.1)	(0.5)	(0.8)	(3)	
Total	100%	100%	100%	100%	100%

* Values in parentheses show ratio of observed frequency to expected frequency

Summarizing the above results, two conclusions can be drawn: first, in the social relations sphere, there is a clear trend of stratification, the middle class, lower class, and self-employed class are all much more likely to select friends from their own class than from others. Second, there are no notable differences within the middle class or the social lower class.

iii) Marriage Matchmaking

To analyze the situation of marriage matchmaking, the status gains analytical framework established by Blau and Duncan can be used, namely by dividing marriage matches into "achieved (status)" and "ascribed (status)" types. The former is when the socio-economic status of both marriage parties is similar, and the latter considers the similarity of the socio-economic background of both the husband's and wife's families.[87] Due to data limitations, this paper will only analyze the "achieved status" marriage matchmaking situation, focusing on situations of similar class status. From this marriage perspective, the existing condition of the middle class and its related traits will be shown.

This paper certainly does not carry out a kind of factor analysis explanation of the marriage choice model, but uses data from respondents already married when surveyed,

---

87   Li Yan and Lu Xinchao, as above.

and describes the marital situation of members of different classes. These married persons include divorcees and remarried widowers. Due to certain limitations of the data, there is no way to carry out description or interpretation of marriage matchmaking when it occurred.

Table 6 shows that intra-class marriage is a relatively clear trend, and the level of class-related matchmaking is quite high, especially between the lower and middle classes. About three quarters of lower class marriages are with members of the lower class.

Table 6 Marriage Matchmaking in Different Classes

Respondent Class Status	Spouse Class Status			
	Middle	Lower	Self-Employed	Total
Middle Class	59.90%	35.78%	4.32%	100%
Lower Class	20.85	73.04	6.11	100%
Self-Employed Class	11.98	38.54	49.48	100%
Total	34.2	54.09	11.71	100%

Correspondence analysis visually shows more clearly these results (see Graph 3): intra-class marriage of the three classes has an extremely strong trend, the only exception being the self-employed class, which is slightly further away from other classes.

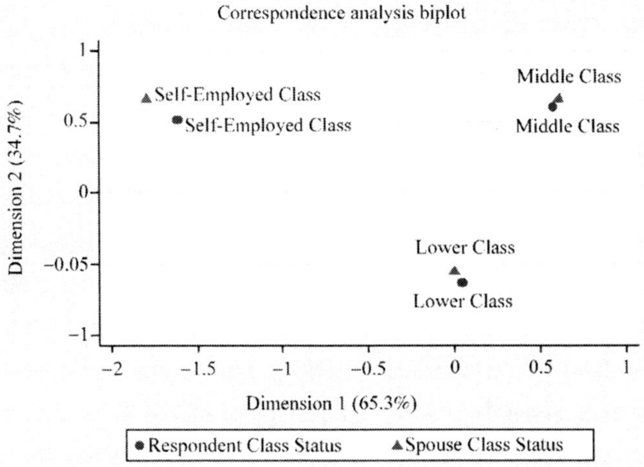

Correspondence analysis biplot

Graph 3

iv) Lifestyle

While lifestyle is often considered a unique trait of the middle class, whether a normal middle class lifestyle form has been formed in Chinese society is the result of conflicting verdicts.[88] This paper thinks that consumption and leisure time are the main forms of lifestyle, and it is the types of consumption and leisure, not their ability or level, that are able to more exactly portray the traits of the middle class. In this paper's distinguishing analysis of the level and characteristics of differentiation in the spheres of consumption and leisure, we determined two simple categories: according to consumption class, consumption is defined as either "common consumption" or "high-end consumption", and according to leisure type, leisure is defined as either "common leisure" or "avant-garde leisure". The "high-end" refers to the relatively higher cost of consumption, and also has a fashionable meaning, while "avant-garde" mostly refers to a kind of "taste" or "choice". At the same time, the respondent's enjoyment of life was also inquired about.

Table 7 is of different consumption and leisure types, life-enjoyment traits, and class relations organized according to corresponding analysis. Regardless whether it is "accordant" or "discordant", if a corresponding class is shown, it signifies a notable connection between a class and that choice. If a cell is empty, it signifies that this choice has no notable class characteristics (responses were scattered). From the table below, it can be seen that in the sphere of lifestyle, characteristics of differentiation show a complex scene, and have similarities with the sphere of political ideology. 89 For instance, in terms of common consumption, the middle class and lower class show notable differences – the lower class and self-employed class are always far from high-end consumption. But, the middle class only shows difference from other classes regarding shop selection, while in regards to the other two high-end consumption aspects, they have not formed notable class traits.

In the sphere of leisure, there is no notable connection between the middle class and the two kinds of common leisure forms that are attributed to the lower class and self-employed class. But the middle class does exhibit clear class characteristics in terms of its leisure style, although in terms of the other two aspects it does not. If the middle class is subdivided into the upper- and lower-middle classes, it can be seen that the lower-middle class mostly correlates with gym-related activities, and the upper-middle class corresponds much more to art and home decoration. This might be related to the different middle class levels of income and work conditions. From these results, it can be concluded that, of the lifestyles most indicative of the middle class, only part of the middle class shows

---

88 See Zhang Wanli, Li Wei and Gao Ge, "Xianjieduan zhongguo shehui xinzhongjian jiceng goucheng tezheng yanjiu". *Beijing Gongye Daxue Xuebao* (Shehui Kexueban), 2007(2). And Li Chunling, "Zhongguo dangdai zhongchanjieceng de goucheng ji bili". *Zhongguo Renkou Kexue*, 2003(6).

89 See Li Lulu and Wang Yu, above.

differentiated class characteristics, and in many regards this class has still not formed its own characteristics. Furthermore, the lower and self-employed classes show clear class lifestyle and other traits. The middle class in China is actually still in the formation process.

Table 7   Categories of Different Class Lifestyles

Lifestyle Type	Lifestyle Characteristics	Class Characteristics	
		Accordant	Discordant
Common Consumption	1) Except when necessary, my family and I never impulse buy non-necessity products	Lower Class, Self-Employed	Middle Class
High-end Consumption	2) When my family and I celebrate birthdays and other special occasions, we always go out to eat	Middle Class	Lower Class, Self-Employed
	5) Whenever I go out, I take a taxi or drive myself		Lower Class, Self-Employed
	6) Long-lasting products in my home are all brand name and high-quality		Lower Class, Self-Employed
	3) I always go shopping at well-known shops	Middle Class	Lower Class, Self-Employed
Common Leisure	11) Most of my leisure time at home is spent watching television	Lower Class, Self-Employed	Middle Class
	12) On weekends or when I have free time, I often play cards or Mahjongg	Self-Employed	Middle Class, Lower Class
Avant-Garde Leisure	13) I often go to specialized gyms to work out		Lower Class, Self-Employed
	7) My home is full of good art, and paintings decorate the walls		Lower Class, Self-Employed
	10) During leisure time, I always listen to music or enjoy artwork	Middle Class	Lower Class, Self-Employed
Life Enjoyment	9) I feel life is good right now, I don't often feel stressed by things	Middle Class	Lower Class
	4) My work is always high-pressure	Middle Class	Lower Class, Self-Employed

Lifestyle is favored in analysis of the middle class because compared to objective class status, lifestyle is much more a characteristic constructed by society, regardless of whether it's a product of status structure or a cultural values "construction". This paper attempts to analyze the main factors influencing lifestyle, including employment, education, and income, etc. But the results show that lifestyle differences are not able to explain much. One aspect of this might be due to problems in the structure of the statistical model, or another aspect might be due to society as a whole, including the middle class, and its currently rapidly changing state, meaning that no stable style has yet been formed. In terms of the trends distilled here, income plays a relatively large influence on consumption style, and aside from income influences, leisure style is even more influenced by education level and employment. But in this paper's analysis these factors did play a notably clear role. Some researchers have emphasized that the "consumption class" perspective, the "consumer middle class" concept that has been formed, needs to highlight that these conclusions are mostly the result of consumption level or consumption ability analysis, not from analysis of consumption style or behavior (tendencies), of which the latter is considered a middle class characteristic. Regarding consumption style or consumption behavior, class differentiation is not notable – whether consumption style differences depend on class status or other factors is still a highly contested question.[90]

3. Conclusion

The middle class of the social life sphere is similar to the middle class of the political ideology sphere, showing middle class characteristics on a few aspects. On other aspects, the middle class has not yet formed its class characteristics.

In terms of homes and residence, the middle class does not at all show a unique pattern. But the appearance of residential differences deserves attention, namely: compared to the lower class, the middle class has relatively more members living in higher-priced, better-situated typical commercial neighborhoods, and the lower classes have more members in unchanged, old neighborhoods.

In terms of lifestyle, while the data shows the existence of a middle-level consumer class, in terms of consumption patterns and behavior, the middle class has not yet formed its own style. That is to say, it has not formed a middle class consumer pattern distinct from other classes.

The difference between the two above aspects is that in terms of social relations, a clear trend in social stratification is clear, as the highest likelihood in each class is that social relations occur between members of like-classes, much higher than the likelihood of social relations with different classes. Social relations are greatly limited to within one's class. Furthermore, simple marriage matchmaking analysis shows the existence of the "intra-class marriage system". Here there is a clear line between the middle and lower classes.

In the opinion of the authors, the result of the interrelated differences above is that, as a transforming society, the characteristics of Chinese society are already decided, namely:

---

90   See Li Chunling. *Duanlie yu cuipian — dangdai zhongguo shehui jieceng fenhua shizheng fenxi* [Fragmentation and Rupture: Empirical Analysis of Contemporary China's Social Class Stratification]. Shehui Kexue Wenxian Chubanshe, 2006(05).

China's social transformation is continuous, urban-focused, and rapid. The so-called "continuousness" primarily refers to the fact that during the process of transformation no interrupting changes have occurred, and so the "legacy" of the system of reallocation is still largely present in current society. This legacy can be clearly seen in the residential sphere. The transformation towards a market system has made status based on "market conditions" and "market power" (Weber) extremely influential in social relations and marriage decisions, thus characteristics of stratification have appeared. If this is explained according to a class order perspective, rapid social transformation has meant that consumption patterns based on class status in the social life sphere are far from widespread, and the middle class patterns are still unformed, but the process of stratification has already begun, and the lower classes have already formed class lifestyle characteristics. Of course, this paper does not at all deny that lifestyle might be a "self-constructed" product. As a research analysis series, in our next paper we will carry out analysis of the heterogeneity of socio-economic characteristics of China's middle class.

Chapter 12

The Moral Order of a Middle Class Community

Tai-lok Lui and Shuo Liu

> "In doing, they came to be middle class, making their own definitions of what was correct – for who was to say if they were or weren't?"

Young (2003: 10)

Introduction

Thirty years' economic reform in contemporary China has brought about a transformation of its social structure. Among all the important changes in its social structure, the emergence of a middle class (or for others, the middle classes) is no doubt a social phenomenon carrying significant social and political implications. Largely a response to this emerging middle class, there has been a proliferation of relevant research, focusing on its definition, composition, and politics (just to quote a few examples, Dickson 2003; Li 2005; Li 2010a; Pearson 1997).[91] Despite a growing, academic as well as political, interest in China's middle class, the focus of discussion remains rather narrow. Definitional debates continue. Speculations of the political role of the middle class (a 'social buffer' of growing class contentions or a vanguard of liberalization and democratization), largely based upon its situation in the changing socio-economic and political environment, are plentiful. But few attempts have been made to look at the emerging middle class in their social milieu and to understand how they gradually develop their style of living, identity, as well as their normative orientation.

Of course, research on the rise of the middle class and the political outlook of this emergent class is most relevant to our analysis of social and political changes brought

---

91 It is quite obvious that different researchers adopt different definitions of the middle class and include people in rather diverse backgrounds – from professionals and managers to private entrepreneurs to the self-employed – in their discussions.

about by economic reforms in the past decades. Yet, prior to our understanding of the political outlook of the middle class, it is crucial for us to examine how class formation is carried out among the middle class. Without a closer look at the class formation process, it is difficult to understand how China's middle class is developing their identity, shared social perspective, and an articulation of common interests. This study, based upon ethnographic interviews and participant observation in a middle class residential community in suburban Beijing, is an attempt to fill this gap in the existing research on the middle class in contemporary China. It is an attempt to examine how the middle class is formed in contemporary China. Of course, the processes of class formation are multi-dimensional and multi-layered, and it is beyond the scope of the present chapter to examine all the different aspects of the class formation process.[92] In this chapter, we shall primarily focus on the cultivation of a middle class style of living and the constitution of a moral order in a middle class community (Baumgarter 1991). Social changes in contemporary China have provided us with a good opportunity of observing the rise of a middle class as well as the way this middle class is developing their culture and style of living. What we observed in a middle class community in suburban Beijing was a prototype of a middle class way of life. It is our contention that the relevance of our observations is not confined to that particular community. Rather, as a prototype, the way the residents lead their lives there will, sooner or later, be seen in other middle class communities in China. Through participant observation, intensive interviews, and following the residents' discussions on their internet forum, we shall report on how the middle class residents are forming their expectations about how one should live like a middle class in their own community.

Becoming Middle Class

Current research on the middle class is primarily driven by three theoretical concerns, namely its definition (to a large extent, the repeatedly and heatedly debated boundary problem), the political outcome (i.e. its political orientation, action, and, in the case of developing and/or democratizing countries, their future role in critical political change such as democratization), and (to connect the two) the process of class formation (for a summary, see Abercrombie and Urry 1983). To some extent, the growing literature on the middle class in contemporary China largely follows the debates in the broader academic circle of

---

92   There are few theoretical discussions of the formation of the middle class. For one of the few attempts, see Archer and Blau (1993). Regarding the conception of class formation, consult Katznelson (1986).

social class research. The definitional problem is one of the leading themes of current discussion in China (Li 2010b). Discussions on the size and composition of the middle class and debates on the political character of the middle class (as rearguards in politics, reluctant radicals in defending their property rights, or rather vested interests in existing economic reform, etc.) are growing in importance as they respond to the public's concern of the implications of the rise of the middle class. But few attempts have been made to look into the process of the formation of the middle class.

This neglect of the class formation question is not difficult to understand. Given the rapid rise of the middle class in contemporary China, particularly since the late 1990s, the focus of attention, journalistic as well as academic, has been placed on issues concerning the composition of the middle class, its size (vis-à-vis other social classes in the entire population), as well as their political demands.[93] Answers to these questions would inform the concerned parties about how the middle class is going to shape the course of social and political development in the immediate future. As a result, relatively less attention has been paid to the investigation of the formation process of the emerging middle class.

This neglect of the processes of middle class formation is also found in the literature of class analysis in British and American sociology. Whether they take the Marxist position or not, most researchers have shared the same assumption that once the class boundary is clearly defined, class interests would be automatically identified, and accordingly they can, more or less, predict the political orientations of different classes (Crompton 2008; Hindess 1987). The prevalence of this structure-based analytical framework partly explains why the process of class formation does not gain much attention in current debate. Furthermore, with the assumption that structural class locations naturally entail class interests (as the classification of structural class locations simultaneously identifies class relations), it is easy to jump to the conclusion that class actions are political actions that protect different classes' political interests. As a result, class formation process is frequently treated as a process in which objective interests of middle class are transformed into political interests and actions, and consequently related discussion mainly concentrate on the political role played by the middle class. Indeed, quite often discussions of political orientations and actions are based upon the above-mentioned deductive reasoning of the position of (and thus the related material interests of) the middle class in the social structure (e.g. the middle

---

93 Similar questions were raised in the studies of the East Asian middle class when the so-called 'Four Little Dragons', namely Hong Kong, Korea, Singapore and Taiwan, were undergoing rapid socio-economic changes and political liberalization in the early 1990s. See Hsiao (1993) and Robison and Goodman (1996).

class will perform the function of 'shock absorbent' of social tensions given its 'middle-ness' among contending classes). Class actions taken by the newly formed middle class in China, which are contextualized in the mundane world of their everyday life and do not immediately articulated to specific political agendas, have been largely neglected.

It is our intention to go beyond the framework of existing discussion and thus do not confine ourselves to political mobilization of the emerging middle class in China, and focus on the class formation process from a different perspective. Particularly, utilizing the methodology of community study from urban sociology, we emphasize the class formation process observed in daily life. Despite our focus on class and class formation process, we recognize that the analysis of residential community—especially those in suburbs—and the ethnographic methods in urban sociology would better equip us to understand class in the everyday life context than traditional approaches in class analysis. Our emphasis on contextualizing class action in the everyday life context is closely connected to some of the classical studies of the middle class and their communities. Whyte's study of 'the organization man' (1963) is one of such important classical texts we are referring to.

By adopting this everyday-life-context approach, our study highlights the significance of two issues:

First, the process of class formation includes different dimensions and layers. In general, most researchers are interested in looking at three aspects of class formation:

1. The political: politically speaking, class formation refers to the process wherein structurally defined class interests are materialized into actions taken by social and political actors. As stated above, this has been the focus of traditional class analysis and yet little efforts have been made to bridge the gap between structure (i.e. defining the middle class and mapping its position in the class structure) and action (i.e. the political outcomes).

2. The relational: this aspect of class formation focuses on class relations, and more specifically the distinctions that separate different social classes.[94] Here class formation refers to the social processes through which members of a certain class establish a distinctive identity of their own by, consciously or unconsciously, drawing upon symbolic means to construct class boundary. Current research on status and consumption can be considered as attempts in this direction (e.g. Zhang 2008). There are also some discussions of distinction and exclusion by establishing gated residential communities with tight security measures in Chinese cities (Pow 2009). Seeing class action as grounded on local social activities (such as the formation of a residential community), these attempts have

---

94 See Bourdieu (1984; 1989).

probed the production and reproduction of class culture.

3. The way of living: this aspect of class formation is closely related to the previous one. The questions concerning how middle class people express their class position and status by means of leading a certain lifestyle and constructing a particular mode of consumption are surely important to our understanding of how the class itself is shaped. However, that said, the process of middle class formation is not confined to consumption and the expression of symbolic power. The focus on one type of class strategy (of constructing class distinction and maintaining social distance) leads to the under-emphasis on other equally important daily life experiences in building commonalities among the middle class. Indeed, their shared experience in social mobility and work life and their propensity of owning property and making investment constitute the social foundation of building middle class values and norms in their everyday life context. To say so is not to understate the significance of social differentiation and exclusion that have been carried out in middle class residential communities. No doubt, through case studies (for instance, Pow 2009), we have observed how the middle class have constructed a sense of other-ness and a 'purified landscape' in order to exclude outsiders from their premises. But a one-sided emphasis on differentiation and exclusion leads to an unwarranted assumption: that the middle class have already developed their well defined way of life and culture so that they are conscious of the presence of the non-middle class people in their community. And built upon such an assumption, few attempts have been made to find out actually how do the middle class work out their culture and lifestyle in their daily life. It is our contention that, before jumping too quickly to the conclusion there has already existed a middle class identity, culture and lifestyles (and thus some kind of social barrier to exclude others), we need to take a serious look at how the middle class are developing their way of living. Of course, our investigation of the middle class way of life and the class practice of distinction and exclusion are not two totally separate issues. Indeed, they are connected and would interact.[95] To draw an analytical distinction between the two is to underline the fact that prior to the consolidation of a class culture and subsequently boundary of class distinction, there is a process of the emergence of shared expectations and values among the middle class. Upon the basis of normative common ground, there arise tacit understandings among members of the same social class. Class identity would be reinforced and the middle class would express their shared class-ness in their daily community life.[96]

Second, by locating the class formation process in the everyday life context, this gives

---

95 For an application of Bourdieu's perspective to a study of the constitution of a middle class way of life, see Young (2003).

96 The interactions among the subjective and objective factors are underlined in Bourdieu's framework. The works of Boltanski (1987) best illustrate how they interact and reinforce each other.

us an opportunity to reflect on our understanding of class politics. Existing discussion of class politics tends to focus on identifying the political character of a particular social class, probing whether their political orientation is liberal or otherwise. We argue that such discussions are overly simplistic in their understanding of class politics. They are particularly problematic either in assuming a gradual and almost unidirectional process of political maturation (i.e. becoming more and more rights conscious and active in political participation once they have participated in social conflict or organized action) or in overstating the strength of the formal and/or informal institutions in accommodating tensions and conflicts arising from everyday life concerns of the middle class.[97] Not only have the participants in these debates forgotten that society oscillates and people shift in their public involvements (Hirschman 1982), more importantly most people, in a way the middle class in particular, do not necessarily pursue further actions in the public domain once their grievances have been adequately redressed. The political outcomes of middle class politics cannot be deduced from a calculation of the interests of the middle class and a description of its changing position in the class structure. Instead, we should thoroughly investigate how middle class get involved and deal with issues in the public domain. What we want to point out here is that the political issues that the middle class are concerned about are not necessarily those on organized politics or 'big issues' (i.e. democracy and freedom); rather, it is more often the case that they are concerned about everyday community tensions and conflicts, which Wolfe (1999) calls 'below politics': it is interpersonal, related to everyday life, and about moral judgment of right and wrong in an ordinary context. It is not just about material interests. Nor would it touch upon political ideology. It is buttressed in their daily life and yet it comes to form a moral and civic order regulating social life in the community.

We believe that we are witnessing the formation of a new social class, namely the middle class, in contemporary China (also see Hsu 2007). It emerges in the context of a once de-stratified society and is quickly forming its own identity and culture. The cultural practices adopted by the middle class residents have not yet been codified and socialized as expected behaviours and manners. That is, the middle class culture under observation in contemporary China is prototypical. They are, as noted by Williams (1977), 'still in

---

97 Tsai (2007) emphasizes the significance of the adaptive informal institutions in accommodating the grievances as well as demands of the emerging middle class. While the significance of such institutions should not be under-stated, it is also important to recognize their limitations.

process'.[98] It is exactly because such practices are 'still in process' that we find them intriguing and informative. Through an examination of such everyday practices, ranging from managing barking dogs to dealing with nuisance related to improper dressing in the community, we come to see how a micro civic and moral order comes into being. Through observing daily practices and reviewing the gossips circulating in the community (i.e., examining social life in the community under an ordinary circumstance), we shall be able to know how a micro social order is undergoing its formation.[99] More interestingly, such a moral order expresses a way of living the middle class residents desire. Indeed, one of the most important reasons for them to move into the community is that, in addition to finding a comfortable accommodation, they go there to look for a desirable living environment defined in the broad sense of the word.

With this consideration, we believe that the best ways to investigate a middle class residential community are participant observation and in-depth interview that are frequently adopted in community studies. Variation in terms of the social background of the residents is expected. The middle class residents acquire their property through the market mechanism and thus the composition of the community would be different from those housing blocks provided by the work units. But such heterogeneity within the community does not affect our analysis (for the heterogeneity of middle class community, also see Zhang 2008:34). In fact, we did find that there are considerable similarities in social background among the residents (see Diagrams 1-2). More importantly, it is exactly because of the existence of differences among the residents that our study would allow us to observe how middle class people coming from different industries and occupations would gradually converge and develop an increasingly similar lifestyle and expectation.

---

98   In Williams's words, by structures of feeling: "We are talking about characteristic elements of impulse, restraint, and tone; specifically affective elements of consciousness and relationships: not feeling against thought, but thought as felt and feeling as thought: practical consciousness of a present kind, in a living and inter-relating continuity. We are then defining these elements as a 'structure': as a set with specific internal relations, at once interlocking and in tension. Yet we are also defining a social experience which is still in process, often indeed not yet recognized as social but taken to be private, idiosyncratic, and even isolating, but which in analysis (though rarely otherwise) has its emergent, connecting, and dominant characteristics, indeed its specific hierarchies." (Williams 1977: 132; original italics)

99   Willmott and Young (1967:112) pointed out the subtle class character of a suburban community in London: "A newcomer to a street …will not necessarily be accepted into a neighbourhood group. She has to show she is worthy of it, be the right sort of person, have a decently furnished home of her own, speak with the right accent, be neatly dressed, enjoy living in Woodford but not so much that she would mind moving, have a readiness to engage in conversation, and, above all, be rather extroverted, able to march out and meet people without being too shy about it." Sociability and the normative order evolving from it shows the class character of a community.

The Setting and Fieldwork

Our research was conducted in a suburban residential community in Beijing called KC (Liu 2009). It is located on the eastern edge of the city, about 10 kilometers from the business district and 15 kilometers from downtown. KC provides stacked townhouses which have two units vertically, each with its private entrance from the street. Each unit has a private parking lot. Houses in KC range from 180 to 250 m^2 with an average price of 7,000 RMB/m^2. It offers more living spaces than the average in Beijing, which is merely 32.68 m^2 (National Bureau of Statistics of China 2005). KC also tries to distinguish itself by the provision of quality community facilities and environment. It contains not only 2.7 hectares of public green area, but also a 7 km^2 artificial lake. Besides, KC provides community-wide facilities, including a community club house, playground, a swimming pool, a sports centre, a driving range for golfing, tennis courts, barbeque facilities, etc. The property developer aimed to attract middle class urban residents, and this marketing strategy was clearly shown in its slogan: 'The Private Garden of CBD'. Many residents living in the community are high level employees working in joint ventures, private enterprises, universities, and community and social services like TV stations, hospitals and local government. Detailed information of residents' composition can be found in the following diagrams (Diagrams 1–2):

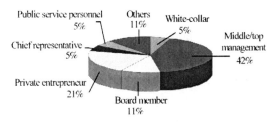

Diagram 1   Occupation of KC Residents

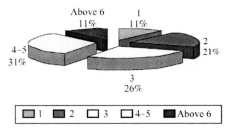

Diagram 2   Family Structure of KC Residents

The ethnographic fieldwork consisted of both participant observation and in-depth interviews. It was conducted in KC from June to August 2007. Participant observation included two components. Part of the observation was carried out on the community's online forum. Unlike other residential communities whose community online forums were usually attached to major property developers' websites, KC's online forum was set up and completely controlled by KC's homeowners. Aiming at providing a carefree environment for discussions among neighbours, this forum required every user to register by submitting their personal information such as real name, cell phone number, and most importantly, their address in KC. Also, their contacts were posted on the forum for the facilitation of communication among members of the residential community. In this sense, KC's online forum was not an entirely virtual world. Residents' behaviors and interactions in this semi-virtual world largely reflected their real expectations and ideas of everyday life in the community. More than 150 households in KC registered on this forum with identity verification, which made up 40% of total households in KC. Considering that, at the time of the fieldwork, there were more than one third of the owner households had not yet moved into the community, we had reason to believe that those registered on the forum were the majority of KC residents. For this reason, we believe that the contacts on the forum constituted a reliable sampling frame for our sampling of internet communication and the selection of respondents to the intensive interviews. And with the help of this forum, we were able to identify the most active residents in KC. This assisted us in finding a good mix of active and not-so-active residents for interviewing.

In addition to the online observation, residents' activities and interactions in real life situation were also closely followed. Through participation in informal neighbourhood gatherings, residents' home parties, and casual chats with homeowners while working out together in the community clubhouse, walking dogs and buying groceries, we are able to develop a sketch of homeowners' everyday life in KC. Following an initial period of participant observation, 23 in-depth interviews, totaled 45 hours in length, were conducted with 22 households in the later period of the fieldwork. The composition of the interviewees' age, education, occupation was consistent with the general description of KC's residents (see Diagrams 1-2). Besides, the manager of the property management company was also interviewed for an understanding of KC from a different perspective.

The Emerging Moral Order in the Community

KC is a peaceful suburban community. However, this is not to say that ownership rights and related matters have not been sources of contention. Indeed, in the early stage of its development, many owners got themselves mobilized and joining organized action in order to negotiate with the management company about the quality of the buildings as well as details of internal decoration. Their actions were reported in the news media. However, with the actions of property rights protection gradually subsided, the middle class residents in KC returned to their homes and did not take further action. Contrary to the conjecture that rightful property protection and resistance would energize the concerned participants to take further action, life in KC quickly turned quiet and calm after the initial round of organized actions. When the residents' interests in confronting KC's developer gradually faded, mundane, and sometimes trivial, matters in daily life again became people's focus. Like any other residential community, barking dogs, improper occupancy of car parking space, and a variety of other nuisances and minor offences were commonplace. These trivial and mundane matters were by no means unimportant as they might appear. Quite the opposite, it is exactly by dealing with such mundane issues that middle class residents gradually established their expectations of living in a newly developed middle class community. In other words, what we observed here is how residents in a middle class community construct their way of life and a moral order at the community level.

During the three months' fieldwork at KC, the issues that triggered the most intensive discussions among residents were not some big 'political' items. Rather, they were about how to make a balance between private and public interests in their daily life.

One of the hottest issues in KC residents' exchanges was how to keep dogs properly in order to minimize disturbance to their neighbours. When one of the residents, Mr. Li, posted his complaint on the community forum about his sleeping problem due to dog barking at midnight, it immediately received a lot of attention. Discussions among the residents covered not only how to deal with dog barking problem at midnight, but also other related issues, including whether it was appropriate to keep dog in private courtyards, the proper way to walk dogs, and how to deal with dog wastes in common areas in the community.

Generally speaking, there were two dominant views. On the one side, a large number of residents believed that they could not simply turn a blind eye to such nuisance and expect the problem would go away. They believed that this was just a false hope. For those whose lives were disturbed by the barking dogs should try to deal with the problem either by negotiating with the dog owner directly or through KC's property management office, or directly reporting to and seeking help from the police. On the other side, there were residents who considered dog keeping a private matter. As long as the dog was kept in private space, others were not supposed to have the rights to interfere. As one resident named Spark posted on the forum:

> "I really can't understand why people have so many opinions on other people's lifestyles. How to keep a dog, indoor or outdoor, is the dog keeper's own business. Is there anything that needs to be 'understood' by others? Too many restrictions and too much interference mean stepping into other people's private lives?"

During the interviews, we also encountered many residents with their views on dog keeping. As put by some interviewees, these were no trivial matters. Indeed, they were not simply about individuals' own personal preferences and lifestyles; rather, they reflected the delicate balance between personal freedom and public's interests in a community. Ms. Zhang said:

> "Take dog keeping as an example. I think the online discussion is vigorous, and personally I am against dog keeping. I can understand the way that they [dog keepers] behave, but at the same time, I think it's important that no one is imposing his/her view on others. We need to have mutual respect. I think my bottom line here is my life not being disturbed. I'm not a person with a very strong sense of social responsibility. As long as you are not disturbing my life, basically I won't confront you. This is my bottom line."

Theoretically, property owners were entitled to freely lead their preferred way of life within their premises. These were private space owned by the property owners. However, their homes were parts of a broader communal environment. That they were living in a community meant they had to take into account of what other members of the same community thought of. Simply put, there were something called public interests. Of course, in many occasions, it was found that grievances would not turn into conflicts. It was shown that there was a certain level of tolerance among the residents:

> "…I totally understand the frustration of my neighbours about dog barking at night. It's very annoying. I know some of my neighbours have sleeping problems and are very sensitive to noise. If my dog barks and wakes them up, they won't be able to fall asleep again. How can they get their expected peaceful life of living in this community? So I've never allowed my dogs to stay in the balcony by themselves, as they may create noise and make my neighbours unhappy. As a dog owner, we should love our dogs, but it's equally important that we also respect our friends living in this community…"
>
> "All of us have just moved in, having rather high level of expectation of the quality of living here. We are easy to get 'irrational' [when such expectations are not met]. Perhaps a few years later when we are familiar with each other, we can expect a certain level of tolerance. After all, there are not many households living here. " (Interviewee Ms.

Ma)

> "One of their neighbours living next door once told the Nians (dog keepers) that she was afraid of dogs. Then they try not to go near her courtyard when they walk their dog. That is how we deal with this kind of problem. There's really no need to make a big fuss out of it." (Interviewee Mr. Wang)

> "In a community like KC, dogs are often found outdoor. Given that we share the common areas within this community, it's inevitable that the dogs would somehow affect the residents' lives. If we were to live in apartments, as long as you can keep them quiet that would be OK. How you actually keep your dog in your apartment would be none of our business. No one would bother to care about how you keep your dog. But we are here in KC, a community which contains a lot of common areas. Your way of dog keeping would affect others and some of them may raise their complaint. There'll be lots of such complaints. I think it's not a problem between the residents and the animals. Rather, it's a problem among the residents. To deal with such problems, I think the 'soft' options would be more appropriate than simply staging confrontation. The point is to find a solution to the problem. I think it's quite stupid if we sacrifice our relationships with neighbours just because of some arguments about the animals. I think mutual understanding is important: dog keepers should keep their non-dog-loving neighbours in mind, and at the same time, we who do not have a dog at home should be more tolerant towards dog keepers." (Interviewee Ms. Zhang)

Of course, some of the residents' grievances and discontents would bring about arguments and conflicts. There were also occasions that they ended up in open confrontation and police officers were called in to settle the conflicts among the residents:

> "From what I heard, it wasn't the first time that police officers came to deal with problems arising from dog keeping. Last Sunday, I saw two police vehicles in KC, responding to a resident's call. One of our neighbours called 110 (i.e., the police emergency number in China), as his kid was frightened by an unleashed dog while taking a walk in the community. The dog owner didn't show any sign of regret and told other people that her dog was quite gentle and would not attack people. The offended neighbor couldn't hold his anger and called the police. Staff of the property management company also tried to play the role of a mediator between the two parties. But our angry neighbour simply didn't listen to any of them. He would only follow orders from the police, as they are officials having the authority to handle such problems." (Interviewee Ms. Zhu)

Although local police was quite an effective agent in dealing with neighborhood nuisance, many residents were reluctant to approach them and would do so only in the very last resort. The main reason for them to do so was that seeking intervention from a third party was perceived as a confrontational move. It would discredit and embarrass the concerned parties in front of other neighbours living in the same community. Indeed, when they decided to seek intervention from the outside, the disturbed residents might need to consider the wider implications of their action for interpersonal relationships in the neighborhood. Not only that it would create embarrassment, it might also bring about retaliation. In the eyes of many residents, tolerance and mutual accommodation were expected. As long as nuisances were not totally out of control and problems were confined to a limited scale, they would prefer handling the problem in person and not to bring in the police authority. As summarized by our respondents, police intervention could only remove the symptoms but would not provide a long term solution to conflicts among the residents. For most KC's residents, it was more important to create a kind of mutual understanding and respect among the neighbours than to rely on formal authority in order to handle their conflicts.

> "If I find cat waste in my yard and I know it's because my neighbours are feeding abandoned cats around my house, I would approach them and see what could be done to deal with this matter. If my neighbour showed his compassion and tried to work things out with me, I'll be fine with it. It may need some time to solve the problem and I won't expect immediate action. But, at least, I know he's trying hard and is willing to help. He's aware that I suffer. Thus, I won't take any radical action. However, if there is no change at all, then I must give him some warnings. Then definitely I'll take some actions." (Interviewee Mr. Chen)

Despite such readiness of taking action, the dominant thinking was about being considerate, having self-control, and developing mutual understanding. Accommodation was the word that cropped up frequently in their discussion of how to deal with nuisance.

> "From my own perspective, what I can do is to be a considerate resident, and hope that my behaviours may in turn affect my neighbours. For example, when I see neighbours leaving the dog wastes behind, I'll give him/her a poop bag and say 'Maybe you forgot to bring one, and here it is'. People may feel embarrassed and next time they won't forget to clean the dog waste. We are all members in KC community, and if each one of us is doing our best, there won't be any problem at all. It may be more appropriate to deal with such issues in an indirect and subtle manner." (Interviewee Ms. Ma)

> "I think what we need to reinforce in this community is that of a moral order. It's about people following the rules. It's about enhancing people's quality. If there were no rules to follow, we won't be able to deal with the problems. Some dog owners may know how to breed dogs, but they have little knowledge of how to educate their dogs. So I posted that message on the web. I didn't write that article by myself. I found it online. You know, they are your neighbours, and sometimes you can't say things to your neighbors

directly. For most of the time, what we need in this community is self-control. I posted that article because I hope to remind some of our neighbours that they should control themselves and follow the rules and guidelines. You can say it is a kind of 'soft struggle', or a rather indirect way to influence or to educate your neighbours." (Interviewee Ms. Zhang)

"In my opinion, pet keepers in KC should have more self-restraint and be more considerate than those living in other type of housing. There is no other option, simply because most of the people living in this community are not pet keeper. The majority rule. Pet keepers have to be more considerate so that, in return, more people will also become more tolerate towards them and their pets. If you upset your neighbours, this won't do any good to the pets at all. This will only drive many angry residents towards calling the police once there's an argument. This will only intensify the conflict. In the last resort, the management office would only impose restrictions on pet keeping. So, what can you do? You'll have to bear the loss." (Interviewee Nancy)

As we can see from the residents' comments on how to keep pets in KC, it was evident that they did have their expectations. These were expectations regarding KC as a middle class community. They were also expectations about how the residents in a middle class community should behave. This concerned the kind of quality of life they expected to enjoy for living in KC. The quality of life they were referring to was not just about the physical structure and the facilities of the community. They had in mind a set of behavioural code that would guide the residents to enjoy their own chosen lifestyle and to adjust to the expectations of their neighbours'. Accommodation, requiring mutual adjustment as well as self restraint, is the main theme of their discussions. How to respect others and public interests was underlined. Furthermore, how to handle arguments and conflicts in everyday life in a civilized manner became a major concern among the middle class homeowners in KC.

A Balance between Private and Public

Besides dog keeping, another topic that had been widely discussed in KC concerned the code of proper clothing and behavior in private courtyards. At the first glimpse, it might appear that this issue was unquestionably a private matter, simply because courtyards in KC are essentially private properties. However, most of these backyards were semi-open, and hence residents' behaviors in their private yards were, to a large extent, semi-public. It was not so much about whether individual residents would mind if they had been seen in their private courtyards by others. It was about how residents in KC would expect their neighbours to behave in a 'civilized manner':

"The walls fencing the courtyards in KC are not that tall. So, our courtyards are, in fact, quite exposed. In this regard, I think there should be some dress code to follow here. For instance, to me, the way our half-naked male neighbour dressed, with only a boxer putting on his body, while hanging out in his own yard is definitely not acceptable. We should not treat our courtyard as purely private space. Instead, even in our private space, we should also consider how other people feel. Besides dress code, another thing that we should pay attention to is our conduct in the courtyard. For instance, I can't tolerate people yelling in their yards very early in the morning. Others have not yet woken up and you yell 'Get up! Get up!'. This is unacceptable. Some other details also deserve our consideration. For example, living in a community like KC, it is not appropriate to hang and dry your clothes, including underwear, in open area. But unfortunately, many residents here rarely pay attention to such issues. I can't see how to deal with it." (Interviewee Ms. Zhang)

"My neighbours are quite different from my own expectation. I feel very uncomfortable when seeing male neighbours being half-naked in the summer. I may try to appreciate if they have a great body. But no, they're not even close to any acceptable standard of fitness. What we see in the summer is they, in groups, gather in courtyards or common areas, with their half-naked bodies. I find it difficult to adjust to such behaviours. But there're plenty of them behaving like this. There're also neighbours who raise rabbits in their courtyards. They're treating their courtyards as garbage collection stations. On our way here, did you see that there are chickens out there? They even use coal briquettes in winter! That's terrible! It's like living in rural villages." (Interviewee Ms. Cai)

What was reflected in the above discussion was the residents' expectation of developing a kind of public awareness in the community: even in private space, residents should still consider feelings and opinions of the others. More interestingly, such expectations were not necessarily confined to issues that would touch on their personal and immediate interests (i.e. behaviours that might bring damages community facilities or those, such as setting up illegal or improper structures, that might affect property price). Rather, these expectations of public awareness were more often related to the culture and manners of their neighbors in KC.

Other issues that caught the residents' attention included how some of their neighbors failed to take care of communal facilities and public space (e.g., improper car parking practice), and whether they should tolerate noises created by their neighbours during midnight. All these mundane issues were concerned with how to draw the line between private and public. The general opinion among KC residents was that they should learn to be aware of the private/public interface:

"Actually, in my opinion, everyone has his/her own personal freedom. As long as he/she is not affecting other people's lives, we should not judge their behaviours according to our own preferences and habits. For instance, some may say keeping dog is against the law. I think such hostile attitude is completely unnecessary. First, the dog is walking on leash, and it's not likely to get anywhere close to you; and second, it's simply passing by in front of you. I think it's not about the pets; rather, it's about showing respect to our neighbors. If you are offended, for instance, you are harmed by the dog, then you can blow it up and make any complaint you want to. Other than that, I think it's always an over-statement. People over-react. Be more tolerant to your neighbours and they will be more tolerant to you. Then, it's done. Case settled. Communication is important. Try to understand and respect other people. There is no need to think that other people are intentionally trying to take advantage of you. Things aren't that serious. It's far more important to maintain a kind of harmonious relationship with your neighbours. Don't always put your own rights in front of everything else. You aren't alone in this community. There're other people as well. You help others and they help you in return. OK. Imagine that you're able to uphold your rights so that no dogs would be allowed to pass your front gate. Is this a good thing to you? What we have now, with all these arguments among neighbours, is the outcome of an over-emphasis on individual rights." (Interviewee Ms Bai)

"KC is one of the two experimental communities in Beijing where dog owners are free to decide the number and breed of dogs to keep at home. As a result, there is no clear regulation on either species or number of dog that can be raised in this community. Some residents may think that the courtyards are their own, so they can do whatever they want as long as they are doing that inside their own premises. It doesn't work this way. Whenever you open your gate, you are in the public area: even your courtyard is in public domain. Of course, no one can enter your courtyard without your permission, but your behavior in it or the view of your courtyard is inevitably becoming part of the public environment in this community. Therefore, [how to behave in the courtyard] is not your personal call. [The courtyard] is in fact a place which is shared by other residents in this community. You may have the property right of owning the courtyard, but all that entails is you are allowed to use the courtyard or decorate it in certain way, and other people can't just walk into the yard without your permission. Even when that's the case, the courtyard is still part of the community. Maybe legally speaking, your neighbors can't tell you how to behave in the yard, but morally, you have to consider your neighbors' opinion. This is the character of this community. Every action in the courtyard, including ugly design or careless yard maintenance, is in fact some kind of damage to the broader community environment. Unfortunately, not many people recognize the importance of this point, and most of them still believe that as long as they are on their own property, then it's none of your business. It really shouldn't be the case." (Interviewee Nancy)

The main point in the respondents' comments was about how to strike a balance between the private and public. Private property ownership guaranteed homeowners their rights to lead their life according to their own preference and taste. Yet, they were not expected to do whatever they liked. Our discussion above is not simply about the existence and application of civic mindfulness. It is also about the expectations espoused by the individuals as well as the community as a whole about the kind and quality of life in KC. What the KC residents did was more than simply taking into consideration how others felt. They were, in a way, joining a process of constructing a new collectivity. This collectivity was different from the kind of collective unit found in their work unit prior to economic reform in contemporary China. Rather, this was a new collectivity based on homeownership and personal choices. They could choose (through the market mechanism) and yet they were willing to adjust and accommodate other residents' expectations. They were leading a new life in this kind of new collectivity. It was a collectivity built upon private property and a chosen way of living.[100] The way of life they were living was their own choice.

Discussion

We believe that we are witnessing the formation of a newly constituted middle class in contemporary China. It rises in the context of a marketized economy and is quickly forming its own identity and culture. It is undergoing a social process that the middle class on the two sides of the Atlantic had gone through in the 18th and 19th centuries (see, for example, Archer and Blau 1993). From the clustering of people of different occupational and socio-economic backgrounds, there emerges "a life style, set of cultural codes, behaviors, and conventions" (ibid: 30). In 19th century America, Britain and Australia, in the process wherein the middle class developed its lifestyle and codes of behaviour, the evolving cultural practices were codified into etiquette books and household manuals (Young 2003). Manners were gradually institutionalized. The significance of such a formation of class culture is that "Believing like the middle class, performing like the middle class, consuming like the middle class, constituted agents *as* the middle class." (ibid: 20; original italics)

As discussed above, KC was a community showing the prototype of a middle class community. The residents there were forming their expectations of the neughbours: being members of KC, one should have these understandings and awareness. All the mundane issues they discussed among themselves were about a loosely defined code of behaviour in the neighborhood. The emphasis was placed upon being reasonable and sensible (e.g. being

---

100   Fleischer (2010:109) also underlines the notion of preference in his analysis of a suburban community in Beijing.

considerate to your neighbors, taking care of communal facilities). One was also expected to be decent and polite (so that being half naked in one's own living room was not very proper). There were certain expectations and standard of behaviour that KC residents were about to meet (though they had never been told to do so). Details of these expectations were essentially about the level of civility of being KC residents.

In KC we observed the constitution of a structure of feeling on how one should lead a decent life in a middle class community. The moral order in this community emphasized the maintenance of a balance between the private domain and the public domain. The prerequisite of this moral order was the freedom of choice: with reform of the housing commoditization, the middle class could choose their ideal or desired place to live. To choose a decent life, their consideration was shifting from property value and market price to the composition and quality of the neighborhood. In other words, they choose to live with people who share certain common social attributes. Their references included not only economic indicators such as income and occupation, but also common understanding of a middle class lifestyle and its related moral order. By living like a middle class, espousing middle class decency, the residents of KC had built their own middle class community.

References

Abercrombie, Nicholas and Urry, John. (1983) *Capital, Labour and the Middle Classes*. London: George Allen & Unwin.

Archer, Melanie and Blau, Judith R. (1993) 'Class formation in nineteenth-century America: the case of the middle class', *Annual Review of Sociology*, 19:17-41.

Baumgarter, M.P. (1991) *The Moral Order of a Suburb*. New York: Oxford University Press.

Boltanski, Luc. (1987) *The Making of a Class*. Cambridge: Cambridge University Press.

Bourdieu, Pierre. (1984) Distinction. Cambridge: Cambridge University Press. (1989) 'Social space and symbolic power.' *Sociological Theory*: 7(1).

Crompton, Rosemary. (2008) *Class and Stratification* 3rd Ed. Cambridge: Polity Press.

Dickson, Bruce J. (2003) *Red Capitalists in China*. Cambridge: Cambridge University Press.

Fleischer, Friederike. (2010) *Suburban Beijing: Housing and Consumption in Contemporary China*. Minneapolis: University of Minnesota Press.

Hindess, Barry. 1987. *Politics and Class Analysis*, Oxford: Blackwell.

Hirschman, Albert O. (1982) *Shifting Involvements*. Princeton: Princeton University Press.

Hsiao, Michael H.H. Ed. (1993) *Discovery of the Middle Classes in East Asia*, Taipei: Institute of Ethnology, Academia Sinica.

Katznelson, Ira. (1986) 'Working-class formation: constructing cases and comparisons', Ira Katznelson and Aristide Zolberg (eds) *Working-Class Formation*. Princeton: Princeton University Press.

Hsu, Carolyn L. (2007) *Creating Market Socialism*. Durham: Duke University Press.

Li, Cheng. Ed. (2010a) *China's Emerging Middle Class*. Washington DC: The Brookings Institution.

Li, Cheng. (2010b) 'Chinese scholarship on the middle class', Cheng Li (ed.) *China's Emerging Middle Class*. Washington DC: The Brookings Institution.

Li, Chunling. (2005) *Duanlie yu Suipian: Dangdai Zhongguo Shehui Jieceng Fenhua Shizheng Fenxi* (Cleavage and Fragment: An Empirical Analysis on the Social Stratification of the Contemporary China. Beijing: Social Sciences Academic Press.

Liu, Shuo. (2009) 'The ordinary middle class in an ordinary community: the formation of the new middle class in China". Unpublished Ph.D thesis, Sociology Department, Chinese University of Hong Kong.

Pearson, Margaret M. (1997) *China's New Business Elite*. Berkeley: University of California Press.

Pow, Choon-Piew. (2009) *Gated Communities in China*. London: Routledge.

Robison, Richard and David S.G. Goodman. Eds (1996) *The New Rich in Asia*, London: Routledge.

Tsai, Kellee S. *Capitalism Without Democracy*. Ithaca: Cornell University Press.

Williams, Raymond. (1977) *Marxism and Literature*. Oxford: Oxford university Press.

Willmott, Peter, and Michael Young. (1967) *Family and Class in a London Suburb*. London: The New England Library.

Wolfe, Alan. (1999) *One Nation, After All*. London: Penguin Books.

Young, Linda. (2003) *Middle-Class Culture in the Nineteenth Century: America, Australia and Britain*. Houndmills: Palgrave Macmillan.

Zhang, Li. (2008) 'Private homes, distinct lifestyle: performing a new middle class', Li Zhang and Aihwa Ong (eds) *Privatizing China*. Ithaca: Cornell University Press.

Zhu, Jianggang. (ed.) (2008) 'Collective action regarding homeowner rights in China', *Chinese Sociology and Anthropology*, Vol. 40, No. 2.

This book is the result of a co-publication agreement between Social Sciences Academic Press (China) and Paths International Ltd (UK).

Title: The Rising Middle Classes in China
Chief Editor: Li Chunling
ISBN: 978-1-84464-094-2

CPSIA information can be obtained at www.ICGtesting.com
Printed in the USA
BVOW04*2033040515

398503BV00003BA/11/P

9 781844 640942